WORK, SOCIAL STATUS, AND GENDER IN POST-SLAVERY MAURITANIA

WORK, SOCIAL STATUS, AND GENDER IN POST-SLAVERY MAURITANIA

Katherine Ann Wiley

Indiana University Press

This book is a publication of

Indiana University Press
Office of Scholarly Publishing
Herman B Wells Library 350
1320 East 10th Street
Bloomington, Indiana 47405 USA

iupress.indiana.edu

The paper used in this publication meets the minimum requirements of the American National Standard for Information Sciences—Permanence of Paper for Printed Library Materials, ANSI Z39.48-1992.

Manufactured in the United States of America

Library of Congress Cataloging-in-Publication Data

Names: Wiley, Katherine Ann, author.
Title: Work, social status, and gender in post-slavery Mauritania / Katherine Ann Wiley.
Description: Bloomington : Indiana University Press, 2018. | Includes bibliographical references and index.
Identifiers: LCCN 2018014997 (print) | LCCN 2018023311 (ebook) | ISBN 9780253036254 (e-book) | ISBN 9780253036216 (hardback : alk. paper) | ISBN 9780253036223 (pbk. : alk. paper)
Subjects: LCSH: Muslim women—Mauritania—Social conditions. | Muslim women—Mauritania—Economic conditions. | Social status—Mauritania. | Mauritania—Social conditions—21st century.
Classification: LCC HQ1815 (ebook) | LCC HQ1815 .W55 2018 (print) | DDC 305.4869709661—dc23
LC record available at https://lccn.loc.gov/2018014997

1 2 3 4 5 23 22 21 20 19 18

For Pat, Ken, and Mike

Contents

Acknowledgments

THIS PROJECT NEVER would have happened if not for the wonderful women, men, and children who not only befriended me but incorporated me into their social circles and families in Kankossa. I do not name them here to preserve their privacy, but I will be forever grateful to them for all they taught me about my research questions and, more importantly, life in general. This book exists because of them.

Many other Mauritanians were generous with their time and taught me more than I ever could have hoped for. Mohamedou Mohameden Meyine and Fatimetou housed me in Nouakchott and provided me with access to the *Centre d'Etudes et de Recherches sur l'Ouest Saharien*. Mohamedou also graciously helped me gain permission to conduct my research. El Hassen Ould Ahmed, Zekeria Ould Ahmed Salem, Mariem Mint Baba, Mohamed Khattar, and Cheikh Saad Bouh Kamara provided much helpful guidance on my work. Thank you to the staff at the *Institut Mauritanien de Recherche Scientifique*, especially the director Jiyid Abdi for helping to facilitate this project. A special thanks, as well, to others in Nouakchott who welcomed me into their homes, especially Soukeina Allaf, Siham Babana, Daouda Diallo, and all my friends from Kankossa who ended up settling there. I am so lucky to have Brahim Bilal Ramdhane as a friend and teacher. His assistance with my research was invaluable, and his and his family's company made my time in Nouakchott very pleasant. The same goes to Cheikh Sidi Ahmed and Mustapha Ould Sedeti who taught me so much about Hassaniya and life in Kankossa. Thank you also to officials in Kankossa who helped facilitate my stay, including the head of the gendarmes, Sidi Mohamed Ould Haida, and the department governor, Sidi Ahmed Ould Ahmed Ould Houeibib.

This book has also been shaped by many generous and insightful individuals who read portions of it or commented on papers I presented over the six years I worked on it. These include Mara Bernstein, Kate Bishop, Lewis (Addison) Bradford, Elizabeth Burbach, Geert Castryck, Sarah Dillard, Tara Deubel, Brigittine M. French, Dinah Hannaford, Itohan Idumwonyi, Susan N. Johnson-Roehr, Cole Louison, Adeline Masquelier, Susan McKinnon, Erin Pettigrew, Wendell Schwab, Nadine Sieveking, Susan Slyomovics, Beverly Stoeltje, Devorah Shubowitz, Annie Wainscott, and Bruce Whitehouse. Monica Foote and Sarah Gordon's feedback and commitment to keeping us all on track greatly contributed to the start of this work. I am also grateful to participants in the 2010 Paris conference on Ḥarāṭīn, especially E. Ann McDougall, Bruce Hall, and Alessandra

Giuffrida for their comments and suggestions. E. Ann McDougall and Hsain Ilahiane's reviews of the manuscript greatly improved it and pushed me to think more deeply about these topics. At Indiana Press, thank you to Paige Rasmussen for answering all my questions and to Dee Mortensen for her helpful guidance and feedback. I am also very grateful to Casey Wiley for reminding me to focus on the writing, not just the content, and to Pat and Ken Wiley for providing encouraging feedback and helpful questions.

This project was funded by several generous organizations including the Wenner-Gren Foundation, the Social Science Research Council with funds from the Andrew W. Mellon Foundation, the Project on African Expressive Traditions, and the West African Research Association. After returning from the field, a College of Arts and Sciences Dissertation Year Fellowship from Indiana University gave me the time I needed to move forward in my analysis and writing. Much of the project's development occurred during a postdoctoral fellowship at the University of Virginia's Carter G. Woodson Institute. I am grateful to Deborah E. McDowell and Lisa Shutt for their support, as well as all the fellows, especially Celeste Day Moore, Jonathan Forney, David Morton, and Erin Nourse for their thoughtful feedback on my work. Thanks to the anthropology department at PLU for all their support as I finished the manuscript, especially Jordan Levy for reading much of it, Ami Shah for many conversations about Africa, and Amanda Taylor and Jennifer Spence for helping me remain moderately calm through it all.

Thank you to Melanie Thurber, Obie Shaw, and Lauren Lewis, who housed me in Nouakchott; conversations with them, as well as with Alassane Ba and Jacque Seeley, greatly shaped my thinking about these issues. Bruce Hall, Timothy Cleaveland, Mohameden Ould-Mey, Ghislaine Lydon, and Ben Soares provided logistical advice about conducting research in Mauritania. Thanks to Khaled Esseissah and Matthew Steele for answering questions on Hassaniya and Arabic.

Finally, this book would not look the way it does without some key individuals. They include my committee at Indiana University: Beth Buggenhagen, Gracia Clark, Maria Grosz-Ngaté, and John Hanson. As my chair, Beth was extraordinarily generous with her time. She taught me much about anthropological theory, was a careful reader whose comments and questions pushed me in exciting directions, and counseled me on how to navigate all stages of the process from grant writing to job seeking to maintaining a healthy life and work balance. Ellie Lapp kindly read the entire manuscript and provided invaluable suggestions and feedback. Finally, thank you to Michael Rings, who reminded me I could do it at every stage of the process and who helped me to revise, plan, and take breaks from the manuscript.

* * *

Two of the chapters have been published elsewhere in slightly different versions. Chapter two appeared as "Joking Market Women: Critiquing and Negotiating Gender and Social Hierarchy in Kankossa, Mauritania" in *Africa* 84(2014): 101–118© (reprinted with permission). Chapter five appeared as "Making People Bigger: Wedding Exchange and the Creation of Social Value in Rural Mauritania" in *Africa Today* 62(2016): 49–70©. Permission to publish this material here is gratefully acknowledged.

Note on Transliteration and Language

In transliterating Hassaniya for this manuscript, I rely on the system of the *International Journal of Middle Eastern Studies.* I decided to retain the diacritics to aid specialist readers; I hope they will not detract from the text for broader audiences. As an oral language, Hassaniya is sometimes difficult to transliterate and words are not always uniform across texts (e.g. Ḥarāṭīn may also be written as Ḥrāṭīn). In some cases, I choose a spelling that may be easier for English speakers to pronounce. Note that pronunciation in Hassaniya varies slightly from Modern Standard Arabic, and I try to follow the Hassaniya conventions in the text. Throughout the book, I generally employ the English "s" for the plural to avoid confusion for the reader. I do not use diacritics for Arabic words that commonly appear in English (e.g., haram), for the names of persons, or for place names.

One of the challenges in analyzing a category like "Ḥarāṭīn," whose meanings are slippery and contested, is determining how to refer to the people one is writing about. I have considered several options, including "black Hassaniya speakers" and "sūdān" (a Hassaniya term that encompasses slaves and Ḥarāṭīn). I rejected the former since it presumed racial categories that may not have meaning locally and the latter because it overemphasizes Ḥarāṭīn's connections with slavery. In the end, I decided to use the term "Ḥarāṭīn" but with the caveat that it means different things to different Mauritanians and may sometimes be used to refer to people who do not consider themselves part of this category. Despite my interlocutors' use of other terms I discuss throughout the text, they most commonly referred to themselves as "Ḥarāṭīn," which also influenced my choice of terminology. It is also the case that sometimes the term "Bīẓān" can also refer to and include Ḥarāṭīn. I try to be clear in the text when I am employing it in this sense. Finally, I treat Ḥarāṭīn and Bīẓān as proper nouns and capitalize them.

WORK, SOCIAL STATUS, AND GENDER IN POST-SLAVERY MAURITANIA

Introduction: I Will Make You My Servant: Social Status, Gender, and Work

One hot afternoon Toutou, a middle-aged *suwāqa* (market trader), sat on a brightly colored plastic mat in the living room of her partially finished concrete home divvying up a large bag of spices into smaller packages. She and her husband, Brahime, had been funding their house's construction in stages, as their financial resources allowed. Three rooms were completed, but others awaited roofs, doors, and floors. Their home is near the lake in Kankossa, a town of about 10,000 people in south-central Mauritania. While much of Mauritania is in the Sahara, Kankossa is located in the southern part of the country that transitions into the greener Sahel.

Using an empty rectangular matchbox as a makeshift spoon, Toutou carefully scooped teaspoons of spice, transferring them to tiny plastic bags the width of her thumb. The daughter she had talked into helping her—one of her others had begged off, claiming a headache—tied them into tight bundles Toutou would sell tomorrow at her market table, charging a coin for each. Beyond spices, she also sells vegetables—tomatoes, eggplants, peppers, and carrots—she carefully cuts into halves or quarters to sell by the piece. Toutou hoped to finish bagging the spices quickly so that she could also work on her second business, dyeing cloth. She would make a dingy yellow *malaḥfa* (Mauritanian veil) wearable again by dyeing it black and turn a white malaḥfa maroon with bright orange circles across one end, as her client had requested. As she bent over her work, Toutou let her own cotton malaḥfa—six-yards of colorful fabric women wrap around themselves partly as a sign of their Muslim faith—slip off of her head, something she only does around close family and friends. Like most people in this Islamic Republic, Toutou is Muslim.

Toutou's husband, Brahime, lay on a thin mattress near the back of the room, half watching an action-packed Bollywood film while intermittently dozing off. The living room was also occupied by several children—both Toutou's own and those of relatives and neighbors—who sat or lay close to the corner television, absorbed in the film. Brahime had returned from work an hour ago; he had one of the rare salaried administrative positions in Kankossa. Toutou glanced at her husband and then turned to me. "Look," she said. "If I married a Bīẓān he wouldn't let me sit here bagging spices. He would get me a maid who would do all this work."

The Bīẓān are one of Mauritania's major ethnic groups; its members have long dominated the country economically and politically. Like most of the other vegetable traders, Toutou and her husband are Ḥarāṭīn, a term used to refer to former slaves or descendant of slaves of the Bīẓān.[1] Mauritania's government legally abolished slavery in 1981, making it the last country in the world to do so. Estimates place 40 to 45 percent of Mauritania's population as Ḥarāṭīn (McDougall 2010, 259).[2] While most Bīẓān claim Arab or Berber descent, most Ḥarāṭīn are of black African descent, so their associations with slavery are marked by their skin color and the fact that they share language (Hassaniya) and cultural attributes with their former masters. Today, Bīẓān and Ḥarāṭīn are colleagues, friends, and, occasionally, spouses, but tensions persist between some members of these groups. By threatening to marry a Bīẓān, Toutou thus contends that she could marry someone of high social, and possibly economic, standing.

Brahime smiled slightly at her claim that marrying a Bīẓān would free her from work and then warned, "That would only depend on his money. Not all Bīẓān are rich. Some have nothing." His comments remind that not all Bīẓān occupy privileged positions. This group is organized around a hierarchical structure; lower-status members are often not well-off. However, his contention also speaks to broader economic challenges that affect much of the country's population, including high inflation and unemployment rates. Toutou laughed and asked him, "Would you come and serve us tea if I married a Bīẓān?" Keeping the tone light, Brahime retorted, "What are you talking about? Make *you* tea?" He promised he would leave her long before he served any beverages.

Both Toutou and Brahime laughed during this exchange—he less than she. They frequently joked together and many of Toutou's jokes, like this one, revolved around her imaginings of other life paths. Sometimes she would laugh, saying she aspired to be the minister of finance and then would make Brahime her servant. He could bring her tea and cold beverages. Even more frequently, perhaps because it made me laugh, Toutou described how she and I would travel to Turkey to find Muhened and Murad—the handsome stars of two popular Turkish television serials that had been airing in Mauritania. She liked Murad best, so she planned to marry him, while I could have Muhened. When Murad returned to Kankossa with her, she explained that Brahime would either become their servant or she would send him away to work on the edge of town. Murad would never know they had been married. These imaginings sent her into fits of laughter.

This interaction captures some of the central questions that motivated my ethnographic research—questions that focus on the intersections of social status, gender, and work. What is it like to be a slave descendant in the country that most

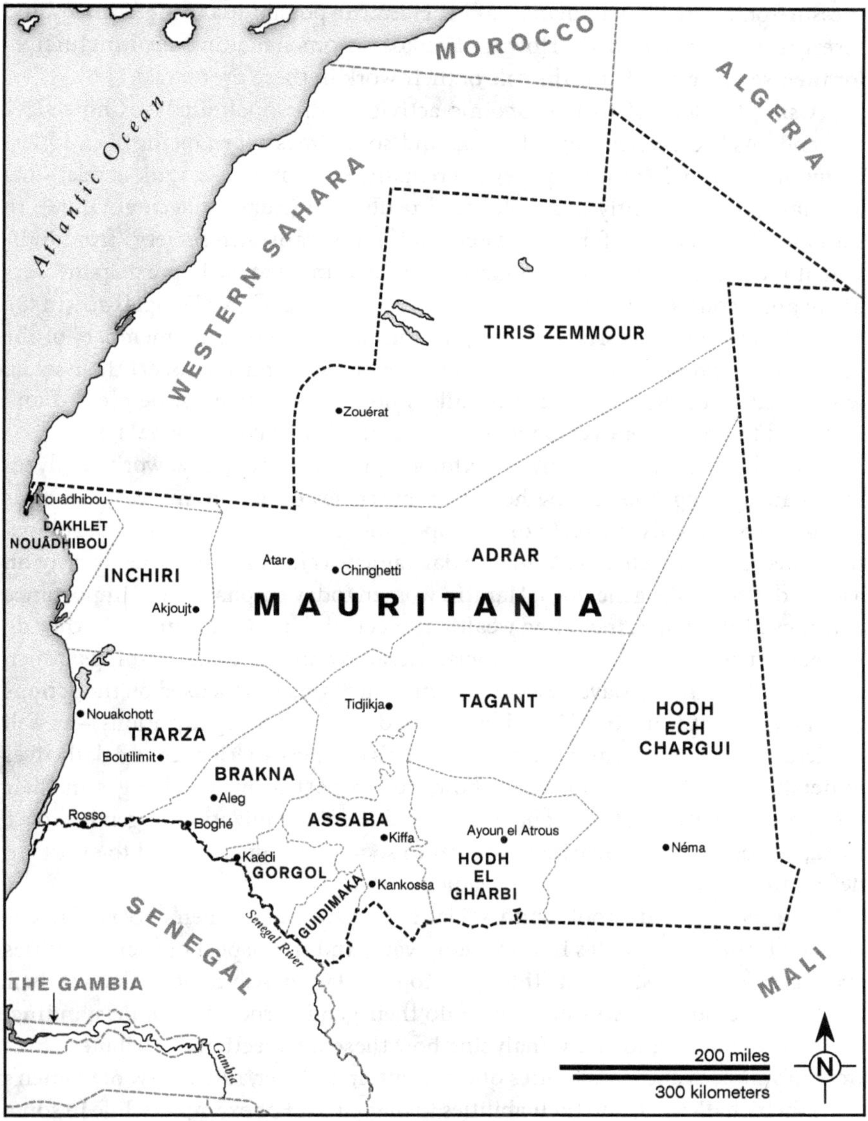

Mauritania. Map by Martin Lubikowski, ML Design, London, England.

recently abolished slavery and that is ranked among the highest for prevalence of slavery in the world? How do female slave descendants navigate their social positions while being disadvantaged in many ways by both their genealogies and gender? How does the neoliberal moment—characterized by increasing economic pressure on many Mauritanians—affect Ḥarāṭīn's possibilities for getting by and asserting their social worth? How are Kankossa women making meaningful lives for themselves, and what is the role of their work in these processes?

Using the lens of their economic activities, this book analyzes how slave descendants are challenging, altering, and sometimes reproducing social hierarchy in a place where slavery's legacy remains evident. Social rank is relational and has to be constantly negotiated and reaffirmed (Buggenhagen 2012, 48). In the case of Mauritania, former masters and slaves transform society "from individual more than collective negotiations, rooted in what each 'participant' sees as advantageous and honorable in his/her new contexts" (McDougall 2015, 258). Central to women's efforts to claim positions as free and equal members of the polity and build meaningful lives is how they understand and assert their social worth and value. Social value, after all, is not static, but "must be created and recreated to prevent or overcome dissipation and loss" (Weiner 1992, 15).

Based on twelve months of ethnographic research, my work analyzes this maneuvering, illustrating how such processes occur on an everyday basis through women's discourse, bodily comportment, dress practices, and participation in economic exchange. While social value was historically based largely on ascribed factors like genealogy, Ḥarāṭīn women today emphasize the importance of achieved attributes, including wealth, respect, and industriousness. As they do so, women challenge the broader social hierarchy and its underpinnings. Much previous literature on slave descendants in Mauritania has focused on the actions and advocacy of Ḥarāṭīn political parties and antislavery organizations—as well as hierarchy more generally—leaving women's unique experiences and daily lives understudied. My work illustrates how, due in part to major changes in their economic activities in the neoliberal era and the reorganization of gender roles, Ḥarāṭīn women are increasingly central to social reproduction and to efforts to define and assert social worth and value.

The focus of this book is on social hierarchy, but women's social rank is affected by other attributes in important ways, and this aspect of their identities is not always the most salient. Their positions as slave descendants influence their opportunities and constraints, but so do their gender, socioeconomic standing, religion, and generations. By analyzing how these intersectional attributes affect women's choices and possibilities one may attain a richer, fuller view of women's lives, their challenges, and their abilities to maneuver. For example, while in some ways their gender serves as a constraint—that is, women do not typically own profitable shops that sell bulk foodstuffs in the market since this is men's work—it can also be an asset since they are at times able to break into lucrative new areas of work that are not appropriate for men, such as dyeing cloth. Although I focus on women, I also consider men's lives, since their experiences are often intertwined. Paying attention to men's and women's varying economic opportunities is essential to understanding how gender and social status intersect.

Despite her constraints, Toutou has achieved a lot in her life. She has purchased land, which she controls herself and thinks of as a valuable asset. While she had limited formal education, she is proud that she is able to send her children to school and hopes they will have important jobs someday. She is a respected and, comparatively, well-off member of her community, which consists of relatives as well as her friends and their families. But Toutou's story and those of the other women I introduce throughout the book are not neat, upward trajectories of social achievement that end with them being considered equal to their freeborn counterparts. Despite her gains, Toutou sells vegetables in the market, an activity Bīẓān in Kankossa avoid because it is "dirty." Likewise, while Toutou's dyeing business has been lucrative for her, Bīẓān women do not engage in such work. I am interested in contradictions like these and how women make meaningful lives for themselves among them. In the process, Ḥarāṭīn women assert new understandings of what constitutes social value and challenge the basis of hierarchy in general.

Social Hierarchy and Legacies of Slavery

Toutou self-defines as Ḥarāṭīn and her membership in this category is evident in the kind of work she conducts and the composition of her social networks. "Dirty" work, like selling vegetables and dyeing cloth, is associated with lower-status groups and many of the other women who do this work are also Ḥarāṭīn. Toutou sets up her market table near other Ḥarāṭīn women, and when she sits under her family's *limbar* (a permanent tent many people have outside their homes) she can easily call to the nearby Ḥarāṭīn relatives and friends who occupy her neighborhood. Her closest friends are Ḥarāṭīn, most of whom were also born in Kankossa. These women support each other; they help organize their daughters' weddings or provide financial assistance when relatives fall ill and have to be taken to the capital, Nouakchott, for treatment.

Overcoming their connections with slavery is difficult for women like Toutou because they remain marked as slave descendants by their generally dark complexions.[3] They are also marked by the fact that they share a language and cultural attributes with their former masters. It is also the case that others often know their genealogies. Although the exact etymology of "Ḥarāṭīn" is unknown and has caused considerable discussion for decades (Marçais 1951; Nicolas 1977), this term also indexes the group's connections with slavery. Potential Arabic derivations include *ḥurr thānī*, meaning "free person of a second class" or "a person who has become free" (Ould Cheikh 1993, 183) or, as interlocutors suggested to me, *ḥurr ṭarī'* (new freedom) or *ḥurr 'āṭanī* (freedom he gave me).[4] The linguist Catherine Taine-Cheikh argues the term likely derives from the Berber word *ḥarḍanən* or *āḥarḍān*, which has the connotation of mixing and thus suggests the idea of mixed blood between slave owners and slaves (1990, 96), and others have seconded this translation, meaning "mixed" or "unpure" (McDougall 2015, 253). All of these possibilities reference the term's connotations with slavery. While

Toutou describes herself as Ḥarāṭīn, she rarely speaks about her family's history of slavery. Avoiding such topics is common and speaks to the enduring stigma slave descendants face.

Beyond slavery's visible legacy, antislavery activists and international organizations contend that slavery itself still exists in Mauritania to some extent. Although Mauritanians disagree about what constitutes a slave, in 2013 the Walk Free Foundation designated Mauritania as having the highest prevalence per capita of contemporary slavery in the world.[5] The Foundation dropped the country's ranking to number seven in 2016, but this classification reflects Mauritania's post-slavery condition. The term post-slavery, which was first used in the context of American and Caribbean histories of slavery, refers to a period after the legal abolishment of this institution, during which structural inequalities and unequal power relations developed under slave systems continue to impact people's lives (Lecocq and Hahonou 2015).[6] The legacy of slavery remains a major issue in Mauritania, and Ḥarāṭīn continue to face discrimination in the economic, political, and social realms. For example, they are largely excluded from powerful political positions; since independence from France in 1960, every president has been Bīẓān. In 2015, 30 of 35 government ministers hailed from this group, as did all but one of the regional governors (Kamara 2015).

Toutou's position as a slave descendant coupled with slavery's enduring legacy make her earlier comments to her husband, Brahime, especially charged. While the women I worked with contended that slavery was no longer practiced in Kankossa itself, they and others noted that it did occur in surrounding villages and elsewhere in the country. When Toutou tells her husband she will marry another, richer man and make Brahime her servant, she references how the kind of labor men and women conducted historically corresponded to and reinforced their social positions. For example, slaves worked for others and were responsible for tasks free elites avoided, including domestic work. By contending that her husband will work for her, Toutou not only suggests that he will occupy a lower social position than herself, but she also presents herself as being powerful enough to employ him. She thus draws attention to her aspirations to improve her life while claiming the ability to do so.

How serious her threat is, however, remains ambiguous. On the one hand, it functions as a joke because it is clear these dreams are likely out of her reach. The fact that she threatens to leave while she is bagging spices that will sell for a handful of coins highlights the impossibility of her buying a plane ticket to Turkey, just as her gender, slave genealogy, and lack of formal education make her claim to becoming a high government official virtually impossible. On the other hand, although elites have historically avoided marrying Ḥarāṭīn or other lower-status groups, including dependent Bīẓān (Freire 2014), Toutou's claim that she could leave her husband warns Brahime of possible repercussions if he fails to adequately provide for her family. She openly draws attention to his own lack of economic resources and implies he is not living up to his responsibilities, a claim illustrated by his dozing while she works in the midday heat.

Toutou's story demonstrates the complexity of negotiating one's position in a place where hierarchy continues to substantially impact women's and men's daily lives. Bīẓān have long had a hierarchical system where elite nobles occupied the highest positions, with slaves occupying the lowest.[7] Historically, status was partly based on ascribed factors, especially genealogy, and elites often claimed common ancestry with the founder of their *qabīla* (lineage groups that historically served as the basis of Mauritania's social and political organization) and sometimes even with the Prophet Mohammed.[8] Elites also drew upon achieved factors to reinscribe their social positions by claiming military strength, religious knowledge, or wealth, as well as by garnering honor and respect. Elite women indexed their social rank by avoiding manual labor and nurturing larger body sizes; their leisure signified they had the wealth and power to have others work for them. Men and women's positions in the hierarchy were not fixed, and they could alter their status by marrying into other groups, reworking genealogies, and garnering (or losing) wealth or dependents. Similarly, slaves could gain freedom by purchasing it, running away, gaining religious knowledge, or seeking manumission.

Though slavery has diminished in Mauritania over the past century, the fact that legal abolition occurred just a few decades ago makes it an ideal site to consider how people like Toutou and Brahime are negotiating their social positions. Elsewhere on the continent, slavery's abolition is more distant, occurring, for example, in Zanzibar in 1897 and Morocco in 1922. The French did abolish slavery in 1889 in Saint Louis and later French West Africa, but they only started implementing this policy elsewhere in West Africa in 1905 and then only slowly and unevenly (de Bruijn and Pelckmans 2005; Klein 1998). Continuing resistance to French expansion in northern Mauritania into the 1930s made colonial administrators especially reticent to drastically alter social organization there; they feared that doing so would alienate their Mauritanian allies and upset their own economic interests (Acloque 2000; Robinson 2000). Although slavery had long been diminishing in Mauritania, its legal abolishment did not come until 1981, two decades after independence.

Due to such recent abolition, Mauritania is an excellent place to analyze how slave descendants negotiate their positions on a daily basis, something not always evident in the historic record. This book contributes to the rich, historic work that has considered how slave descendants maneuvered around the continent in the decades after abolition.[9] Along with government and personal archives, historians have explored court cases, colonial reports, literature and poetry, life histories and interviews, musical recordings and song lyrics, and censuses. While such sources yield valuable evidence, they are constrained by gaps in the historic record and provide a limited view of the everyday lives of slave descendants.

Ethnography is thus a powerful tool for investigating social hierarchy because it provides insight into the multitude of ways through which women and men negotiate social rank on a daily basis. As a cultural anthropologist, my research relied heavily upon participant observation—the principal method of this discipline in which the researcher accompanies people throughout their daily pursuits, learning about life as it unfolds. By participating in women's mundane activities, I discerned nuances and intricacies in the meanings of hierarchy and social value that do not always emerge in written sources or interviews. For example, my work demonstrates how everyday jokes like Toutou's, many of which occur publically, are a powerful way for women to critique hierarchy and suggest alternatives.

There are many other places in West and North Africa where slavery's legacy endures and effects men's and women's lives, including Mali (de Bruijn and Pelckmans 2005; Pelckmans 2011; Rodet 2010), Morocco (Ilahiane 2001; El Hamel 2008), and Burkina Faso (Bouman 2003). While all of these cases are unique, the Mauritania example speaks to shared challenges slave descendants face more broadly throughout the region and provides insight into how they navigate around them. This case is also singular, however, in that slavery has been a very public issue in Mauritania since the 1970s, largely due to early Ḥarāṭīn politicians and subsequent antislavery activists' efforts to draw attention to it. This situation contrasts with many parts of the continent, where the enduring legacy of indigenous slavery remains largely out of the public spotlight even while it continues to limit former slaves' possibilities. For example, Lotte Pelckmans has shown how the Malian government attempts to keep this institution's history largely invisible, remaining reticent to acknowledge indigenous African slavery (2011, 27).

While Mauritania's government also tries to downplay the persistence of slavery, recent antislavery legislation and recurring crackdowns on antislavery activists continue to draw attention to it. In 2007, the government passed a law that put measures in place to prosecute slave owners; in 2015 it was replaced by a tougher law that officially made slavery a "crime against humanity" and increased prison terms for offenders. These positive steps contrast with government officials' treatment of some antislavery activists. In 2010, police arrested leaders of the antislavery organization, Initiative for the Resurgence of the Abolitionist Movement (IRA), during their attempt to free two young women who they claimed were slaves. IRA's leader, Biram Ould Abeid, who won the UN Human Rights prize for his work on slavery and was the runner-up in the 2014 presidential elections, was arrested again in 2014 on questionable charges and was eventually sentenced to two years in prison along with three other anti-slavery activists (Hemmig 2015). He was released early in 2016, but other activists who were protesting the treatment of Ḥarāṭīn were arrested soon after.

The fact that issues of slavery and inequality are so visible in Mauritania make it an important setting in which to consider how hierarchy manifests itself and how people challenge it. While the women I worked with do not frequently discuss slavery itself, its presence in public discourse and the media make questions of status prominent in public thought. Likewise, public critiques levied by activists against enduring slavery and inequality emphasize how social hierarchy is constructed and can be dismantled. Against this backdrop, working women strive to display their social worth and assert new forms of social belonging, with some Kankossa slave descendants even adopting a new social category, coming to self-identify as Khaẓarīn (see chapter 1). This is similar to shifts in contemporary post-abolition societies in Africa more broadly, where "status categories have been acquiring new meanings, and new identities and euphemistic expressions have been introduced" (Rossi 2009, 3–4). The term Khaẓarīn has been in use in Mauritania for at least a century, but its widespread use in the east is unique and has yet to be extensively explored. Women's and men's adoption of this term illustrates the malleability of social categories and the important role discourse plays in constituting them. While people employ this term in a variety of ways in Kankossa, many use it to describe slave descendants who have been free for generations and who claim other high-status attributes, including wealth, education, and respect. The fact that some women and men identify as Khaẓarīn is significant not only because by doing so they posit membership in a new social category but because they also highlight the value of achieved attributes and thus challenge the foundations of genealogy-based hierarchy. At the heart of women's claims to be Khaẓarīn lie questions of what constitutes social worth in contemporary Mauritania: What does it mean for someone to be respected and valued?

Kankossa is a fruitful place to investigate such questions since slave descendants there historically had opportunities their counterparts did not necessarily have elsewhere, thus contributing to conditions of increased social fluidity. While scholars often identify urban spaces as places where slaves and their descendants are able to assert new identities and forms of belonging (Brhane 1997) and experience improved conditions (Villasante-de Beauvais 2000, 291), this example illustrates how rural areas are not peripheral to such processes. Early Ḥarāṭīn settlers, including Toutou's father, came to Kankossa in the 1950s and 1960s to work for the French, who had established an agricultural research station beside the lake. Beyond providing them with wages, the move to Kankossa distanced workers from their former masters and gave them the possibility of claiming land, thus granting them autonomy and resources that were not always available elsewhere. This relatively privileged past continues to affect these workers' ancestors today, helping them build wealth, exhibit generosity, and garner respect, as well as contributing to the adoption of the social category Khaẓarīn. That Kankossa's early history provided slave descendants with such possibilities illustrates how developing a more nuanced understanding of how contemporary Ḥarāṭīn conceptualize, rework, and reproduce hierarchy requires looking beyond urban areas.

By exploring how slave descendants navigate and challenge hierarchy, I hope to complicate the often-simplified understanding of slavery in Mauritania that continues to dominate the scant US media coverage of this country.[10] Beyond the obvious shock value, interest in this issue is connected to the somewhat racialized nature of slavery in Mauritania, which resonates with the United States' own history with this institution. In reality, slavery there differed greatly from slavery in the United States; it was never based upon a plantation model and slaves occupied a range of positions, including working as autonomous farmers, domestic servants, and trusted advisors. Furthermore, many Bīẓān never owned slaves, while some Ḥarāṭīn did, and the ancestors of some people who today are classified as slave descendants in reality may never have been enslaved at all. Such sensationalist articles keep international readers' attention, and dollars, focused on a limited definition of slavery, detracting from other pervasive human rights issues—such as widespread poverty—and from the interrogation of what slavery means in this context. Similarly, antislavery organizations may overemphasize the number of slaves and their living conditions to garner international attention and funds (Rossi 2015, 323). Stories like these perpetuate negative stereotypes about Africa as a backwards continent whose challenges greatly diverge from those confronted in the West, overlooking shared challenges like severe economic inequality. I do not mean to imply that slavery is not a problem in Mauritania—the recent arrests of antislavery activists on questionable charges calls into question the government's commitment to ending this institution—however, a better understanding of slave descendants' realities will provide a more nuanced picture of how social categories there are constructed, expressed, and altered. While many Ḥarāṭīn are undeniably oppressed in some way, oppression is situational and needs to be explored in particular contexts.

Getting by in the Neoliberal Era

Toutou and Brahime have been married for over a decade. They generally get along well, often staying up late into the night talking with friends and family members. Compared to many of their Ḥarāṭīn counterparts, they are middle-class—for example, they have a maid who helps with basic household tasks—but money is tight and often causes tension. Toutou's jokes draw attention to Brahime's inability to provide for their family, a concern many Kankossa women share in regard to their own husbands. Although in Islam it is prescribed that men support their households, an edict many Kankossa residents take seriously, this expectation is becoming increasingly unrealistic. Brahime's salary was often not enough to cover his family's needs, particularly because a short-term loan he took to finance construction on the still-uncompleted house continued to drain his funds. While

Brahime did provide Toutou with a monthly stipend for basic food costs, she complained that it barely paid for the necessities. Toutou often supplemented his funds herself, paying for food, clothing, and school supplies for the children.

Many other Kankossa residents share Toutou and Brahime's financial challenges. During my research, the phrase *vaẓa mā khālga* (there is no money) frequently echoed throughout the market, and women and men perceived this moment in history as one of particularly scarce resources. Their observations are not surprising given that Kankossa is located in the Assaba, one of three southern regions of Mauritania that constitute what aid organizations refer to as the "poverty triangle." Though recent macroeconomic indicators show some aspects of the country's economy have improved (Mele 2014), this positive growth is not felt by the majority of Kankossa's population. According to the National Office of Statistics, 44 percent of Assaba inhabitants lived in poverty, with seven percent living on less than one dollar a day in 2004. Furthermore, in 2008, 39 percent of the region's active population was unemployed.[11] These challenges are not limited to this region. Between 2008 and 2009, the country faced escalating food and oil costs, a drop in prices of major exports, a diminishment in oil production, and, after several years of positive growth, a GDP growth rate of -1.1 percent (ADB 2011, 2–3). While inflation held at 5.7 percent in 2011 and Mauritania enjoyed an economic growth of 4 percent, Kankossa residents continued to feel economic strain, which was exacerbated by a severe drought later that year.[12]

Various factors contribute to these economic difficulties, including repeated ecological disasters, such as drought, locust invasions, and flooding, as well as growing consumer desires for imported goods and the global economic crisis. Government instability also exacerbates these challenges. Since independence in 1960, Mauritania has experienced several coups, most recently in 2008. While Mohamed Ould Abdel Aziz, the leader of the 2008 coup and subsequent winner of the 2009 and 2014 elections, has promised he would be the "president of the poor," Mauritanians complain about the lack of state services.[13]

The financial struggles Toutou and Brahime face are also connected to decades of structural adjustment policies and neoliberal reforms put in place by the government, as has been the case throughout much of Africa and elsewhere. While intended to stimulate the economy, these reforms led to increased unemployment, growing poverty, and widening gaps between rich and poor (Ould-Mey 1996). Like similar financial reforms elsewhere, their emphasis on privatization, free trade, and free markets significantly diminished the size of the public sector, meaning people like Toutou and Brahime cannot depend on the government to care for their most basic needs, a challenge also faced elsewhere in Africa (Apter 1999; Ferguson 2006; Kaplan 1994). This fact became painfully obvious when, at a 2011 public meeting with the regional governor, Kankossa citizens listed the town's needs: an ambulance, a more *mitṭawwara* (developed) hospital with better trained professionals and up-to-date medical equipment, a bank, enough desks for their schools, a more reliable water supply (during my stay the water would sometimes cut off for days at a time), a library, adequate numbers of teachers in rural schools, and a paved road between Kankossa and the 90-kilometer distant regional capital.

These reforms have thus made it increasingly difficult for women and men to get by in Mauritania and elsewhere, so it is not surprising that the analysis of neoliberal reforms in Africa has primarily focused on their negative outcomes. While the harmful effects of such reforms cannot be denied, the Kankossa example illustrates that some groups use neoliberal language and ideologies to their own advantage. In Mauritania, such programs emphasize the value of hard work and personal responsibility. This focus on the importance of labor to the modern economy calls into question elite Bīẓān values that favor abstention from labor, especially manual labor. Slave descendants draw on these neoliberal ideologies to revalue their own labor, claiming working hard as an important practice that makes them valuable modern citizens. Their claims have implications for research elsewhere, illustrating how, like other aspects of globalization, neoliberal policies can be interpreted and taken advantage of in local contexts to improve lives and assert agency.[14]

Women Reworking Hierarchy Through Labor and Exchange

While Ḥarāṭīn women in Kankossa have earned income from the early days of the French agricultural research station in the 1950s, increasing numbers of women are entering the workforce and making a living in this neoliberal moment. Although Toutou imagines a future in which her husband will become her servant, her reality is characterized by juggling multiple income generating activities seven days a week. She increases her earning potential by enlisting her, often unwilling, teenage daughters when possible; she has them take charge of household tasks, watch her *ṭābla* (market table) on the weekends while she scours the market for deals on bulk produce, and assist in work-related activities at home, such as roasting peanuts to prepare them for sale.

Toutou started working over a decade ago, beginning by making couscous to sell, and later having a small ṭābla at her home. She saved her earnings from these endeavors to fund her market ṭābla, a trade she learned from her mother as a child. While Toutou's gender limits her work possibilities—in Kankossa some activities, such as selling wholesale, are considered appropriate only for men—she continues to expand her income generating activities. For example, she begged her way into the training a local non-governmental organization (NGO) organized on dyeing cloth. She sends malaḥfas to Nouakchott to be dyed, which she then sells in Kankossa, and she also participates in a cooperative that grows fruit trees. Her current dream is to open a clothing store, but she has not yet accumulated the necessary start-up funds.

Toutou's experience with work is not unique to Kankossa. Many Mauritanian women support their families, frequently because their husbands have left to

View of Kankossa and its lake from the sand dune that borders the town. Photo by author.

look for work elsewhere or because of the high divorce rate. In the late 2000s an estimated 105,315 Mauritanians, over 3 percent of the population, lived outside of the country (Saleh 2009, 22), although the number of Kankossa men who live elsewhere is much higher since many relocate to urban areas in Mauritania. Many of the women who remain behind serve as *de facto* heads of household. In 2008, 44 percent of Kankossa's heads of household were women; that almost a third of these women were married reflects these migration trends (Fall 2008).[15] Ideally, migrants send back remittances. In reality, these funds are often intermittent, which leaves women largely responsible for supporting their families.[16] While migration can be an avenue through which Ḥarāṭīn make their freedom explicit and enhance their social positions (de Haas 2006; Ilahiane 2001; 2002), I discuss the women who remain behind, analyzing their roles in these processes.

As Toutou and Brahime's situation illustrates, even men who have salaried positions often do not make enough to cover their families' needs. Work has thus become central to women's experiences. When I came to Kankossa in 2009 to conduct preliminary research, I asked women what aspects of their lives were important to them and what they thought I should study. Overwhelmingly, they named *shaqla liʿlayāt* (women's work). This term refers to income generating activities that occur outside of the home that are primarily conducted by women, including salaried employment, such as elementary teaching, as well as informal activities, such as market trading or sewing malaḥfas to prepare them for dyeing. It also refers to general household labor for which women remain largely responsible. How much women work and the kind of work they engage in varies; some groups who are disadvantaged socially or economically, such as Ḥarāṭīn or lower-status Bīẓān, are more dependent on income generating activities than elite Bīẓān. In a survey of 485 Ḥarāṭīn men and women in Nouakchott in the 1990s, 44 percent of Ḥarāṭīn women were in the labor force, as compared to 35 percent of all Mauritanian women (Brhane 1997, 247).[17] My observations in Kankossa also suggest that Ḥarāṭīn have a larger presence in the market than women from other social groups.

Following women's advice, I decided to focus on their work. Over the course of my research, I became increasingly interested in how women negotiated their social rank and gender roles through their economic activities. Work is a powerful lens through which to examine such processes because social status and gender in this region have long been articulated through the kind of work men and women performed (Brhane 1997; Ruf 1999; Villasante-de Beauvais 1991). For example, slaves and lower-status people were distinguished from elites by the fact that they worked for others (Villasante-de Beauvais 2000, 289). Exploring the kind of work women conduct and how it is changing is thus a valuable way to gain insight into how they navigate and alter the social hierarchy. Recently, slave descendants' economic activities have not received much attention in scholarship on post-abolition Africa.[18] The post-abolition literature that has focused on labor tends to examine the gradual move from slave to client to contract relations (e.g., Cooper 1980 or Meillassoux 1991). Historian Frederick Cooper (1980) has illustrated, for example, how in East Africa the ideology of abolition obscured new forms of oppression and coercion that furthered the spread of capitalism; while free, many former slaves became tenant farmers with little economic power, thus expanding and maintaining relations of dependency. In the Kankossa context, work is a central means not just through which women get by but also through which they negotiate social rank and generate social value.

Such maneuverings work in tandem with women's participation in exchange networks, which makes it important to consider their diverse economic repertoires (Guyer 2004, 128) to more fully understand how they conceive of, reproduce, and challenge social difference. I analyze slave descendants' participation in the market and gift economy, both of which play important, and often intertwined, roles in their negotiations of social difference. For example, Toutou uses her earnings to participate in family ceremonies, where she slips carefully folded bills into the hand of a new bride's mother or presents her with shining metal bowls as a gift for her daughter. Such acts help women create relations of credit and debt that protect them and their families in difficult economic times

(Buggenhagen 2012; Cooper 1997; Masquelier 2009). When Toutou suddenly had to fund a naming ceremony for a child of her nephew who was abroad, women who were indebted to her helped pay for the event. Despite the fact that she was unsure whether her nephew would repay her, Toutou's insistence that the ceremony be lavish, with copious gifts for the new mother and ample food and drink for guests, speaks to the important role such events play in cultivating positive reputations for women and their families as generous, wealthy people. Analyzing women's work in tandem with exchange processes provides insight into how Ḥarāṭīn negotiate hierarchy and belonging.

Exploring Ḥarāṭīn exchange practices also illustrates how such processes may have different meanings for lower-status individuals. Anthropologists have considered how "keeping-while-giving" can be a major way through which participants authenticate their authority and family histories by preventing inalienable items associated with their families from circulating in exchange networks (Weiner 1992). By keeping such valued items, people attempt to associate themselves with these objects, thus improving their reputations (Malinowski [1922] 1984). As a group, whose relatively recent access to wealth means few former slaves own inalienable objects, Ḥarāṭīn expand the social value generated through exchange processes in other ways. For example, members of the bride's family frequently return a portion of the bridewealth back to the groom's family; this action makes visible their generosity and associates both parties with this valuable gift, thus magnifying their social value. My work illustrates how historically lower-status groups are innovative in their exchange practices and that exchange can be a generative process for exchange participants.

Women's work and their accompanying exchanges are ways through which women attempt to improve their financial standing, work to create positive reputations for themselves and their families, and maneuver their social positions. Their stories also illuminate aspects of the modern economy and our shared experiences within it. I began writing my dissertation, which would become the basis of this book, a month before the start of the Occupy Wall Street movement and continued working on it through the enduring global economic crisis, events that drew attention to the severe economic inequality in the US, my home country. In the final year of my graduate work, I too pieced together a variety of income generating activities—including teaching classes, designing curriculum, working in an administrative position, and organizing a conference—all of which barely covered my living expenses.

I completed the book while in a tenure-track job that offered some stability, but I had to watch my husband struggle to find adjunct work, which is underpaid and characterized by uncertainty.[19] The widespread sense that the contemporary economy has left them behind is one reason many voters turned to Donald Trump in the 2016 election, though some of his policy priorities—dismantling the Affordable Care Act and implementing tax reforms that benefit the wealthy and corporations—suggest his administration will likely only increase income inequality. Much of the book was also written during the protests in Ferguson and the birth of the Black Lives Matter movement, events that have highlighted the ongoing structural racism and deep inequality in my home country.

My personal experiences and these events suggest that many of the challenges Toutou and her counterparts face are not unique to them. As anthropologist Roger Botte (2005) has argued, while slavery has been abolished everywhere, the contemporary era is marked by new forms of coercion that reflect vestiges of this institution, including forced migration, precarious employment, and tenant farming. The point of this book, then, is not to see Ḥarāṭīn women as apart from the world but rather to consider the unique configurations of their challenges that readers elsewhere may share in other forms.

Gender and Hierarchy

Women's increased earning potential and positions as heads of household have translated into their claiming more responsibility and power within their families, thus destabilizing power relations and upsetting definitions of gender roles (Babou 2008; Buggenhagen 2012). Amidst these changes, men and women debate what constitutes appropriate gendered comportment. By imagining she will marry a rich Bīẓān, Toutou criticizes Brahime's lack of financial contributions to her family. She also calls into question his masculinity, which in Kankossa is linked to men's abilities to provide food, clothing, and shelter for others, and punctuates her point by contrasting him with a hyper-masculine character on a popular Turkish television series who exhibits little emotion even when executing his enemies. The fact that Toutou voices her critique while she labors as Brahime half-sleeps nearby further emphasizes her point.

Many other women share Toutou's concerns that men are failing to uphold their social responsibility. As another market trader put it, "Going into a house you feel that men are now taking the old roles of women—watching TV, doing nothing, idling, chatting—while women are working." This trader critiques men's behavior and also suggests women have abandoned their "old roles" of remaining idle since they now actively participate in the economy. Women's earnings affect their positions in their households and their relationships with their husbands. As one woman put it, "Your husband can't tell you what to do if you have money."

While uttered as a joke, Toutou's threat emphasizes her own agency and independence, particularly her assertions that she could leave her husband for someone else and send Brahime away. Not everyone, of course, is happy with such contentions or the power women's incomes may provide them. Men and some women critique working women, arguing that they are becoming "like men" and are neglecting their husbands and children. I analyze these tensions, examining both how women's and men's shifting participation in productive activities is unraveling gender roles and also how women and men struggle to control these definitions and their opportunities against the backdrop of shifting responsibility.

My own experiences in Kankossa helped illuminate women's shifting positions. As a childless, unmarried, thirty-three-year-old woman, I had by Mauritanian standards very different life experiences than many of my Kankossa peers. Most of them had been married at least once—some for close to twenty years—and had several children, both of which contributed to their becoming women. I thus occupied a liminal position. I was a woman but was also like a man since I had traveled extensively and was pursing higher education. I was also childlike since I had not undergone some of the typical major transitions to adulthood, including marriage.[20] There were many times when I grew tired of my in-between status, but it also afforded me access to people and events I might not have had otherwise. I was able to befriend men and children, all of whom provided me with many insights into Mauritanian life. My own ambiguous position also pushed me to pay attention to other ambiguities in regards to gender, such as working women's concerns over how to remain women, despite the fact that their participation in productive activities makes them "like men."

Gender does limit women's opportunities; aside from elementary school teachers and nurses, men hold most salaried positions in Kankossa. Most Ḥarāṭīn women of Toutou's generation received limited education, and some, including Toutou, are virtually illiterate. But as the above tensions between men and women suggest, Ḥarāṭīn women are exercising significant authority in their households and among other women. Women often support their families, weigh in on or make important household decisions, build social networks that will help sustain them in times of hardship, and strive to generate positive reputations for their families. While women have always played a part in social positioning, their growing financial power means their roles in asserting their own and their families' social value are increasingly significant. Considering their contributions to social positioning is essential to understanding how the meanings of social value and hierarchy are shifting more generally in contemporary Mauritania.

While much excellent scholarship has investigated how slave descendants have negotiated their positions and identities in Mauritania, it has largely overlooked the role of women. This may in part be due to men's greater visibility in public life, as well as assumptions that women are peripheral to such processes due to enduring patriarchy.[21] This work has focused on how men have contributed to shaping slave descendants' possibilities on the national level through their participation in politics or the antislavery movement, as well as their attempts to claim land or adopt new economic roles. These male leaders' contributions have undoubtedly impacted Ḥarāṭīn's lives, but, with a few notable exceptions (Brhane 1997; Ruf 1999), scholarly work has not extensively explored women's essential roles in generating social rank on a daily basis or in helping men attain positions in society. My attention to women at the local level reveals more nuanced understandings of rank and status that are often not visible at the national level where groups push particular agendas. For example, women occupying public space in the market and their willingness to joke openly about hierarchy and shifting gender roles means it is they who often raise these issues publically. Exploring such daily positioning provides insight into how power is configured and the mechanisms through which it shifts, as well as how it endures. Similarly, while there has been significant work on Bīẓān women, Ḥarāṭīn women have been peripheral to most literature, which thus overlooks their influence on both public and private life.[22] While much of the literature on slave and post-abolition societies in Africa has failed to recognize lower-status men's and women's agency (for a critique, see Klein 1998), the Kankossa example illustrates how Ḥarāṭīn women actively redefine their social positions, with varying results.

Ignoring women's contributions is especially problematic in Mauritania, since women there have long occupied powerful positions as compared to some of their counterparts elsewhere in the Muslim world. At the time of independence in 1960, the government created a *Conseil supèrieur des femmes* and nominated one of the first female ministers in Africa (Simard 1996, 65); more recently, in 2006, a quota was implemented to ensure that 20 percent of officials elected to municipal councils are women. How much the quota has actually increased women's public power has been called into question since it only pertains to local government. Women remain underrepresented at the highest levels of government, and most who hold positions within it are confined to domains considered appropriate for women, such as women's rights, health, and social affairs (Lesourd 2016). Despite challenges in the political realm, Mauritanians boast of how women in their country can divorce, speak their minds, work in public, and resist polygynous marriages. Scholars have speculated that Mauritanian women's privileged positions may be attributed to the lingering impact of the matriarchal systems of their Berber and Tuareg ancestors (Lydon 2009; Simard 1996; Tauzin 2001), the country's long history as a center of Muslim learning which led to more liberal interpretations of Islam (Simard 1996), and women's own knowledge of Islamic law (Lydon 2009). While slave women would not have benefited from such freedoms in the same way as their elite counterparts and while women still do not occupy equal positions to men in public life (Lesourd 2016), this precedent of strong, powerful women supports Ḥarāṭīn women in their efforts to define and assert social value.

This book thus also challenges assumptions about Mauritanian women prevalent in Western media by exploring their diverse experiences and abilities to exercise agency. While coverage of Mauritanian women is rare in the United States or Europe, the stories that appear often focus on force-feeding, child marriage, and marital abuse.[23] Such experiences are unfortunately true for some women, but the prevalence of coverage of negative topics like these reproduces orientalizing discourse that makes Mauritanian women the "other." It also portrays women's experiences as uniform and overlooks the ways they creatively navigate around structural constraints. Through stories like Toutou's, I work to counteract such depictions, providing three-dimensional portraits of Mauritanian women while being careful not to generalize about all women and their experiences.

Finally, it is important to note that Islam both provides avenues for women to assert their social worth and reinforces social inequality. Some Ḥarāṭīn women, for example, highlight their piety through modest dress and their comportment, which indexes their respected status. Likewise, since Islam and its tenets provide women with the ability to, theoretically, control their own resources, it gives them some economic advantages. However, religious leaders' contentions that women should not overspend at ceremonies challenges women's attempts to assert their social worth through exchange processes.[24] While their faith greatly influences Ḥarāṭīn women's lives and choices, I analyze their Muslim identities as one of many identities. This intersectional approach helps avoid both overemphasizing the importance of this faith in defining women in an ongoing process of orientalization (Lazreg 2005; van Santen 2010, 275) and also portraying Muslim women's positions as static (Newcomb 2009, 24). Islam works in tandem with other attributes to shape women's understandings of social rank and difference and their possibilities for earning income. I illustrate the importance of examining women's religious identities in tandem with other identity categories, rather than privileging their positions as Muslims.

Through sharing these women's lives and words, I also aim to follow other post-9/11 works (Abu-Lughod 2013; Masquelier 2009; Newcomb 2009) to illustrate the complexity of Muslim women's lives and to help combat stereotypes of them as oppressed and voiceless. Women's participation in income generating activities illustrates their engagement with the world and their agency. As with so many parts of the Muslim world, Mauritania provides an example of how Muslim women can circulate easily in public, earn income, and make important decisions that impact their families. This is not to say women do not face barriers and ongoing systems of oppression, but such challenges cannot be neatly attributed to Islam and need to be examined and considered alongside other aspects of identity.

Methodology and Fieldwork

My methods—particularly the long-term participant observation amongst a community of women who are connected by kinship, friendship, and overlapping professions—facilitated my investigation into how women negotiate social hierarchy in everyday life. The fact that I had previously lived in Kankossa as a Peace Corps Volunteer from 2001 to 2003 helped this process. During my service, I became close friends with many women, some of whom later helped facilitate my research by becoming interlocutors or introducing me to others. The bulk of my twelve months of research occurred between 2010 and 2011, and it also included shorter visits to Kankossa and Mauritania's capital Nouakchott in 2008 and 2009.

During my research, I spent hundreds of hours with market traders, paying attention to their interactions with customers and each other. When the market quieted down in the late afternoons, I would visit friends, sitting with them as they conducted a variety of tasks—sewing malaḥfas, making couscous, and minding children. As I got to know the women better, I attended weddings and naming ceremonies with them when invited. I lived with a trader, spending my evenings at her home and gradually coming to know well most of her family members and their social circles. During all of these activities, I paid attention to how conceptions of social value and hierarchy manifested themselves in women's daily lives since social rank remains a sensitive issue people are often uncomfortable discussing directly (Freire 2014, 427; Klein 1998, xiii). My use of participant observation sets my work apart from earlier studies on the Ḥarāṭīn, many of which depended on data primarily collected in interviews that, while valuable, cannot get at the complexity of how social hierarchy unfolds in daily life.[25]

While my time in the Peace Corps helped me make initial contacts and eased my acculturation process, my history as a high school English teacher also led to challenges. Since women and men already knew me in another capacity, many believed I had returned as a teacher (and I did teach an English class through a women's organization). This assumption made it difficult to explain my research to others, which was compounded by the fact that anthropology is not a common discipline in Mauritania, although many women had encountered NGO or government researchers before. To avoid confusion, I explained my role frequently to others and my closest interlocutors did so as well as they became more familiar with my work. My experience illustrates, however, the challenges anthropologists can face in making our research clear to our interlocutors and how this difficulty can be compounded by having already worked with them in another capacity.

My focus on women was partly due to necessity, since, in this loosely gender-segregated society, it was much easier, and expected, for me to develop personal relationships with women than with men. Since market traders tended to sell to and sit near women whom they know well, many of my interlocutors were neighbors, friends, members of common age groups, and relatives—and sometimes all four. They were thus part of a social community whose members attend each other's family ceremonies, provide financial support in times of crisis, pool resources in the market, and socialize together. As I got to know these women better, I met their daughters, mothers, and, in some cases, grandmothers, so my interlocutors expanded to include multiple generations. I also came to know women who pursued other forms of income generating activities, which helped expand my focus. This book does not attempt to speak for all Ḥarāṭīn women in Kankossa, but since my interlocutors include women from a variety of neighborhoods, socioeconomic statuses, generations, qabīla, and geographic origins, it sheds light on these issues for them and also the wider Ḥarāṭīn community in Mauritania.

I chose to focus primarily on one community of women who were linked through relatedness, their work, and friendship (c.f. Abu-Lughod 1986; Buggenhagen 2012; Pelckmans 2011). This approach had some shortcomings; for example, I had limited contact with Bīẓān women, though throughout the book I try and address their divergent experiences when possible. However, developing close relationships with women was essential to exploring sensitive topics, such as social rank, and to understanding the complexity of their economic activities. Most Kankossa residents have a primary social network—though they know many people outside of it—so aligning with a particular group of women and their social circle was normal behavior.[26]

There were also some practical considerations in developing my research focus. Al-Qaeda in the Islamic Maghreb (AQIM) has been operating in the region for several years, mainly in the large desert area that includes parts of eastern Mauritania, Niger, northern Mali, and Algeria, and has a history of kidnapping foreigners.[27] While local officials kindly approved my request to conduct research in Kankossa, they asked that I limit my movements within and outside the town. While they did permit me to take a few trips into the region, having my Mauritanian friends aware of my general location was key to maintaining my safety and authorization to live in Kankossa. This limited my ability to conduct interviews with Bīẓān, many of whom live on the periphery of town, or with Ḥarāṭīn communities elsewhere.

During the last six months of my research, I conducted formal, recorded interviews with twenty-five of my interlocutors in which I explored some of the themes that had emerged during participant observation. I focused on collecting women's work histories, asking open-ended questions that allowed them to touch on a variety of topics that were important to them, including work, family life, money, and marriage. Due to the sensitivity of slavery and social rank I did not ask about these topics directly, but I explored them when women brought them up, as they often did (for a similar approach, see Strobel 1979, 5). I primarily interviewed people with whom I had interacted before and whom I knew well and tried to select a sample that was representative of the diverse experiences and attributes of my interlocutors. I also recorded formal interviews with five Kankossa men who discussed their life and work histories, as well as one who talked about social status. I supplemented these interviews with many informal discussions with men about life in Mauritania, which provided important insights to the project. I conducted all these interviews myself in Hassaniya and later reviewed words and phrases I did not understand with my research assistant in Nouakchott.

The following chapters explore how women assert, challenge, and sometimes reinscribe social rank in their everyday lives. Chapter 1 provides the historic context of social difference in this region, examining circumstances that contributed to the increased fluidity of social rank, including the region's growing integration into the market economy. This section also explores the meaning of the social category Khaẓarīn and its implications for hierarchy in general. Chapter 2 turns to the market, exploring how traders navigate social difference and gender relations there and considering how they draw on a variety of ideologies to assert social rank, including neoliberal values. Their championing of the independent worker suggests neoliberal reforms have benefited some disadvantaged groups in unanticipated ways. The next chapter analyzes women's speech in the market, particularly jokes that involve gender and social rank. While women's jokes publically critique gender roles and social hierarchy, their impact is ambiguous since they can easily be dismissed as "only jokes." Chapter 4 analyzes women's economic strategies, including their participation in group savings associations and their creation of relationships of credit and debt. Although neoliberalism emphasizes the independent worker, in Kankossa, nurturing wide ranges of social networks is an essential way through which women navigate this economic moment. Chapter 5 explores the meaning of gift exchange at a Ḥarāṭīn wedding, including the back-and-forth exchange of bridewealth. These gifts are an important means of creating social difference, as they literally "make people bigger" and thus increase their social worth. I argue that discourse is an essential part of exchange processes, especially in making its effects endure. The final chapter analyzes how women's consumption and production of the Mauritanian veil not only indexes their Muslim identities, but also their social positions and gender. Dressing modestly has important meaning for Ḥarāṭīn women as an index of their piety, but women's participation in the production of veils reinscribes their lower social status, since Ḥarāṭīn conduct "dirty" tasks like dyeing.

Throughout the book, I try to bring my interlocutors and their worlds to life. Most chapters focus on one or two women, while incorporating the words and experiences of many. I focus on a few people in-depth to give readers a better sense of their varying experiences and to bring them to life. In this way, I hope to draw on anthropology's ability to craft "narratives that connect readers to writers, triggering mutual understandings that make the world a little bit sweeter" (Stoller 2014, 8).[28] I follow Toutou throughout the book to more fully develop her singular story and to give readers a sense of how she navigates the many aspects of work and life the book addresses. Since some of the topics I engage with are sensitive issues, I employ pseudonyms and at times change details of these women's lives to prevent them from being identified.

The women who I knew in Kankossa did not only self-identify as slave descendants. They were mothers, friends, sisters, wives, and businesswomen who were actively working to achieve their dreams and the lives they desired. While many Ḥarāṭīn face dire economic circumstances, I hope this book conveys these women's creativity and perseverance and the fun that they have in their everyday lives. Their resourceful strategies help some women like Toutou to not only get ahead in the market but also to contribute to the development of their families and nation. When crafting policy or aid decisions, I urge policy makers and development workers to avoid making assumptions about the economic or social status of slave descendants. Rather, they should carefully assess the vulnerability of social categories and individuals within them, not assuming their experiences are uniform across regions or within groups. I also encourage government officials to take real measures to improve women's and men's livelihoods across social categories, which would increase their opportunities and give newly freed slaves more avenues to improve their lives. Investing in women's businesses would be one way of doing so. This book is not intended to show the plight of Ḥarāṭīn in Mauritania; rather, I hope to provide insight into women's rich, complex identities.

Notes

1. Not all Bīẓān owned slaves and some Ḥarāṭīn say that their ancestors were never enslaved. For a discussion, see chapter one. Other ethnic groups in Mauritania include the Wolof, Halpulaar, and Soninke, all of whom are also hierarchical. Historically, members of these groups also owned slaves.

2. The president abolished slavery in 1980, but the subsequent law that affirmed his actions passed in 1981 (Brhane 1997, 91). Note that it is difficult to estimate the number of Ḥarāṭīn in Mauritania because no statistics on the ethnic makeup of the country have been produced since 1963 (Ould Ahmed Salem 2013, 45).

3. Phenotype is not always a good indicator of one's social category in Mauritania. See chapter one for a discussion.

4. Another potential Arabic meaning is *ḥarrāth* (ploughman, laborer) (Villasante-de Beauvais 2000, 300; Ruf 1999).

5. See "The Global Slavery Index 2013," *Walk Free Foundation*. Accessed May 17, 2016. http://www.ungift.org/doc/knowledgehub/resource-centre/2013/GlobalSlaveryIndex_2013_Download_WEB1.pdf. Benedetta Rossi rightly cautions about uncritically accepting headcounts of slaves in Africa since it is often unclear how such information is obtained or whether a clear definition of slavery was agreed upon amongst researchers who collected such data (2015, 323).

6. For additional discussion on "post-slavery" societies in Africa in general, as well as the meaning of this term, see the International Journal of African Historical Studies' 2015 special issue on post-slavery in Africa. Brown and Johnson (2014) detail similar processes in the United States. They trace the historical discourses surrounding black males from the fifteenth century up to the present, arguing that they have shaped contemporary negative perceptions of African-American men and have contributed to continued stereotyping and discrimination.

7. See the following chapter for a more detailed discussion of social organization in Mauritania.

8. The Arabic term qabīla is often defined as "tribe" in English and Mauritanians use the equivalent term *tribu* in French when discussing it. It refers to federations that are roughly geographically based and whose members may trace descent from a common ancestor. Today some qabīla continue to play a role in politics and settling disputes. Scholars have shown how "tribe" can be a reductive term that does not adequately capture the nuances and varied meanings of this institution across Africa (Cleaveland 2002; Villasante-de Beauvais 1998, 243–44). To better capture its meanings in the Mauritanian context I employ the term qabīla throughout this work.

9. There are many examples of this excellent historic literature (Cooper 1980; 2005; Fair 2001; Klein 1998; McDougall 1988; McMahon 2013; Strobel 1979).

10. Reports on Mauritania in Western media often focus on this topic. As their titles suggest, they are often alarmist in nature. For an example see Monica Mark, 2012. "Slavery Still Shackles Mauritania, 31 Years after Its Abolition." *The Guardian*, August 14. Accessed August 15, 2012. http://www.guardian.co.uk/world/2012/aug/14/slavery-still-shackles-mauritania#start-of-comments. The comments on this article capture some of the readers' feelings about slavery as well as the sorts of generalizations such news coverage breeds. See also, Max Fisher, 2011. "The Country Where Slavery is Still Normal." *The Atlantic*, June 28. Accessed March 7, 2017. https://www.theatlantic.com/international/archive/2011/06/the-country-where-slavery-is-still-normal/241148/. This article, as many do, overestimates the percent of slaves in Mauritania, putting it at 20 percent, and plays up the racialized dimensions of slavery which, as explored in chapter two, are more complicated than they are typically portrayed. See also, John Sutter, 2011. "Slavery's Last Stronghold." *cnn.com*. Accessed May 17, 2017. http://www.cnn.com/interactive/2012/03/world/mauritania.slaverys.last.stronghold/index.html. This story is accompanied by a documentary which aired several times on CNN. This project received a lot of attention in the United States, but some of its claims are exaggerated or misconstrued. For a response to the CNN project and a general critique of Western news coverage on this issue see Erin Pettigrew, 2012. "The Complex Problem of Slavery in Mauritania, A Response." *Opalo's Weblog*, March 20. http://kenopalo.com/2012/03/20/the-complex-problem-of-slavery-in-mauritania-2/.

11. This number may be misleadingly high since the report is unclear as to whether it counts informal sector work—that is, market vendors, home-based producers of hand-dyed veils, prepared food sellers, herders—as employment, which is how many Kankossa residents make their livings. Despite the lack of clarity, it illustrates the general paucity of work in the region.

12. The *Office National de la Statistique* (ONS) offers helpful data detailing Mauritania's economic and social climate. For more national data, see ONS (2011); for regional data on the Assaba, see ONS (2008). For macroeconomic data, the Ministry of Economic Affairs and Development (2013) is also helpful.

13. Protests occurred in Mauritania following the start of the 2011 uprisings throughout the Arab world. They have continued on and off since then, sometimes garnering thousands of participants.

14. Anthropologists have increasingly emphasized how global processes are interpreted and co-opted in distinctly local ways. James Ferguson illustrates how, while many theories of globalization have been about worldwide convergence, "Africa has proved remarkably

resistant to a range of externally imposed projects that have aimed to bring it into conformity with Western or 'global' models" (2006, 27). Similarly, Karen Hansen (2000) demonstrates that Zambians do not just wear Western used clothing in an imitation of elsewhere; they rework the meanings of these garments to make them distinctly Zambian. Charles Piot (1999) also shows how increasing integration into the global capital economy does not suppress exchange processes; rather, the Kabre in northern Togo seem to be expanding these. Likewise, I argue that groups use neoliberal ideologies in sometimes surprising ways.

15. Earlier research found similar situations among Ḥarāṭīn who occupied peripheral neighborhoods in Nouakchott (Brhane 1997, 248) and in the central Tagant region where Ruf's (1999) survey of eleven villages showed that women led more households than men.

16. This situation is not unique to Kankossa, but is widespread throughout the continent (Clark 1994; Hansen 2000; Hodgson 2011; Osirim 2009; Pietila 2007).

17. It is unclear what this difference can be attributed to: possibilities include a lack of stigma attached to Ḥarāṭīn women working, greater poverty amongst Ḥarāṭīn, or particular marriage patterns. Brhane's survey also showed that 55 percent of Ḥarāṭīn marriages end in divorce, as compared to 37 percent nationally (1997, 249), which would suggest that more Ḥarāṭīn than Bīẓān women have financial responsibility for their households.

18. Recent scholarship has focused on a wide variety of productive areas, including on how former slaves and their descendants have negotiated their social positions through popular culture (Fair 2001), involvement with local and national politics (de Bruijn and Pelckmans 2005; Ould Saleck 2003), marriage and land ownership (Botte 2010), antislavery activism (McDougall 2010; Ould Ahmed Salem 2009; Tidjani Alou 2000), reworking conceptions of honor and respect (McMahon 2013), and migration (Ilahiane 2001; Pelckmans 2011).

19. He did eventually find a lecturer position that offered a better salary and benefits while still having the uncertainty of a year-to-year contract. Academic positions are increasing filled by contingent faculty; over 50 percent of faculty occupy such positions today. See the American Association of University Professors for more details: https://www.aaup.org/issues/contingency/background-facts.

20. For a comparison see Abu-Lughod (1986) who gives a very thoughtful discussion of her liminal position as a researcher in a patriarchal society that relies heavily on marriage and child-bearing as important markers of adulthood for women. Other researchers have also emphasized the importance of marriage and children to adulthood in this region (Bouman 2003; Popenoe 2004; Rhine 2016).

21. Studies have focused on how Ḥarāṭīn, especially men, have attempted to improve their social positions through participating in the political realm (Brhane 1997; Leservoisier 2000; Ould Ahmed Salem 2009; 2013; Ould Jiddou 2004; Ould Saleck 2000; 2003; Villasante-de Beauvais 1998) claiming land (Leservoisier 2000; Ruf 1999), working with antislavery NGOs (Ould Ahmed Salem 2009; 2013), and adopting new economic roles (McDougall 1988; Ould Cheikh 1993). Urs Peter Ruf's (1999) work is a clear exception; his book provides a detailed look at Ḥarāṭīn life in the Tagant, including two chapters on gender. Meskerem Brhane (1997) also pays attention to gender in her dissertation on Ḥarāṭīn involvement in politics.

22. There is a rich history of scholarship focusing on Bīẓān women which has explored their roles in economic, family, and religious life, as well as their conceptions of gender, beauty, and sexuality (Cleaveland 2000; Fortier 2001; Frede 2014; Lesourd 2014; Simard 1996; Tauzin 1986; 2001).

23. Such articles often draw on sensationalist language that others their subjects. One article reports that girls are "brutally force-fed" and this practice is described as "the custom of funneling rich food into young girls like geese farmed for foie gras" (Haworth 2011). Another article's title "Surviving Violence in the Sahara: The Women of Mauritania" suggests that all Mauritanian women live in dire conditions, as does a woman quoted within it as saying "In Mauritania there are no rights for women at all" (Higgs 2017). While this may be her perception, it again furthers stereotypes that all Mauritanian women are oppressed. See also Duval Smith (2009).

24. This is similar to processes elsewhere in West Africa where religious leaders have critiqued women's participation in exchange as wasteful and unproductive (Buggenhagen 2012; Masquelier 2004).

25. Ruf's (1999) study on Ḥarāṭīn and slaves in the central Tagant region is a notable exception. He conducted extensive participant observation, although his research was broader in nature than mine, focusing on people throughout several communities. His project thus provides more breadth, while my focus on a single community provides more depth. Brhane (1997) also conducted participant observation with Ḥarāṭīn communities in the capital, although her work was more heavily based on a survey and interviews.

26. While my Ḥarāṭīn interlocutors frequently interacted with Bīẓān women and many knew them well, they were not core members of their social circles. I felt that spending too much time with Bīẓān would jeopardize my relationships with my Ḥarāṭīn interlocutors by giving the perception that I was neglecting their communities. However, I did form friendships with some Bīẓān women, including in the capital, and these relationships helped me gain a clearer sense of where their lives overlap with Ḥarāṭīn and where they do not. As discussed in the following chapter, Bīẓān themselves are not uniform so at times lower-status Bīẓān women's lives intersect in interesting ways with those of Ḥarāṭīn (thank you to E. Ann McDougall for reminding me of this). I try to point out these convergences throughout the text.

27. At the time of my research little was known about the structure of AQIM, its leadership, or its connections with Al-Qaeda elsewhere. Many people in Kankossa felt that the kidnappings that occurred were actually carried out by "bandits" who wanted to sell the foreigners to AQIM. See Thurston (2011) for a timeline of the kidnappings in the region beginning in 2007. The Inter-University Center for Terrorism Studies has also published seven annual reports on "Terrorism in North Africa and the Sahel": http://www.iucts.org/publications/reports/.

28. I am inspired by Paul Stoller's (2014) discussion of anthropology. He acknowledges the importance of furthering theory and method, but also argues for the value of bringing one's interlocutors to life and the power of anthropology to make their stories resonate with readers from diverse backgrounds. Many excellent students have also reminded me that they benefit from ethnographies that help them step into women's and men's worlds and life experiences.

1 From Black to Green: Changing Political Economy and Social Status in Kankossa

Kankossa is a sprawling town nestled between a large orange sand dune and a long, thin, year-round lake that was once a branch of the Senegal River. The town is primarily composed of one-story cement dwellings, many of which are comprised of a single room. Some of them are accompanied by *limbars*, semi-permanent tents whose tops are lined with layers of old cloth and plastic to keep out the rain and sun's heat. Such tents are reminiscent of the period before independence in 1960 when the majority of Bīẓān were nomadic. There are also increasing numbers of larger cement homes with multiple rooms, wide verandas, and stairways leading up to flat roofs. As with Toutou and Brahime's home, construction on these houses often occurs in stages and may stall for many months while the owner waits for sufficient funds to continue financing the project. Despite the varying stages of completion, these larger structures attest to the financial success of some of Kankossa's residents.

The oldest structures in Kankossa were built during the time of the *Institut des Fruits et Agrumes Coloniaux* (IFAC), or the Colonial Institute of Fruit and Citrus, a French agricultural research group that started a research station there in the 1950s.[1] An ambitious project, IFAC was part of growing colonial interest in agriculture; along with conducting research on dates, administrators aimed to produce this fruit for export. Despite its departure in the early 1970s, many remnants of IFAC remain. Men and women inhabit the rows of crumbling, pale yellow buildings along the lake that were once worker housing, and the police station occupies one of the larger buildings. On the edge of town, an abandoned factory still stands, and remnants of an irrigation system stretch across a now arid field. This is bordered by a runway of hard-packed earth and stone that is reminiscent of a time when planes landed here to deliver mail and supplies, although today it is mainly used by young men as a place to exercise in the late afternoon.

These remnants of IFAC recall a different era, as do its remaining date palms that line the lake. These trees represent a small percentage of what once grew there, since many have long been lost to the desert. Today, Kankossa residents reminisce about how the French projected movies outside on a still-standing

Former IFAC building on the edge of Kankossa. Photo by author.

concrete wall and attest to the former beauty of IFAC's buildings and abundant crops. One man said IFAC, at its heyday, was "*le petit Paris*" (little Paris), noting that, when the French were present, IFAC's grounds were cooler than elsewhere in Kankossa. This memory illustrates the nostalgia with which many Kankossa residents remember IFAC.

While these decaying structures remind residents of this failed and relatively short-lived experiment, they also index the profound changes the project engendered for some slave descendants. The formation of IFAC provided Ḥarāṭīn with wage labor, distance from their former masters, the possibility of land ownership, and, subsequently, the expanded potential for claiming improved social positions. While these were unintentional results of the project, they continue to affect the lives of Kankossa residents today. This example illustrates that the shaping of identity can be profoundly local; IFAC's existence gave Kankossa Ḥarāṭīn access to new sources of income and power many of their counterparts did not have elsewhere and thus helped some to improve their social positions. Similarly, other episodes in Mauritania's history, including severe drought and economic changes fostered by neoliberal reforms, impacted the organization of labor and social hierarchy as well as Ḥarāṭīn's abilities to maneuver in Kankossa and Mauritania more broadly.

One important outcome of these changes is the fact that some slave descendants in Kankossa today identify themselves not as Ḥarāṭīn but rather as Khaẓarīn. While this term is employed elsewhere in the country, especially in the east, its meanings have not been extensively explored nor is it particularly common.[2] In Kankossa, people use it in part to signify improved social rank, as its meaning suggests distance from slavery and an ability to claim other valued attributes, including wealth. That "Khaẓarīn" derives from the word for "blue" or "green" furthers these connotations. It does not literally suggest people are blue or green but rather implies dark skin and thus distinguishes the bearers from the blackness that is associated with slavery in this context. This term's widespread use in Kankossa reflects how this town's unique history has provided residents with increased potential for social mobility.

All of these episodes—IFAC, drought, the neoliberal era—illustrate how slaves and their descendants have long sought new opportunities that might better their lives and how varying political, economic, and social conditions helped or hindered their possibilities. These processes have not been perfectly equalizing; indeed, many Ḥarāṭīn, including in Kankossa, continue to live in extreme poverty and the very fact that Ḥarāṭīn have to assert their status at all demonstrates that discrimination endures in the Assaba region and beyond. But this history illustrates the fluidity and flexibility of social rank and how people's abilities to maneuver within social hierarchy may occur at surprising moments. This chapter complements the larger focus of the book—the dynamism of social rank and how Ḥarāṭīn navigate and negotiate it in contemporary Mauritania—by laying out the historic conditions that help make the contemporary moment in Kankossa a time of significant social fluidity.

This history suggests the events that are often flagged in African history as having the largest impact on the continent—including colonial conquest and independence—have not affected all sectors of the population equally and, in fact, have had minimal impact on some. As historian Richard Roberts has argued, it can be helpful to think of colonialism as a "fog" that flowed unevenly "over a highly variegated landscape. The fog lies deepest in the areas that open themselves most to its influence. The fog covers other zones thinly and bypasses some outcroppings altogether" (1996, 16). This is not to say these major events had no impact on people's social positions; the factors that have affected Ḥarāṭīn's abilities to alter and manipulate status are overlapping and complex. In the case of Kankossa, however, it was these other episodes—the formation of IFAC, drought conditions after independence, and neoliberal reforms—that primarily provided the Ḥarāṭīn with opportunities to modify configurations of social difference. Many of these episodes, especially drought conditions and neoliberal reforms, are not typically associated with increasing equality or the potential diminishment of poverty. Indeed, both of them had devastating effects on much of the country's population and economy, including Kankossa's. But they also resulted in increasing numbers of slaves gaining independence and expanded former slaves and their descendants' possibilities for autonomy and employment. Likewise, they significantly altered gender relations; as Mauritania became increasingly integrated into the capitalist economy, growing needs for cash and increasing male migration led to more women working outside of the home and serving as heads of household.

Conceptions of Work and Status in Precolonial Mauritania

To understand how social status and labor have changed over the past century in Mauritania it is necessary to consider earlier forms of social organization and productive activities. I provide a brief overview of precolonial Bīẓān society, paying special attention to how social hierarchy was asserted and reproduced through the kind of labor men and women conducted.[3] This overview is not to imply that precolonial Bīẓān society was static; rather, it is meant to provide a contrast with current social and economic life. Contemporary Bīẓān and Ḥarāṭīn discourse and ideologies surrounding social positioning sometimes draw upon or contrast with a version of a fixed past (Villasante-de Beauvais 1998, 37). Exploring some key characteristics of social organization in this era helps illuminate such assertions and gives context for more recent changes.

Bīẓān society has long been hierarchical and organized around a continuum on which Bīẓān elites and slaves occupied opposite ends. Social organization in this region was influenced by the Beni Ḥassān, a nomadic group of Arab origin, who had conquered the region by the seventeenth century. They introduced Hassaniya, the dialect of Arabic spoken today. They also introduced powerful emirates that had a hierarchical social organization based upon patrilineality and employed a tributary system. Freeborn men and women claimed Arab or Berber descent and were organized hierarchically.

The term Bīẓān, then, is an umbrella term for a variety of status groups. Within this category, the *ḥassān* and *zawāyā* were the most powerful, with *znāga* (tributary groups), *mu'allimīn* (craftspeople), and *īggāwen* (singers and musicians) falling below them.[4] Historically, the *ḥassān*, or warrior statute, exercised significant political and military influence and garnered prestige and authority by exhibiting strength and courage and adhering to a code of honor. The *zawāyā* wielded ideological and economic power; they were highly educated in Islam and controlled wells and pastures. Lower-status Bīẓān groups relied upon nobles for protection from raiders in exchange for tribute. Freeborn people accumulated slaves through raiding and trade, as well as from forming relationships with the black cultivators already inhabiting the region who might pay tribute or work for them in exchange for resources or protection.[5]

Table 1. An overview of social categories in Mauritania. More of the complexity of these categories will be explored throughout the book.

Social Category	General Meaning
Bīẓān	Umbrella term; generally used for people who claim Arab or Berber descent and who speak Hassaniya (dialect of Arabic); can also include their slave descendants
	Category "Bīẓān" includes various hierarchical groups:
	ḥassān: warrior statute; historically exercised political and military influence; often elites
	zawāyā: religious statute; historically exercised power by controlling religious knowledge; also had significant economic role; often elites
	znāga: tributary groups; provided payments to elite groups in exchange for protection
	mu'allimīn: craftspeople, including people who work with wood, metal, and henna
	iggāwen: singers and musicians
	'abīd: slaves
Ḥarāṭīn	Generally used for slave descendants of Bīẓān; often of black African descent, though there has been much intermixing between groups; speak Hassaniya and share many cultural practices with Bīẓān; sometimes called Bīẓān when term is used in a cultural sense
Khaẓarīn	Slave descendants of Bīẓān who claim generations of free status and other valued qualities, such as wealth, respectability, and education; they thus differentiate themselves from Ḥarāṭīn
Kwār	Umbrella term in Hassaniya for black Africans who do not share Bīẓān culture. These groups speak their own languages and have unique cultural practices, though there has been much cultural exchange within the region. They inhabit various parts of Mauritania and greater West Africa and include the **Halpulaar**, **Wolof**, and **Soninke**.

The term "Bīẓān," which derives from the Hassaniya word for "white," was used by people to distinguish themselves from neighboring black African ethnic groups; such difference was linked not simply to race but to status as defined by patrilineal descent (Webb 1995). Pre-colonial ideas on race were closely connected to ideas of lineage so the "absence of genealogical connections to Arab Muslim ancestors was what rendered one 'Black'" (Hall 2011a, 67–68). Colonial administrators were interested in categorizing and classifying the residents of their colonies and, in the process, often simplified the complexity of the racial and ethnic make-up of the population.[6] Administrators thus ignored the ways local people's conceptions of race might differ from Western understandings, that centuries of intermarriage between groups had blurred racial categories, and that black African groups in Mauritania and Ḥarāṭīn themselves had owned slaves (McDougall, Brhane, and Ruf 2003).[7] While most Mauritanians argue that slave lineage is a defining feature of the Ḥarāṭīn social category, some men and women argue not all Ḥarāṭīn have slave ancestry and people tell stories of various groups who are Ḥarāṭīn but were never enslaved, instead adopting Bīẓān language and customs by living beside them (Ruf 1999, 40, note 31; Brhane 1997, 57–58). Today in Kankossa, blackness is used as both a racial category and also a signifier of one's personal history and ancestors.

While race did play a part in identifying some Bīẓān slaves and blackness has long been stigmatized in the region (El Hamel 2013), slaves' (*'abīd*) and their descendants' (Ḥarāṭīn) positions were defined by various factors, including the kind of work they conducted. Slaves and dependents occupied the bottom of the social hierarchy, but, like free Bīẓān, they also occupied a variety of social positions, meaning they had the potential to alter their social rank. Slaves' statuses varied depending on their origins, with slaves who were born in their masters' homes often having higher rank than those who had been captured. The kind of work they conducted and the relationships they had with their masters also affected slaves' rights, privileges, and social positions, which ranged from "beasts of burden" to confidants (Ould Cheikh 1993, 184).

Slavery in Mauritania was never based upon a plantation system; slaves carried out a range of productive activities that came with varying responsibilities, and they thus exercised differing levels of power and autonomy. Some lived independently in farming communities and only saw their masters when they came to collect a portion of the harvest. Others worked in the caravan trade, sometimes traveling relatively unsupervised for months. Female slaves had unique possibilities for altering their social positions. Women who acted as wet nurses for Bīẓān might garner social capital since the free children they nursed were, in theory, considered their own children's siblings and were supposed to treat these women with respect (Brhane 1997, 75; Ruf 1999, 98).[8] Similarly, women who bore their masters' children were technically supposed to be manumitted at the time of their masters' deaths, although this was not always the case in practice (Ruf 1999; El Hamel 2013).

Given this range of experiences, coupled with the fact that many lower-status Bīẓān were also dependent upon elites, it was often challenging to disentangle the free from the slaves. Social difference between lower-status groups and nobles was partly articulated by the kind of work they conducted, and slaves' productive activities often overlapped with those of free dependents. Higher-status groups largely abstained from manual labor, which was a marker of low social status. Elite women's inactivity signified their femininity and social rank since their wealth allowed them to abstain from physical labor.[9] Slaves' or lower-status people's activities included more physically demanding work, such as farming, digging wells, tending herds and date palms, hunting, working in salt mines, cooking, and collecting gum arabic. That slaves labored for others indexed their dependence and low social rank, something that also defined the social positions of lower-status Bīẓān, including the muʿallimīn and iggāwen (Villasante-de Beauvais 2000, 289). Elite groups reinforced their social positions by redistributing wealth to poorer individuals and controlling land they would allow dependents to farm in return for a portion of the harvest. Lower status, then, whether freeborn or slave, was connected to having to ask others for resources and support in order to survive.

What largely separated slaves from other forms of dependents was their inability to form enduring kinship relations (Coquery-Vidrovitch 2007; Ruf 1999). Slaves were separated from relatives in their homelands, and they also lost "control over every crucial element of existence, starting with the capacity to control social relations (and therewith the capacity to define themselves relationally), the control over their sexuality, and especially the resulting family relations" (Lecocq and Hahonou 2015, 182). Given this, Meillassoux's argument that slaves are defined in the African context partly by "*the social incapacity of the slave to reproduce socially*—that is, the slave's juridical inability to become 'kin'" (1991, 35, emphasis his) resonates in Mauritania where *nasab*, or genealogy, was an essential part of people's identities and their positions in the hierarchy. Precolonial Bīẓān society was divided into political federations known as qabīla, which were organized geographically and varied in the amount of power and influence they wielded. Their freeborn members could ideally trace their descent to a common ancestor. Slaves and other dependents might be attached to qabīla, but their inabilities to claim genealogical ties with members prevented them from enjoying equal membership or exercising the political power that depended upon such links (Villasante-de Beauvais 1998, 215).

While other freeborn dependents might also not share ancestry with a qabīla's founder, slaves were further distinguished from these groups because their owners could control aspects of their relationships in general. Slaves could marry but needed their owners' permission to do so; their owners also retained the right to dissolve these marriages (Ali 2010). Children from such unions would become their owners' property. Their lack of access to kin relations kept slaves legal minors (Ruf 1999, 28). This was quite different from the znāga, who could marry and retain rights over their offspring. While slaves certainly formed close bonds with others, the fact that they or their children could be traded, sold, or relocated made it difficult to maintain or depend upon these relationships. Slaves' relationships with their masters might sometimes have been constituted in terms of kinship (Brhane 1997), but the fictive nature of these relationships excluded slaves from the rights and privileges their masters enjoyed.

None of these social categories were rigid, and people moved between them by reworking genealogies, shifting alliances, and contracting strategic marriages.

Whole groups could also shift their positions. For example, Ahl Sīdi Mahmūd, the dominant qabīla in the Assaba region where Kankossa is located, claimed both warrior and religious status; in the 1800s, they identified as ḥassān, while in the 1900s they identified primarily as zawāyā (Villasante-de Beauvais 1998). Likewise, individuals and groups could move in and out of dependent status as they gained or lost wealth and power. For example, historian E. Ann McDougall (1988; 2005) traces the life history of Hammody, the son of a former slave, who in the first half of the twentieth century became a wealthy merchant, wielded significant power in a qabīla, and owned slaves himself.

Slaves also could, and did, seek freedom in a variety of ways, including by fleeing, by buying their freedom, or by becoming highly knowledgeable of Islam. The transition to freedom was often gradual, with many Ḥarāṭīn renegotiating their relationships with their masters and remaining in some form of dependent relationship. Slaves could also improve their social standing and increase their autonomy by performing their duties well and gaining their masters' trust (El Hamel 2008; Hall 2011b), so while some slaves certainly sought freedom, others tried to improve their positions within the system of dependence rather than leaving it (Hall 2011b). Therefore, social rank in this region has long been fluid and the kind of labor people conducted was one way they maneuvered within it. Such fluidity continued into the colonial period, which provided new possibilities for shifting one's social rank, some of which continue to resonate in the present.

The Colonial Period and New Social and Economic Opportunities for Ḥarāṭīn

The colonial period impacted social hierarchy in Mauritania by straining elite resources and furthering slaves' possibilities for emancipation. French conquest of Mauritania—motivated by their desire to control and contain Morocco—was incremental; the conquest began in 1902 and largely finished by World War I, though they continued to face resistance in the north into the 1930s. During their rule, French administrators taxed livestock and agricultural harvests to fund the colonial enterprise. Payments had to be made in cash, which increased Mauritanians' needs for money, as did a growing demand for imported consumer goods (Bonte 1975, 73; Ould Cheikh and Bonte 1982; Ruf 1999, 184). Farmers and pastoralists found it difficult to garner the cash needed to pay such taxes, particularly during drought years. These policies thus contributed to the gradual diminishment of slavery as it became increasingly difficult for slave owners to care for their dependents. Subsequently, many former slaves began to migrate south seasonally to work in the peanut basin in Senegal. Changing laws about land ownership also made it possible for freed slaves to become landowners, since administrators granted land to those who worked it, rather than exclusively to Bīẓān collectivities. Despite this change, most land remained under control of the qabīlas, and many Ḥarāṭīn cultivators maintained ties with Bīẓān, giving them a portion of their harvests.

The fact that French administrators did not dramatically reform land ownership reflects colonial reticence to alter social organization more broadly in Mauritania. Despite pressures from the metropole to end slavery, colonial officials remained ambivalent about abolition, which they feared would negatively impact their political and economic interests.[10] French administrators did not want to upset delicate relations with Bīẓān leaders, many of whom owned slaves, or foster additional opposition to the colonial project. Slaves were also a major labor source and thus benefited the empire economically. So while the French did ban slavery in their colonies in 1848, they also made it possible for inhabitants to continue such practices. In the 1850s, for example, they issued a decree that gave French subjects the right to retain their slaves; only French citizens, inhabitants of land added before 1849, could not (Klein 1998, 28). The move toward abolition proceeded slowly in the following decades. In 1905, for example, colonial leaders issued a decree that abolished the enslavement, sale, exchange, and gift of persons but did not abolish slavery itself, meaning current slaves were not freed (136).[11] Abolition, then, had a limited impact on entrenched systems of slavery and inequality (Lecocq and Hahonou 2015, 187).

Slaves did experience increasing possibilities for agency and autonomy during the colonial era, but the results of these endeavors were often mixed. Across French West Africa, slaves could seek protection in *villages de liberté* (liberty villages) the French established in the late 1800s. These villages offered them shelter, land to cultivate, and employment, as well as emancipation, but they often failed to deliver on these promises. Many slaves were in fact returned to their masters, although slaves used various tactics to avoid such fates, claiming they did not know their masters' names or where they came from or hiding if their masters appeared (Clark 1995, 320). While some refugees did obtain freedom, these villages were largely intended to help French administrators solve their own labor problems; residents supplied colonizers with food, worked as soldiers and porters, and constructed roads and railroads (Bouche 1968; Clark 1995, 319). Workers were not always paid, and while inhabitants received land in theory, often there was not enough to go around or it was of poor quality. Even if they obtained land, residents often did not have the time to work it since they were responsible for conducting other tasks.

Similarly, Bīẓān hierarchies in the Assaba were only modified slightly during the colonial period and being "free" often did not look very different from being enslaved. The French gave slaves protection in colonial posts, including the Assaba's capital, Kiffa; however, many of Kiffa's "freed" residents maintained links with their former masters, becoming quasi-legal clients and continuing to cultivate land for them or other Bīẓān elites (Villasante-de Beauvais 1991,

194). Likewise, from 1907 to 1942 the leader of the Ahl Sīdi Mahmūd, one of the major qabīlas in the Assaba region, freed and then enrolled slaves in his qabīla. This strategy helped enlarge its economic role and power by expanding available laborers and increasing its membership, which helped assert its authority vis-à-vis the French, but it also kept many former slaves in dependent positions (Villasante-de Beauvais 1998, 89–90). Other former slaves sought protection among southern villages occupied by Halpulaar, one of the black African groups inhabiting the region; in some cases, these refugees integrated and became low-ranking Halpulaar themselves (Leservoisier 2012, 154). While technically free, many former slaves remained in dependent relationships, such as by farming for others. It is not necessarily the case that all slaves sought freedom; for some, dependence may have been desirable, helping them to survive economic hardships and maintain community (Rossi 2015). However, the limited options during this period kept many slave descendants who desired social mobility in low, and often exploited, social positions.

The French did provide Ḥarāṭīn with some expanded work possibilities, hiring them to work as soldiers, tend date palms, or labor on infrastructure projects (Brhane 1997; McDougall 1988; Ruf 1999). Such opportunities were gendered, with women having fewer economic possibilities than their male counterparts. Women worked for wages as servants or prostitutes or improved their status by becoming wives of colonial administrators or soldiers (Ruf 1999; McDougall 1988; Robertson and Klein 1983). Social tensions emerged as slaves and their descendants gained increasing autonomy; one way this manifested itself in the north was through accusations of bloodsucking in which generally Bīẓān accused Ḥarāṭīn, often women, of exercising dangerous magic over others. Levying such allegations against those who threatened to transgress racial and social orders was one way people tried to preserve the status quo in the face of great change (Pettigrew 2016).

Though these expanded possibilities for wages certainly provided some Ḥarāṭīn with new opportunities, their reach remained limited, and many former slaves and slave descendants found themselves in continuing dependent relationships. Colonial impact, however, was not uniform, and in Kankossa it provided slave descendants with more positive outcomes and opportunities than it did in many of the liberty villages or colonial posts. Fisherman from Mali had previously migrated seasonally to the area to fish in the lake, but a permanent settlement was first formed by the French when the colonial research institution, IFAC, established an agricultural research station in 1952. The organization was founded in France in 1942 with the aim of professionalizing scientific research in the colonies and producing agricultural products for export (Tourte 2005, 122). Its establishment was connected to France's growing interest in increasing its contributions to the colonies' economic development and in the role science could play in this pursuit; such aims led to an explosion of colonial organizations focusing on agricultural production (Glenzer 2002; Thompson and Adloff 1957, 336).[12]

IFAC's Kankossa research station was part of a larger colonial project that aimed to extend date palm production from the Atlantic coast to Chad. Mauritania was known for its dates—a sweet, fig-like fruit. In 1944, it produced 45,000 tons of dates yearly, and researchers hoped they would become a major cash crop (Tourte 2005, 497). Beyond producing dates for export, IFAC established the Kankossa station with the aim of investigating treatments for diseases that were ravaging date palms elsewhere in North Africa (Thompson and Adloff 1957, 336). At the height of its existence, IFAC consisted of a factory, storehouse, and worker housing as well as housing for the French and a laboratory (IFAC 1974). IFAC workers also constructed small dams, dug wells, built motorized pumps and irrigation systems, planted agricultural products that did well in close proximity to dates, and introduced a variety of date palm species from Morocco, Algeria, and California (Toupet 1959; Tourte 2005). By 1963, workers had planted 7,000 date palms and researchers were conducting a variety of scientific studies.[13] Two years later, IFAC had cultivated seventy hectors of land, opened a packaging plant for dates (Daddah 2003, 601), and obtained government permission to construct a runway to transport dates and supplies by air (Journal Officiel 1965, 151–52).

Most significant for the Ḥarāṭīn was their role at IFAC as manual laborers. When discussing potential workers for the institute in his 1952 feasibility study, Pierre Munier identified Ḥarāṭīn and other black African groups, referring to them as the "*population laborieuse*" (working population) and estimating they comprised 9,800 of the 11,800 male workers in the Assaba (1952, 66–67).[14] According to Munier, 2,000 of these laborers worked in herding, 3,000 in agriculture, 2,400 in date palmeries, and 1,100 as traders or in salaried positions, which left 3,300 available for employment (67). Munier reported that Ḥarāṭīn work as "servants in the nomadic camps, employees of the Administration, domestic manual laborers, but the vast majority take care of palmeries or participate in seasonal agriculture (millet)" (41). His assessment suggests some Assaba Ḥarāṭīn enjoyed a level of autonomy, particularly those who earned wages, although his findings also indicate that the bulk of Ḥarāṭīn remained in some form of dependent relationship—probably not owning land themselves.

Ḥarāṭīn experience with manual labor and tending palmeries made them ideal candidates for employment, and IFAC officials hired Ḥarāṭīn from Kiffa and surrounding villages to work at the station. Relatives of these early employees remember IFAC workers as being primarily Ḥarāṭīn with a few Bīẓān. The work was not easy; in the first few years, laborers readied the area for an irrigation system, planted windbreaks, leveled land, and built roads, along with planting

Remaining IFAC building near Kankossa's lake. Photo by author.

and tending thousands of date palms (IFAC 1957). Many workers eventually relocated their families to Kankossa to live in the worker housing the French provided. Selma, the Ḥarāṭīn wife of an IFAC employee, noted that the women were responsible for cooking and other household tasks, and she remembered the French testing her food. This memory suggests French supervisors kept close watch over workers' family lives, as does the fact that workers were only supposed to house their immediate families, a rule the French supposedly instituted to minimize the number of people administrators had to feed.[15]

While in some ways performing low-status work such as manual labor at IFAC reproduced Ḥarāṭīn's low social rank, their involvement in the institute gave them possibilities for getting ahead, such as earning income.[16] Since wage labor was limited in the Assaba, the salaries IFAC provided were attractive. Workers were given food and clothing and were paid monthly; Selma remembers her husband receiving 6,000 CFA a month. While this may be more than he was actually paid—the cost of a cow in 1958 in the Senegal River Valley was 9,000 CFA (Ould Cheikh and Bonte 1982, 39)—her recollection of this substantial sum suggests employees were paid fair wages or at least more than they might have earned elsewhere.[17] Worker's salaries allowed them to participate in the cash economy, obtaining the imported goods that were increasingly central to status and social reproduction. Workers' incomes also allowed some to send their children to secondary school in Kiffa. Today, their descendants work as teachers, doctors, traders, and development workers; the success of many is partially connected to the opportunities their parents had as IFAC employees.

To some extent, such economic gains were limited to men. Administrators did not, for example, hire Ḥarāṭīn women to help with manual labor despite the fact that many lower-status women participated heavily in agricultural activities elsewhere. IFAC officials thus imposed a particular understanding of gender roles, one in which women were primarily occupied with domestic tasks. This practice constrained women's potential earnings, but it also associated them with the kind of elite femininity characterized by abstention from manual labor or working for others. Slave descendants thus had the possibility of claiming new forms of femininity to which their counterparts elsewhere might not have had access.

Many Kankossa women did not ultimately remain at home. Selma, for example, sold vegetables in the market, and her husband's income provided her with the necessary start-up capital. Other women gardened. Such pursuits allowed women to potentially expand their resources, and they also gave lower-status women the possibility of engaging in independent labor, which further differentiated them from slaves. IFAC's advantages, then, were not limited to its male employees but extended to at least some of their female relatives as well.

While many of IFAC's early workers and their families were likely already free, this work also provided them with geographic distance from their former masters and new possibilities for autonomy. Anthropologist Mariella Villasante-de Beauvais notes that relations between individuals and groups in Bīẓān society are often reinforced through residential proximity, along with marriage alliances, genealogical connections, and common religious membership (1998, 45). Similarly, living near their masters in Mali limited slaves' abilities to free themselves or to avoid expectations for comportment and behavior that reinforced their lower status (de Bruijn and Pelckmans 2005). This would have also been true in Mauritania; recall how many of Kiffa's Ḥarāṭīn maintained some form of dependent relationship with their former masters. Geographic proximity could also make accumulation difficult for slave descendants since their former owners might claim their possessions and collect portions of their harvests. The high migration rates of slaves and Ḥarāṭīn to urban areas in the twentieth century were thus partly due to their attempts to escape their masters' or former masters' fields of influence.

Relocating to IFAC provided Ḥarāṭīn with distance from their former masters, helping to weaken or sever their dependence on them. One Ḥarāṭīn man, for example, noted that before his father worked at IFAC he had "been in a camp," and salaried work was a new opportunity for him. Certainly not all IFAC workers would have left behind dependent relationships but, as this man's story illustrates, working for IFAC provided some with the possibility of greater control over their own resources. Such independence was reinforced by IFAC workers' lack of extensive participation in their own agricultural activities, which meant they did not produce harvests their masters might claim. The French policy that dictated workers could only house immediate family members also would have discouraged Bīẓān from spending significant time with their former slaves. Another advantage of life in Kankossa was that, as a new town inhabited mainly by slave descendants, the rules of social comportment would not have been as strict as in other more established areas with more sizeable elite populations.[18]

Working at IFAC also provided Ḥarāṭīn with the possibility of forming new kinds of community. As detailed above, slaves and Ḥarāṭīn's lack of genealogical connections with other qabīla members made it difficult for them to claim equal positions to Bīẓān. Their masters' ability to control some aspects of slaves' kin relationships also helped maintain their lower social rank. Just as urban areas provided Ḥarāṭīn with new means of belonging outside of the qabīla, workers in Kankossa created their own communities, bringing family members to join them and encouraging male relatives elsewhere to seek employment at the institute. Many of these relatives did end up working for IFAC and, as time passed, these communities expanded, with some workers or their children intermarrying with other IFAC families.

These networks challenge ideas that portray wage labor as a break from older patterns of accumulation and security. For example, anthropologist Urs Peter Ruf has noted, "To go out and look for a job to rely on is an astonishing biographic pattern if evoked by a member of a society in which the corollary of social security first and foremost is achieved through family and affiliate networks" (1999, 84). The Kankossa example demonstrates, however, that getting a job did not necessitate undermining such networks; rather, it helped reinforce them for Ḥarāṭīn since recruitment at least in part drew upon workers' relatives. By inviting relatives to join them and through marriage with members of other IFAC families, Ḥarāṭīn leveraged their knowledge of employment to build their own social networks. They thus nurtured older social ties and created new ones. These kin networks, which now stretch back several generations, indexed their free status. They also continued to provide kin-based social security since relatives could help support each other in times of hardship.

Finally, while new French laws that provided the possibility of land ownership to those who worked it were not widely enforced, such rulings had more meaning in towns like Kankossa that were directly under the purview of French administrators. The security the French provided eased residents' transitions to becoming landowners. Some IFAC employees or their families had gardens or erected homes of their own outside of the worker housing, thus vivifying the land. After IFAC closed, some workers remained in Kankossa and continued to inhabit this land. The spatial composition of the town reflects this history, since many descendants of IFAC workers occupy one of the central neighborhoods not far from IFAC. These residents describe their land acquisition as a simple process, which required registering it with the local government for a small fee. IFAC workers' relation to land contrasts with the situation of former slaves elsewhere; in 1960, for example, few Ḥarāṭīn who settled along the Senegal River owned land themselves. Forty-eight percent paid usage fees to Bīẓān, 8 percent rented the land from Halpulaar, and only 14 percent did not pay any rent, which implies that they owned the land or at least had more control over it (Vergara 1979).[19]

Modern-day Kankossa Ḥarāṭīn have enjoyed decades of autonomy, relative wealth, and distance from their masters. This is not to imply IFAC was a benevolent French project designed to help Ḥarāṭīn. As was the case with the liberty villages and colonial officials' position on abolition in Mauritania, the project had the institute's interests in mind, and IFAC administrators likely viewed the Ḥarāṭīn as a source of inexpensive but experienced labor. It is also probable that IFAC workers did not enjoy close relationships with the French, who most likely did not view them as social equals.[20] The workers are largely absent from the station's reports; while one report discusses interns who have come from throughout Mauritania and present-day Mali to train to become part of the "agricultural elite," (IFAC 1957, 57), there are few mentions of IFAC workers, suggesting they were not considered particularly valuable.

The changes IFAC did engender cannot be unilaterally attributed to the institution; it may have been especially bold or entrepreneurial workers or individuals who had already severed ties with their masters who took advantage of this opportunity. Even still, IFAC is an example of how new opportunities arose for Ḥarāṭīn during the colonial period and how particular conditions help make social change possible. These changes facilitated increased social fluidity in which Ḥarāṭīn could assert new possibilities of social worth. Women's and men's abilities to navigate social rank in contemporary Kankossa are impacted by conditions put in place under IFAC; descendants of early employees continue to benefit from land ownership and their longstanding social connections in this community.

Drought, Structural Adjustment, and Women's Shifting Roles and Responsibilities

IFAC was not long-lived. In 1963 the groundwater in Kankossa began to diminish, and when this persisted under growing drought conditions, the station closed in 1972 (Tourte 2005, 167). One man told me it shut down because Kankossa residents allowed their animals to eat its crops, which likely was also linked to the drought. Its closure also corresponded with Moktar Ould Daddah's, the nation's first president, increasing attempts to adopt nationalistic policies, spurred by protests in 1968, which contested France's continuing major role in the economy (Pazzanita 1999, 47). Subsequently, in the early 1970s, Ould Daddah withdrew from the CFA zone and nationalized the foreign-owned iron ore mining company. Such policies, coupled with severe drought, made it difficult for the institute to continue its operations. The drought that contributed to IFAC's departure would also have dramatic consequences for the country's economy and social organization, cementing many of the changes that had begun during the colonial period. In the Assaba, it would advance Ḥarāṭīn's possibilities, including men's and women's pursuit of wage labor and women's increasing participation in the workplace.

The drought began in 1968 and continued through the mid-1970s. It had a devastating effect on Mauritania's agriculture and pastoral industries in which over 80 percent of men and women labored (Ould-Mey 1996, 82). Between 1970 and 1974 the number of cattle in the country diminished by half and cattle prices fell dramatically (Pitte 1975; Vergara 1979). With cattle export a major means of accumulation, the drought dramatically impacted Bīẓān livelihoods. Similarly, while the country's total grain yield in a normal year could reach 100,000 tons, in 1972 it had fallen to 15,000 tons (Pitte 1975, 650). Throughout the drought, Kankossa consistently received more rain than the northern Assaba (Vermeer 1981, 286–87), but, even so, residents remember that one year the lake dried up. As the drought worsened, Mauritanians' growing reliance on imported goods, including food aid, resulted in new patterns of consumption that further integrated the country into the capitalist economy and continued to increase reliance on cash.

The devastating effects of the drought further transformed systems of production from agriculture and pastoralist to wage labor, which provided Ḥarāṭīn with continued possibilities for emancipation. As it became increasingly difficult to maintain a pastoral way of life, many nomads were left with no choice but to become sedentary. While two-thirds of Mauritanians were nomadic at independence in 1960, only 36 percent of the population continued this lifestyle by 1976 and the number continued to diminish over the decades that followed (Ould Cheikh and Bonte 1982, 32–33; Ould Cheikh and Ould Al-Barra 1996). The economic strain Bīẓān faced from losing their herds was compounded by the newly independent state's attempts to impose a new government order modeled off of the French system of administration (Bennoune 1978). Such policies further diminished Bīẓān authority by eroding Bīẓān military power and favoring administrators educated in the French system, rather than the religious system, while supporting foreign economic interests.

Ḥarāṭīn and other lower-status groups struggled during this period; as with many ecological disasters, the drought's effects impacted the poor first. But as increasing numbers of income generating activities flourished and Mauritania became more embedded in the global market economy, Ḥarāṭīn also had new avenues for claiming improved social rank, such as by emphasizing achieved attributes like wealth. As Bīẓān wealth diminished, it became difficult for many elites to maintain their dependents and, subsequently, large numbers of slaves moved to cities looking for work and gaining de facto emancipation in the process (McDougall 1988, 374). People from all social groups relocated to urban areas; Nouakchott's population grew from 5,807 in 1962 to 134,000 by 1977 (Ould-Mey 1996, 82). Growing cities in Mauritania and Senegal provided slaves and Ḥarāṭīn with new possibilities for employment as maids, butchers, bakers, and manual laborers—jobs higher-status individuals avoided if possible (Bonte 1975, 78; Ould Cheikh 1993). Their wages allowed some Ḥarāṭīn to obtain wealth for themselves in the form of imported goods, land, and livestock—items formerly monopolized by elite Bīẓān. While this rapid growth strained resources in cities and towns, the fact that IFAC employees were already settled in Kankossa largely protected their claims to land, as did the French presence throughout much of the drought. They also escaped some of the hardships Ḥarāṭīn who depended on agriculture faced, such as their Bīẓān counterparts pushing cultivators to give them larger portions of their harvests (Brhane 1997, 268).

The departure of IFAC, along with the drought's consequences and growing needs for cash, meant many men left Kankossa to seek work elsewhere. In the 1970s, the onset of the construction of the Road of Hope, a paved two-lane highway that would eventually link Kiffa and Nouakchott, accelerated this process. Some women also migrated to Nouakchott seeking paid labor for themselves, often as domestic workers (McDougall 2015, 264), but many women remained behind and served as de facto heads of household. Some started small businesses since they were unable to depend on their husbands' support. They sold couscous or set up tables in the market selling vegetables or foodstuffs, which women were also doing elsewhere in the country, including Nouakchott (Tauzin 2001, 203–4). As one Mauritanian woman who worked in development in Nouakchott said:

> [Women] need to work because men left, most of them left—if I think of Kankossa, if I think of in the villages. They left; they went into the city. And most of the time what they bring back is just what they are going to use themselves, mostly to show off. And [men] are not the head of household [as they were] traditionally. Women need to work because of poverty, mostly because of the drought. The drought brought . . . if I think of my [home town] there was milk, millet all year long. So you see, it was easy cooking. . . . Nowadays people pay for everything they are getting. From health to education to basic needs.

The increasing integration into the capitalist economy meant people now "pay for everything they are getting." These growing needs for cash and desires for consumer goods also propelled women to work. As one Kankosa market trader put it, "The problems of the family have become many. [We need] clothes, shoes, notebooks, pens, soap, Omo [laundry detergent], things you don't even know what they are." Women's abilities to earn wealth and their expanded roles in social reproduction and the economy have created tensions surrounding men's and women's social positions as women increasingly fulfill roles men did in the past.

Increasingly, goods purchased with cash became symbols of social status, further entangling social rank and monetary wealth. For example, increasing differentiation between rich and poor areas in Nouakchott illustrated "the new social stratification, based more and more on income" although tribal and familial solidarity also continued to matter (Ould-Mey 1996, 210). As imported goods came to symbolize wealth and engagement with the global economy, these products and cash gradually replaced locally-produced goods women exchanged in family ceremonies.[21] Such changes also increased women's need for money.

In the decades following the drought, the government's implementation of structural adjustment programs (SAPs) and neoliberal policies furthered these shifts, expanding women's increasing participation in microenterprises and male migration. As they did elsewhere on the continent, these policies aimed to stimulate economic growth by encouraging countries' further integration into the free market system, but they often had unintended negative consequences.[22] Mauritania adopted these reforms in the mid-1980s to help stimulate its economy, which had suffered from its involvement in a conflict over the Western Sahara, declining prices of its major export iron ore, lingering effects of the drought, and government instability (Ould-Mey 1996). In exchange for loans and aid, these plans devalued the currency, privatized public enterprises, promoted private investment, and liberalized trade and prices.[23] After their implementation, Mauritania experienced a declining GDP, increasing prices along with diminishing purchasing power, growing gaps between the rich and poor, and rising unemployment; by the early 1990s, it had fallen in its World Bank classification to a low income country (Ould-Mey 1996, 191–92; Seddon 1996).

As with the drought, continued impoverishment across social groups furthered the diminishment of slavery; it made it difficult for slaveholders to support their dependents. This leveling came in tandem with the government's formal abolition of slavery in 1981 and subsequent land and political reforms that aimed to improve the rights of lower-status groups. While these measures were not evenly enforced, they did provide slaves and Ḥarāṭīn with a legal framework for claiming rights and further eroded the influence of traditional elites.

As it moved into the 1990s, Mauritania faced the continued contraction of the public sector, deterioration of agricultural and pastoral activities, and devaluation of its currency whose purchasing power diminished by 75 percent (Simard

1996, 59). Women in Kankossa felt, and continue to feel, the effects of these processes and remember how money used to go further. As one trader noted:

> Money was [worth] more in the past than today. With regards to a family, 500 MRO, 1,000 MRO would provide for the biggest family in existence. Today, 2,000, 3,000 will not feed the biggest family. In the past a kilo of meat was 200 MRO. A kilo of rice was 50 MRO. In comparison, today a kilo of meat is 800 MRO, 1,000 MRO... Rice is 200 MRO. Oil is 500 MRO. 2,000 cannot provide for a big family.[24]

The deteriorating economy made it increasingly necessary for women to work outside of the home, as did their growing numbers of dependents as many young people, even the educated, were unable to get jobs. As the number of available public sector jobs decreased, many women and men turned to microenterprises, which in turn made such work increasingly competitive.[25]

As part of its initiatives to encourage private enterprises, the government supported such processes. In the late 1980s it instituted an employment policy that worked to revitalize and promote the formation of small businesses by offering improved access to credit, supply, and marketing (Ould-Mey 1996, 203). By 1988, the informal sector was growing faster nationally than other employment sectors, and between 1980 and 1988 the number of participants in it increased by 8.5 percent yearly (Seddon 1996, 205).[26] NGOs, whose presence in Mauritania expanded significantly in the late 1980s and 1990s, supported similar programs. In the Assaba in the early 1990s, NGOs promoted "private initiative and market relations" by providing trainings and loans to entrepreneurs, thus further integrating them into the market economy (Ould-Mey 1996, 137–45). In Kankossa, some of these NGO initiatives focused on women, and the number of female market traders also increased, fueled in part by continued male migration.

These programs pushed workers to accumulate resources on their own rather than relying on the government and emphasized the value of men and women working for themselves—a focus that remains in the present.[27] While these neoliberal policies increased poverty throughout Mauritania, their emphasis on the worth of productive labor contrasted with precolonial ideologies that valued abstention from work, particularly manual labor. Such ideas challenged the notion that being an active worker signified low social status, suggesting instead that participation in labor was a key part of modern sensibilities and success. While older ideologies endure, this favorable valuing of work continues to resonate today, providing Ḥarāṭīn with a positive ideology surrounding income generation they can use to assert their social worth and challenge older notions of hierarchy; labor becomes a path to higher social status, not a marker of enslavement.

Some of the outcomes of these neoliberal reforms and the preceding drought overlapped with those of IFAC. They all increased men and women's reliance on cash, imported goods, and wage labor. They also all provided some Ḥarāṭīn with new social and economic possibilities, diminishing the prevalence of slavery and increasing the importance of wealth in social worth. During this period, new possibilities for claiming social rank emerged in which social strata "form according to *monetary wealth* while the statutory groups remain based on *genealogic origins*" (Villasante-de Beauvais 1998, 136 [emphasis hers]). Today Ḥarāṭīn continue to emphasize wealth as an important marker of social rank.

While structural adjustment programs and neoliberal reforms have been heavily critiqued in Africa and elsewhere, this example suggests their emphasis on individual accumulation and labor expanded Ḥarāṭīn's possibilities for asserting social worth. SAP's and neoliberal reforms did not have this effect everywhere, and certainly were detrimental to many social groups, including the Ḥarāṭīn; however, just because they had negative consequences does not mean their other, often unintentional, effects should be ignored. As I explore further in the following chapter, we should analyze how these reforms impacted different groups and how people acted within these constraints, often asserting more agency than critics of these reforms ascribe to them. These programs did expand some Ḥarāṭīns' possibilities for social maneuvering, and Ḥarāṭīn in Kankossa today draw upon them in asserting and reshaping their social rank and in presenting alternatives to elite social values.

From Black to Green: New Categories of Belonging in Kankossa

As the opportunities IFAC offered slave descendants and the broader shifts in the political economy indicate, the realities of many slaves and their descendants altered greatly over the past century. While this impacted their livelihoods, it also raised questions of how to define themselves. In the years following independence, Hassaniya-speaking slave descendants throughout Mauritania debated this question; some felt they comprised a unique ethnic group while others contended that they were actually Bīẓān. The best known proponent of the former view is the Ḥarāṭīn political party, *el Hor* (freedom), which formed in the late 1970s to help its constituents gain increased rights and recognition, making slavery a political issue for the first time in the newly independent nation.[28] Party leaders promised to fight against the economic exploitation of Ḥarāṭīn, called for a massive education movement, pledged to help Ḥarāṭīn gain access to local and national political posts, and asserted Ḥarāṭīn property and marriage rights. They premised their platform on the idea that the Ḥarāṭīn were a unified, autonomous group, separate from Bīẓān. Its charter promised el Hor would "fight to maintain the cultural specificity of Ḥarāṭīn," (El Hor [1978] 2004, 187) which it connected to the groups' black African origins and its adoption of Arab-Berber culture, as well as its folklore, musical instruments, and dance. Ultimately, their activities prompted the government's abolition of slavery, as well as reforms in education and land tenure.

El Hor's popularity diminished over the following decades with members forming other political parties and some leaders being incorporated into the government. But even before it disbanded, no consensus was reached among el Hor members or slave descendants in general about how they should define themselves. Some slave descendants rejected the idea of an autonomous ethnic group, instead emphasizing the qabīla as the main unit of organization. They claimed a Bīẓān identity based upon their common language and aspects of shared culture and argued that they could assimilate with the Bīẓān or, in fact, already had. Some former slaves employed the term "Bīẓān" in this sense—not to refer to populations of Arab or Berber descent but as a term that encompassed all native Hassaniya speakers, marking membership in a shared cultural category (Taine-Cheikh 1989). Critics of this position argued an assimilationist stance was dangerous, contending that the qabīla discriminated against Ḥarāṭīn since they could not claim the shared agnatic descent that power within it was based upon.

The government supported the assimilationist position, encouraging slave descendants of Bīẓān to identify as Bīẓān and even eliminating the distinction between Bīẓān and Ḥarāṭīn in its 1988 census (Brhane 1997, 18). Its position was linked to Arabization policies, which emphasized the country's Arab heritage and pushed for education to occur in Arabic. Such policies found support amongst some political leaders in the years following independence (Moore 1965) and intensified in the late 1980s. Pursuing Arabization occurred to the detriment of the sizable non-Hassaniya speaking population, many of whom spoke French and thus had easier access to government employment in the colonial period and following independence. Arabization policies exasperated tensions between Hassaniya-speakers and other ethnic groups and contributed to violent conflict in the late 1980s that resulted in the expulsion of tens of thousands of Senegalese citizens from Mauritania and Hassaniya-speakers from Senegal, as well as many deaths (Stewart 1989). The state's support of a more inclusive Bīẓān identity also helped government officials push for a combined Bīẓān-Ḥarāṭīn voting block in an attempt to weaken the *Front de Liberation des Africans de Mauritanie* (FLAM), a Halpulaar party whose power expanded in the 1980s (McDougall 2010; Ould Ahmed Salem 2009). Government officials aimed to prevent Ḥarāṭīn from drawing on race as an attribute they shared with black African groups like the Halpulaar, since such coalitions threatened Bīẓān political domination.

Proponents of these two stances—those wanting a Ḥarāṭīn ethnic group and those favoring assimilation with Bīẓān—sometimes had overlapping views and their discourse was full of ambiguities (Ruf 1999, 277). Identity on the ground is often much less polarized than in national discourse, with the same person sometimes identifying as a member of Bīẓān society while at other times identifying as Ḥarāṭīn (McDougall 2005; Ruf 1999, 277). Furthermore, the meaning of "Ḥarāṭīn" itself is not homogenous throughout West and North Africa (Rossi 2015, 316).

In contemporary Kankossa, slave descendants claim a variety of forms of belonging, with the same women and men sometimes defining themselves differently depending on the context. When describing social categories, one female trader noted "there are Halpulaar, there are Bīẓān. But, you see, *Bīẓān who are not Ḥarāṭīn*, they don't sell vegetables" (emphasis mine). By singling out "Bīẓān who are not Ḥarāṭīn" this woman indicates that the Bīẓān category encompasses Ḥarāṭīn, but also that Ḥarāṭīn remain distinct within it, in this case because they perform an activity Bīẓān avoid. Her comments illustrate how the two viewpoints—assimilationist and autonomous ethnic group—are not necessarily mutually exclusive.

The basic identity choices this woman named are consistent with other scholars' observations of slave descendants (e.g., Brhane 1997; Ruf 1999). However, when I began asking women in Kankossa about their *ʿunṣur* (origin, ethnicity), I was surprised to find many responded not that they were Bīẓān or Ḥarāṭīn but rather that they were Khaẓarīn. *Khaẓar* in Hassaniya refers to colors that are dark (blue, green, dark brown, blackish), but not black (*'kḥal*) (Taine-Cheikh 1989, 102). One of my research assistants explained that, like most words for colors in Hassaniya (e.g., *ḥamara* [red] or *'ṣfar* [yellow]), this term is associated with a particular color of sand—a dark, but not black sand—he said he could show me in his nearby village. This term has long been used in Mauritania, appearing at least as early as 1936 when a colonial document referred to land being given to a "Khadara clan" in the Assaba region (Villasante-de Beauvais 1991, 194).[29] However, while present throughout the country, its use appears to be limited, particularly in the west, and scholars have not extensively explored it. Analyzing its usage in Kankossa provides insight into how some slave descendants are conceptualizing and actualizing their changing social conditions.

As its derivation suggests, at times in Kankossa, "Khaẓarīn" is used in the sense of color and can designate dark-skinned people regardless of ethnicity or linguistic identity, a use that has been noted elsewhere (Taine-Cheikh 1989).[30] For example, one woman described a Côte d'Ivorian man who visited Kankossa as "'kḥal [black]! He was khaẓarī, 'kḥal!" This term is also used in a more ethnic sense to designate all black Hassaniya speakers—people who might otherwise be referred to as Ḥarāṭīn. One woman, for example, explained this term to me by pointing to her dark skin, saying Bīẓān and Khaẓarīn "are not the same. Right? Our hair is not the same. You see their hair is like your hair. Right?" She paused and pointed to her tongue, implying language. "But that is the same." For her, Khaẓarīn are separated from Bīẓān by their skin color and other physical traits, but their common language connects them. This use of the term suggests some Khaẓarīn are claiming both similarity with and difference from Bīẓān. When employed in this way, "Khaẓarīn" may also be a euphemism for Ḥarāṭīn, avoiding the latter term's connections with slavery.[31]

Most commonly, however, Kankossa residents use "Khaẓarīn" to refer to slave descendants whose status they describe as being above that of Ḥarāṭīn, a use others have observed elsewhere in Mauritania (McDougall 2015; Ould Ahmed Salem 2009; Ould Jiddou 2004; Villasante-de Beauvais 1997). In her study of Ḥarāṭīn in Nouakchott, Brhane noted this term is used in both western and eastern Mauritania, though it has different meanings. While in the west it is used as a euphemism for Ḥarāṭīn, in the east, which includes Kankossa, it designates slave descendants who have been freed for several generations and thus enjoy distance from slave lineage (Brhane 1997, 77–78). Kankossa men and women do use it to signify distance from slave lineage, but they also take it further, using it to emphasize particular valued attributes. As Mahmoud, a Ḥarāṭīn man, noted:

> What's the meaning of Khaẓarīn? Its meaning is . . . some of those [people were] Ḥarāṭīn from a long time ago, but after they became a *khīma kabīr* [big tent, important family]. They came to have money. They had respect. Society came to valorize them. Some of them themselves even had slaves living with them. Because he has money, he has all of that. It became that he had a value in his tribe, a value in his family . . . That's the meaning of Khaẓarīn. That's Khaẓarīn's real meaning. That a Ḥarāṭīn gets wealth and succeeded and after this he is no longer a slave and no longer works for people. It's become that there is a social class above the Ḥarāṭīn a little, but also they aren't yet Bīẓān. They aren't Bīẓān, because their skin is still black.

When employed in this way, Khaẓarīn refers to people who can claim markers of social worth that draw both on older valued characteristics—wealth and respect—and also new ones—long held freedom and education. This understanding of Khaẓarīn celebrates generations of free status, thus keeping genealogy—albeit a different form than connections to the qabīla—central to social rank. But it also illustrates how people are identifying achieved attributes as sources of social difference, including wealth, participation in independent labor, and the garnering of respect. The emphasis of such qualities coincides with shifts in the political economy over the last century that made attributes like wealth and education increasingly important to survival and success.[32]

Although this term is also employed elsewhere in Mauritania, its widespread use in Kankossa reflects the unique trajectories and opportunities of slave descendants there. The decades of freedom and access to land and wages IFAC employees enjoyed contribute to their abilities to claim attributes such as prolonged freedom and material wealth that enable them to draw on these new forms of classification. This suggests that, while colonial administrators often simplified the complexity of the population's racial and ethnic composition, their programs contributed in some cases to social fluidity. While not all those in Kankossa who identify as Khaẓarīn trace their ancestry to IFAC workers, and certainly the term's popularity is not only attributable to this history, that it is widely used suggests Ḥarāṭīn have been able to assert social rank there in ways their counterparts have not always been able to elsewhere. It illustrates how the history of a place impacts how residents understand and assert social status, suggesting that local histories can provide important insight into the conditions that support or limit men and women's abilities to bring about social change.

While claiming to be Khaẓarīn highlights the importance of achieved attributes, the use of this term does not erase hierarchy. Mahmoud notes that while Khaẓarīn occupy a status above Ḥarāṭīn, "They aren't yet Bīẓān." He implies an enduring hierarchy in which Bīẓān are above Ḥarāṭīn and Khaẓarīn, with Khaẓarīn being closer to achieving this higher status. That Khaẓarīn remain "below" Bīẓān is a view shared by others; one woman suggested that many, perhaps all, Khaẓarīn are not rich, noting "Bīẓān are rich, they have money . . . and Khaẓarīn, they want money." Like Mahmoud, she distinguishes between Bīẓān and Khaẓarīn, but she does not indicate that Khaẓarīn necessarily occupy a privileged social position. Mahmoud's claim that Khaẓarīn are "not yet Bīẓān" implies that becoming Bīẓān may be an aspiration for some members of this group. This view, however, is not universal and other people who claim to be Khaẓarīn proudly boast about their social positions.

Distinguishing between Khaẓarīn and Ḥarāṭīn in this way can have serious consequences. For example, a person's distance from slavery is sometimes taken into account during marriage negotiations; one woman told me a young man who was having difficulty contracting a marriage was of slave descent. While presumably all people who claim to be Ḥarāṭīn or Khaẓarīn in Kankossa have slavery in their family histories, her implication was that some people are closer to it than others. Marriage, then, is a moment when people are differentiated, as is also true for Bīẓān who favor endogamous marriages, such as marrying within their qabīla, as well as hypergamy for women, practices that continue to reinforce social difference (Villasante-de Beauvais 1998, 249). This is similar to the experiences of other lower-status groups, including the znāga. While some znāga men have made gains in material wealth and political power in their qabīlas due to their earnings as international migrants, they remain unable to marry Bīẓān women of a non-tributary status (Freire 2014).

The use of the term Khaẓarīn, then, both challenges and reinforces social hierarchy. On the one hand, it expands existing notions of social difference and confirms slave descendants' abilities to claim social value. On the other hand, it reproduces hierarchy by positioning Khaẓarīn above Ḥarāṭīn while also maintaining Bīẓān's superior position. Khaẓarīn's etymology reflects this ambiguity. By categorizing people as blue or green, in effect dark, but not black, it distances them from associations with slavery. Blackness has long had connotations with slavery and lower social rank in the region (El Hamel 2013). In Hassaniya the term *sūdān*, or "blacks," refers to both slaves and slave descendants (Ḥarāṭīn) and thus associates these groups with blackness (Ruf 1999, 38–39). As discussed earlier, racial categories do not have the same meaning in Mauritania as in the United States. For example, phenotype is often a poor indicator of race or ethnicity in Mauritania, particularly given the long history of intermixing due to intermarriage and slaves bearing their masters' children (Brhane 1997; Cleaveland 2000; Leservoisier 2012; Ould Jiddou 2004; Ruf 1999).

Being "black" in this context, then, has less to do with skin color and more to do with one's genealogy and personal history with slavery.[33] I was reminded of the disconnect between physical appearance and social category when I interviewed a light-skinned female shopkeeper to get a Bīẓān perspective on women's work, only to have her tell me that she was "black" and Ḥarāṭīn. While Khaẓarīn are obviously not literally green or blue, their use of this term differentiates them from blackness and the connotations of slavery that come with it and thus indexes their freedom and higher status. However, this term still implies "nonwhite" and therefore continues to distinguish Khaẓarīn from their "white" Bīẓān counterparts—thus reproducing a hierarchy in which Bīẓān occupy the highest positions. Mahmoud, after all, notes that Khaẓarīn are not yet Bīẓān because their skin remains black. His contention suggests an increased racialization of social categories in this context.

Mahmoud's vision is far from the idea of unity and equality between slave descendants the party of el Hor called for. In its 1978 charter, it criticized Ḥarāṭīn for forming their own social ranks of "Khadaras, freed people, and slaves," suggesting this term's use reproduces social hierarchy ([1978] 2004, 187). Similarly, Baba Ould Jiddou discusses the potential danger of this category, accusing Bīẓān of cultivating a sense of superiority in Khaẓarīn that allows Bīẓān to continue to exploit Ḥarāṭīn and slaves (2004, 170). Mahmoud's comments reflect this notion of superiority, in which Khaẓarīn occupy social positions above Ḥarāṭīn. But while the term may not reflect a utopia of equality, it does suggest many slave descendants in Kankossa perceive social categories as dynamic. For them, achieving higher social rank is a real possibility, given the generations of freedom some Ḥarāṭīn claim, along with the respect, wealth, and education they may garner. In Kankossa, at least in the eyes of my informants, becoming successful and claiming higher social rank does not have to entail becoming Bīẓān or even claiming to belong to this group. While discrimination and the vestiges of slavery continue to exist throughout the country as a whole, such redefinitions and complexity of categories imply the existence of multiple avenues to success.

The use of "Khaẓarīn" in Kankossa is not always consistent—some people who call themselves Khaẓarīn also refer to themselves as Ḥarāṭīn or Bīẓān—nor does it signify the presence of an organized local movement advocating for slave descendants' rights. But the very existence of this category illustrates how residents are rethinking social categories and positing new configurations of social rank. Their abilities to do so can be attributed to many reasons. But for some, Kankossa's unique history and the possibilities it offered for distance from masters, land ownership, and wage labor, put individuals on paths that facilitated their abilities to claim the valued attributes that define this category today. Women's and men's use of this term indicates the fluidity of social hierarchy in Kankossa and individuals' attempts to maneuver within it. In the following chapters, I explore how such negotiations play out in practice.

Shifting Social Rank and Status

Mauritania's political economy, as well as the social situations of slaves and slave descendants, have drastically changed over the past century. The colonial period, drought, and structural adjustment programs all furthered the country's integration into the market economy, opening new possibilities for Ḥarāṭīn to claim social value and worth. With wage labor and an ability to garner cash becoming increasingly important throughout the country, coupled with a general weakening of dependent relations between slaves and former slaves and their masters, Ḥarāṭīn had new possibilities for asserting free status. Older ideologies of social rank continued to circulate and have meaning, but Ḥarāṭīn also had different possibilities to draw upon, including the value of hard work, monetary wealth, and education.

Such changes, however, do not apply equally to all regions and sectors of Mauritanian society. The case of Kankossa demonstrates how the French presence in the form of IFAC had surprisingly positive consequences for Ḥarāṭīn, providing them with incomes, the possibility of claiming land, and distance and protection from former masters, which allowed them to cultivate free status. This is not to say all Kankossa Ḥarāṭīn were able to claim valued attributes or even that others recognized them as doing so. Status, after all, is relational and precarious. But Kankossa's unique history did provide many Ḥarāṭīn with greater potential for altering their social rank than they might have enjoyed elsewhere. That some slave descendants in Kankossa self-identify as Khaẓarīn, a higher-status category, reflects in part their early access to some of these valued attributes.

While anthropologist Urs Peter Ruf argues that slaves and former slaves in Mauritania "struggle to *become like the bizan, but not to become bizan*" (1999, 286), the Kankossa example suggests their social positioning is more nuanced than this. For one, what it means to be a valued member of this society has changed dramatically over the past century for all social groups, destabilizing and expanding the possibilities of valued social attributes people can draw upon to claim social rank. The use of the term Khaẓarīn not only supports Brubaker's claim that ethnic groups are not "internally homogenous" but suggests that individuals who to some extent share heritage may define themselves in very different ways (2002, 164). Furthermore, the use of Khaẓarīn in Kankossa illustrates how the attributes people use to distinguish social rank are not explicitly Bīẓān attributes but rather ones that have emerged as valuable in particular economic and political conditions. Contemporary understandings of social categories in Kankossa demonstrate that Ḥarāṭīn have not simply been vying for membership in the dominant group but that they have been debating and (re)defining what it means to be a valued person in general and even creating new categories altogether. Men's and women's use of Khaẓarīn indicates a struggle to define the meaning of social value, as they emphasize the value of achieved attributes and thus challenge the importance of ascribed attributes in determining their places on the hierarchy. In contemporary Kankossa, this struggle occurs in a variety of settings, including the market where female traders attempt to assert their social worth through their labor and by drawing on sometimes conflicting understandings of social value.

Notes

1. Kankossa residents today refer to the project by its acronym, IFAC, and I do as well throughout. In 1956, IFAC changed its name to the *Institut français de recherches fruitières outre-mer* (French institute of overseas fruit research). Note that in 1944, French administrators redefined the border between Mauritania and the French Sudan in this region, sending some Bīẓān who were inhabiting areas in northern Sudan to Mauritania, including Kankossa (Ciavolella 2012, 8). Ḥarāṭīn claim that the first permanent settlement in Kankossa came with IFAC, which suggests that this group—the Ould Zbeyrāt—did not form a permanent settlement there.

2. While scholars and other Mauritanians told me they had heard of this term being used in the capital and the north of the country, they noted that it was employed relatively infrequently.

3. For the sake of length, this section does not go into great detail. For a more complete discussion of this period, see Cleaveland 2000; Lydon 2009; McDougall 1985; Taylor 1995; and Webb 1995.

4. Many scholars have given detailed overviews of Bīẓān social organization (Bonte 1989; Freire 2014; Ould Cheikh and Ould Al-Barra 1996; Robinson 2000; Stewart and Stewart 1973).

5. Slavery in North and West Africa occurred since at least the first millennium and large numbers of slaves were traded throughout the Sahara. While it is difficult to get accurate numbers on past slave populations in this region, Martin Klein estimates that in

1904 at least 40 percent of Sahel residents were slaves, though this varied between different ethnic groups and regions (1998, 252). Though he does not provide numbers for Mauritania itself, he notes that in Kayes—a city south of Kankossa located in present-day Mali—slaves made up 42 percent of the population (254). In 1900, West Africa was the home to more slaves than all of the Americas at any one point in slavery's history there (Lovejoy 1991, 143).

6. Colonial administrators often imposed their own racial conceptions on the population with colonial documents dividing people by race (Acloque 2000). Administrators subscribed to ideas of social evolution popular at the time that viewed white Europeans as superior to the people who they colonized. French colonial officials thus accepted Bīẓān convictions that they were superior to their black counterparts, which helped to reinforce Bīẓān power (Robinson 2000, 5). For more on colonial understandings of race, see Cleaveland (2002), Lydon (2009), and Hall (2011a).

7. See Mercer (1982) for a more recent example of simplification of categories.

8. For a discussion on the meanings and legal underpinnings of milk kinship, see Ruf (1999, 95–99).

9. This is similar to elsewhere in West Africa where women's immobility was a sign of social rank (Curtin 1975; Irvine 1989; 1990; Popenoe 2004).

10. This attitude was similar to colonial officials' attitudes elsewhere in Africa (cf. Cooper 1980; Klein 1998; Roberts and Miers 1988). For more specifics on colonial policies on slavery and French administrators' attitudes toward ending this institution, see Acloque (2000), Klein (1998), Ould Cheikh (1993), and Robinson (2000).

11. Note that French policy towards slavery varied throughout West Africa and colonial administrators sometimes determined policies "on the spot" (Clark 1995, 315).

12. For a discussion of France's increased role in economic and agricultural development in the colonies see Guy Rocheteau (1991) and René Tourte (2005).

13. Examples of this research include studies on optimal growing conditions (Dugain 1958), soil quality (ORSTOM 1959), and the effects of fertilizers (Lossois 1971).

14. Though it is unclear in the report, presumably lower-status Bīẓān comprised the 2,000 additional workers. This illustrates how Ḥarāṭīn and low-status Bīẓān engaged in similar forms of labor, demonstrating the overlap between these categories.

15. For similar examples of colonial officials shaping family life elsewhere, see Mianda (2002) and Hunt (1988).

16. Former slaves also sought opportunities for income in other contexts, such as by forming new villages in Senegal's peanut basin (Rodet 2015).

17. Mauritania withdrew from the CFA zone in 1972, adopting the ouguiya as its currency (Ould-Mey 1996, 84).

18. Laura Fair makes a similar distinction when discussion the Swahili coast, noting social rules on Zanzibar were not as rigid as in older settlements, which gave slaves more freedom to maneuver (2001, 15).

19. Vergara also notes that 14 percent of Ḥarāṭīn paid Qur'anic tithes for working the land; he does not account for the remaining 16 percent of Ḥarāṭīn cultivators.

20. For a discussion of social evolutionary thinking among French administrators in Mauritania, see Acloque (2000).

21. For similar examples from elsewhere in Africa, see Buggenhagen (2012), Cooper (1997), and Masquelier (2004).

22. Many scholars have explored the negative impact of these reforms throughout the continent (Apter 1999; Bayart 2000; Bond 2006; Buggenhagen 2012; Ferguson 2006;

Kaplan 1994; MacGaffey and Bazenguissa-Ganga 2000; Makhulu, Buggenhagen, and Jackson 2010; Smith 2004).

23. Ould-Mey (1996) provides a detailed analysis of how these reforms impacted Mauritania's economy and its citizens' livelihoods, concluding their impact was largely negative and that they failed to achieve their goals.

24. The Mauritanian currency is the ouguiya, which is abbreviated as MRO (Mauritanian Ouguiya). In 2011, one US dollar was worth approximately 285 Mauritanian ouguiyas.

25. These trends are common elsewhere in Africa and women respond creatively to these challenges. Osirim (2009) shows how Zimbabwean women's work in microenterprises has been a way through which they contributed to national development by reinvesting profits, supporting their families, and engaging in innovative practices. Guérin (2006) explores how Senegalese women respond to economic challenges through creative practices, including group savings associations. Such strategies, however, can also perpetuate inequalities. For other examples of women's responses to economic hardship see Makhulu (2010) and Overå (2007).

26. This is not unique to Mauritania; the informal sector may account for fifty percent of the GDP in many countries in the global south and can provide up to ninety percent or more of all employment (Ilahiane and Sherry 2008, 246).

27. For details on current neoliberal programs and policies in Mauritania see the IMF's Mauritania country page, http://www.imf.org/external/country/MRT/index.htm?pn=0.

28. For a detailed discussion of the party, see Brhane (1997), Leservoisier (2000), McDougall (2005), McDougall, Brhane, and Ruf (2003), Ould Ahmed Salem (2009), and Ould Saleck (2003). For a discussion of the opposing assimilationist stance, see Bonte (1989), Brhane (1997), Leservoisier (2000), Ruf (1999), and Villasante-de Beauvais (2000).

29. This document noted the Khadara clan was composed of Ḥarāṭīn who were dependent on the Tajakanit qabīla.

30. See Taine-Cheikh (1989) for an overview of the use of color terms for describing skin color in Hassaniya. The colors green and blue are also used for skin color in Sudan (Boddy 1982, 690).

31. Other scholars have observed this use elsewhere (Brhane 1997, 78; Ruf 1999, 40; Taine-Cheikh 1989, 102; Villasante-de Beauvais 1997, 83).

32. McDougall also notes that difference in status between Khaẓarīn and Ḥarāṭīn might be due to how they were freed, with those who were freed by the government's abolition of slavery not as properly freed as those who were freed by Islamic law (McDougall 2015, 273, n. 104). It seems plausible such ideas play a part in the term's meaning, although my interlocutors did not mention them directly.

33. Associations of blackness with slavery are also true for other groups in the region. Amongst the Fulbe, for example, "*fulbe*" refers to the strata of masters as well as those who claim Arab origins, while *baleebe* refers to blacks, which includes people of slave descent (Botte 1994, 116; see also Pelckmans 2011, 21). This separation is present despite the fact that, in practice, these groups were all phenotypically black. Slave descendants (bellah) amongst the Tuareg are also known as "black" regardless of their skin color (Lecocq 2005). Furthermore, there can be slippage amongst racial categories in the region. In Southern Algeria, Arabs who were descended from the Prophet could be redefined as "black" if they did not live up to the expected behavior of someone of their social rank, including behaving in an exemplary fashion, treating women well, and being committed to scholarship (Scheele 2012, 47).

2 "We Work for Our Lives": Revaluing Femininity and Work in a Post-slavery Market

It was a quiet afternoon in the market and Lakhsara had only made a few sales. Each morning she carefully arranges vegetables and spices upon her squat wooden *ṭābla* (table), and sits behind it on one of the concrete stoops that line the market streets. The market is bordered by administrative offices, an elementary school, the several story high sand dune that stretches out for miles, and one of the older residential neighborhoods. Many Kankossa residents converge here daily, making the market literally and figuratively the town center. As the main market in the southern part of the Assaba region, it also attracts shoppers from nearby villages on a less regular basis.[1]

The market boasts several hundred small shops, where shoppers can buy anything from an intricate, hand-carved wooden bed to cloth imported from China to memory cards loaded with popular songs from around the world that can be played on cell phones. Although people remember times when the market had only a few "*zinc*" (tin) semi-permanent structures, today its streets are lined with cement boutiques that are usually four or five square meters. Most shops have wide front and back doors so they open up to two streets, and customers often enter through one door and exit through another. They are often built contiguously on top of wide concrete stoops where their owners sometimes allow women to set up tables, often for a small fee. While some stores specialize in particular types of goods—women's clothing and lotion or dishes and other household items—many offer a mishmash of merchandise. Sacks of rice are stacked next to piles of plastic ten-gallon buckets, dusty tea sets sit beneath shelves heaped high with malaḥfas (Mauritanian veils), and five-kilo boxes of tea are flanked by shiny soccer cleats and single-size packets of detergent.

Lakhsara is married and in her forties. Before she started her ṭābla with money she had saved through a *kīṣ* (group savings association), she had generated some income by sewing malaḥfas to prepare them for dyeing, an activity she abandoned because it was too tiring. While some Ḥarāṭīn women in Kankossa work in paid positions, such as in the healthcare industry or as employees of NGOs, most, like Lakhsara, work in microenterprises. This reflects larger trends across the continent where, after agriculture, such work is the main way women generate

A vegetable ṭābla with the proprietor sitting on the stoop behind it. Photo by author.

income (Osirim 2009, xiii). Lakhsara's family background also demonstrates the prevalence of intermarriage in this region since her father is Halpulaar and her mother is a slave descendant, who she identified as Khaẓarīn. While historically ethnicity in Mauritania was passed to children by the father, Lakhsara identifies more strongly with her mother's background, speaking Hassaniya and wearing the malaḥfa. In fact, some of the constraints and opportunities women face in the market are not unique to Ḥarāṭīn but are rather racialized, applying to ethnic groups who are perceived as black.[2]

I had asked Lakhsara if I could interview her about her work, and she told me to come to her ṭābla that afternoon, a relatively quiet time in the market. As often happened during interviews, many other people joined our conversation, commenting or expanding upon Lakhsara's answers. Such dynamic interviews are facilitated by the fact that many *suwāqāt* (female small businesspeople; sing. *suwāqa*) set up their tables close together, often only a foot apart, and also because in a town this size, most traders know each other and many are close friends. On this day Ami, an outspoken middle-aged Ḥarāṭīn suwāqa, chimed in repeatedly, as did a middle-aged Bīẓān man, Mohamed, who was sitting on a chair inside the doorway of his shop nearby in which he sold household goods.

At one point the conversation turned away from Ḥarāṭīn women's work to Bīẓān women's work, with Mohamed noting, "They don't work. Listen to what I am going to tell you. They are only looking at their lower bodies." The women laughed, and Lakhsara told Ami to explain his meaning to me. Ami employed an analogy, naming a kind of tree, *amura*, that grows in Kankossa's lake: "Do you know it?" she asked. "Its head is in the sky. It's that really big tree." The women laughed and she continued, "That tree that is in the lake. Have you seen it? Its *aurāk* [roots] are in the water, right? Its head is above in the sky. It's like a Bīẓān. Their aurāk are in the sand, their eyes are in the sky. They don't see anything." Aurāk means roots, but it can also mean hips, haunches, or thighs, thus referring to a Bīẓān's hindquarters (Wehr 1994, 1245). According to the traders, Bīẓān women sit immobile like this tree, rooted to the earth. The women laughed again as Mohamed added, "They don't even think." Ami agreed, noting that Bīẓān women do not get tired. She then used a high-pitched voice to mimic a Bīẓān woman's speech: "Give me a drink," she squeaked. Her imitation drew loud laughter from the surrounding suwāqāt.

In this conversation, the women and Mohamed joked about Bīẓān women and critiqued their way of life. As my research assistant later explained, part of the joke is that Mohamed's contention that Bīẓān are only looking at their lower bodies not only suggests they are stationary but also has a sexual connotation, implying that they are only good for sex. Mohamed thus portrays Bīẓān women as objects of male desire who are incompetent and helpless. Ami's analogy extends his contention, reducing Bīẓān women to pieces of vegetation who are stuck in the mud. They are literally rooted to the ground, stationary and incapable of movement as they stare off vacantly into space. Mohamed takes it even further, contending that, like trees, Bīẓān women do not even think.

This discussion illustrates how traders—Bīẓān and Ḥarāṭīn—discuss and debate what constitutes ideal femininity in a rapidly changing social and economic landscape. Their comparison of the Bīẓān woman to a static tree evokes elite notions of Bīẓān femininity premised on an avoidance of physical exertion or participation in labor; the women's mocking tone and Ami's tree analogy suggest this form of comportment is outdated and undesirable. In reality, the traders' critiques contrast with how they depict their own work since they boast about their active participation in labor that requires physical mobility. They contend that such activities result not only in economic gains but also help them to foster moral personhood. However, despite their apparent rejection of static womanhood, traders also emphasize the seated and stationary nature of their work as positive and thus draw upon, and reproduce, these feminine ideals they themselves also reject.

Here I examine this apparent contradiction, analyzing how women embrace and reject various forms of femininity and social value. In the process, suwāqāt draw upon not just contradictory values but also ones that seem to reproduce their doubly disadvantaged positions in the gendered and social hierarchy. After all, traders' claims that they adhere to elite Bīẓān ideals, which are premised on dependence on men, suggest suwāqāt are accepting passive, submissive roles. These ideals also associate physical labor with slaves and dependents, so the fact that Ḥarāṭīn women actively participate in physical labor implies they continue to conduct work that reproduces their lower social positions. It thus would seem they are conforming to a public transcript (Scott 1990) that reflects both a patriarchal power structure and a social hierarchy that disadvantages slave descendants.[3] However, this example illustrates how the persistence of particular values does not necessarily reproduce dominant understandings of social rank and gender roles but can, in fact, destabilize these configurations and rework their meaning altogether. Women use discourse and draw on alternative ideologies, including neoliberalism, to expand these meanings. By doing so, they enhance their possibilities for involvement in public life and emphasize the value of their participation in active labor as an important marker of modern personhood and citizenship.

Women frame their labor and comportment and assert and define their social worth largely through their discourse. Talking about themselves and others is an important way through which people establish values (Fair 2001, 25); as anthropologist Rachel Newcomb argues, women in Fes use talk and discussion to "attempt to create and define idealized visions of women through various discourses" (2009, 7). Of course, not all Ḥarāṭīn women interpret these values or act on them in the same ways; some, for example, strive to exclusively adhere to elite Bīẓān notions of womanhood. But for many of the market traders I worked with, having a range of values to draw upon is key to their economic success and their abilities to assert their social worth. I focus on these women, analyzing how they reframe femininity in the market, how they revalue individual labor, and how their unique social attributes make them specially equipped to carry out such maneuvering. Ultimately, women's labor does not simply help them get by; it also serves as an important generative process through which they assert and define appropriate gender roles and social values and thus rework the underpinnings of hierarchy.

Reframing Femininity in the Market

As the traders' depiction of the static Bīẓān woman suggests, femininity in precolonial and colonial Bīẓān society was associated with an emphasis on physical immobility and an avoidance of manual labor—attributes that retain meaning today. Elite women's inactivity signified their social status, demonstrating that their wealth allowed them to abstain from work.[4] Noble families encouraged the ideal of the static, seated woman through force feeding, which aimed to produce a larger body type that was strongly associated with Bīẓān femininity. In actuality, Bīẓān women did participate in productive labor in many ways: taking part in the trans-Saharan trade through the organization and financing of caravans (Lydon 2009); producing household items, including tents, mats, and leather water containers (du Puigaudeau [1937] 2002); serving as Qur'anic guides, healers, and midwives (Frede 2014); and managing property and resources as men migrated south to trade (Cleaveland 2002). They also contributed to reproductive activities through raising and educating children. Much of this work, however, did not involve physical labor, which was associated with slaves and lower-status people. Subsequently, lower-status women were differentiated from the freeborn partly because they conducted work elite women avoided, including cooking, serving as wet nurses, and farming. This understanding of femininity is supported by local interpretations of Islam, which contend that men should provide for their families, thus excluding women from physical labor.

While Bīẓān in no way uniformly adhere to these values today, nor did they in the past, this ideal remains salient for many Mauritanians, including suwāqāt. Despite the traders' critique of the stationary Bīẓān woman, they emphasize how they adhere to such comportment in the market. Lakshara, for example, explained she liked her work "because I rest, I'm only sitting. I don't go and walk, I'm only sitting." Like her, many suwāqāt highlight the stationary nature of their work, noting that they sit behind their ṭāblas while male traders stand in their shops. These differences in comportment are reflected in terminology—such as *wāgiv*, a term that can mean someone who is standing but also refers to men who sell things in shops, both shop owners and the male salesmen they employ. Conversely, the term suwāqāt refers exclusively to female traders, particularly those who deal in small quantities of goods. The term wāgiv, therefore, highlights men's activity, while suwāqāt's association with small amounts of merchandise suggests women do not have to be as physically active in their work.

Divisions between male and female labor in the market also suggest women and men adhere to gender ideals in which men provide for their families and thus generate more income. Traders note that men and women each have their *shaqla khāṣ* (special work), which is differentiated by the types of goods and quantities in which they sell. Men tend to sell both retail and wholesale from concrete boutiques they rent or own, and they speak of their wares as *marṣandīs* (merchandise, French)—a term that indicates large quantities of goods. Conversely, the majority of the Ḥarāṭīn and kwār women traders sell retail, including those who have boutiques (the minority of female traders in these groups).[5] Shoppers refer to women's tables in ways that reflect both the low cost and the small quantities of goods suwāqāt deal in. *Tābla isharīn, 'ashra* (twenty, ten table) signifies the low cost of the items women sell since many of their offerings can be purchased with a ten or twenty ouguiya coin, while *ṭābla at-taṣ-*

rār (tied ṭābla) refers to how women bulk-break spices, portioning them off into small plastic bags—something they also do with vegetables they purchase by the kilo and then slice into smaller pieces. This repackaging, an "economy of division, subdivision, and micro-division," helps women to squeeze maximum profit out of products (Jackson 2010, 56) and allows customers to purchase small amounts of goods when money is scarce. The labor of cutting up vegetables and repackaging other goods also reinforces gender distinctions since such actions are associated with cooking and women's work and reflect their responsibilities at home.

Even when men and women diverge from typical gendered work—such as when men have ṭāblas themselves—they tend to adhere to these divisions. The two men who sell vegetables sell them wholesale off of waist-high ṭāblas they stand behind. Similarly, the Nigerien migrants who sell accessories like watches or barrettes either use waist-high ṭāblas or stand beside shorter ones.[6] Likewise, when shopkeepers rest they often use chairs, benches, or stools, an arrangement that reproduces power dynamics by elevating men above women. While two women do sell vegetables wholesale, they both maintain squat ṭāblas that they sit behind, and they also sell vegetables by the piece. One exception to this was a woman who temporarily took over her male relative's waist-high vegetable ṭābla when he was ill; however, shoppers continued to refer to it as his ṭābla and ask after his health, wondering when he would return.

As with gender, the market's organization continues to reflect historic Bīẓān markers of social rank with Ḥarāṭīn women and men often conducting work Bīẓān will not. Lakhsara explained how work conditions vary between groups:

> Only we whose skin is like this [black] sit in the heat. That's true. The only ones who are sitting here selling are we who have skin like this. Bīẓān [women] only sell inside—they sell women's items and clothing and that. We don't have money. They have men who provide for them, who always say to them, "Sit in the shade."

While both Bīẓān and Ḥarāṭīn women work in the market, Bīẓān often work in better conditions inside boutiques where they are shielded from the sun and the market's dust and bustle. Conversely, most Ḥarāṭīn and Kwār occupy exterior spaces since their tables line the market streets. The exception to this is some muʿallimīn, a lower-status Bīẓān caste of craftspeople, who have ṭāblas outside on which they sell handmade leather products (pillows, pipe holders, knife sheaths) and women's accessories. The fact that it is lower-status Bīẓān who have ṭāblas further reproduces the low status of such work. Shop owners who sell Mauritanian veils may display small items on ṭāblas inside or outside of their shops, but they themselves occupy interior spaces. As Lakhsara's comments suggest, the higher prestige of interior work is linked to the greater economic capital it requires, since renting a boutique costs significantly more than renting table space and proprietors must be able to purchase large amounts of merchandise.

Suwāqāts' occupation of exterior spaces also contributes to their work's low prestige; many Mauritanians consider markets to be disorderly, chaotic, and dangerous.[7] A colorful news article captures this view of markets, reporting how two female shoppers in one of Nouakchott's major markets began to fight, "Beating each other like boxers, disfiguring each other like tigers" (Aliou 2012). One reader's comments on the online version of this article suggest such happenings are mundane: "A journalist must tell the facts that are not ordinary. A fight in the market! That happens every day!" This sense of disorder means some Mauritanians consider markets to be unsuitable places for respectable women (Lesourd 2010, 25); for example, some young Bīẓān women's parents rarely allow them to visit Kankossa's market. While food items are available in small shops throughout Kankossa, vegetables and bulk items can only be purchased in the market. Wealthier women often send their maids to do their market shopping and thus avoid visiting it on a regular basis.

Suwāqāt's association with less prestigious work also derives from the fact that they conduct physical labor, including cutting up vegetables, which is considered *mwasakh* (dirty). Work classified as unclean is often associated with low prestige professions (Clark 1994; Ilahiane and Sherry 2008, 249; Hutchinson 1996, 84), and Bīẓān elites express ambivalence about "the practice of manual trades performed for others, activities considered to be 'degrading, dirty, and ignoble,' but at the same time socially necessary, hence, valuable" (Villasante Cervello 2004, 125).[8] Suwāqāt themselves describe selling vegetables as dirty, at times pointing to their stained malaḥfas to prove their point. So while lower-status Bīẓān women sell handmade leather items on tables, they separate themselves from Ḥarāṭīn by not conducting the dirtiest work in the market.

The fact that social status is reproduced by the kind of work people do is not limited to women. Some Ḥarāṭīn men work in salaried positions as teachers, government officials, gendarmes, utility company employees, or NGO workers, while others make successful livings as merchants. But many work in professions that involve manual labor or are considered dirty, including collecting wood for charcoal, tending date palms, or working as butchers, masons, or launderers who wash *darrāʿa*, the flowing robes many men wear. The fact that much of the labor Ḥarāṭīn men perform is reminiscent of work that in the past would have been conducted by slaves contributes to its enduring negative associations. As one young Ḥarāṭīn man who worked in a temporary government position put it, the Bīẓān "are still using us. They are paying us to do something hard."

Such divisions suggest gender and racialized hierarchies have not changed much since the precolonial period with Ḥarāṭīn women remaining the victims

Cement shops lining one of the major market streets at dusk. Photo by author.

of patriarchal structures and oppressive racialized hierarchies. After all, Ḥarāṭīn women passively "sit," acting as proper, immobile women who are conducting less lucrative work than men, and they also perform "dirty" work Bīẓān women avoid. Bīẓān women and men dominate boutique work, which indicates that they have greater access to financial resources. While some Ḥarāṭīn women do have boutiques, few are able to break into more lucrative "male" work in the formal sector due to a lack of education and connections. Bīẓān women are disadvantaged in some ways as well, which is reflected by the fact that men own the most lucrative boutiques in Kankossa, but they still possess relative privilege compared to their Ḥarāṭīn counterparts.

Despite these continuities with the past, Ḥarāṭīn women's social positions and economic roles have drastically shifted in recent decades; they are taking on new positions of power in their families and are sometimes charged with the task of being the sole breadwinners. This means suwāqāt are in many ways not acting like women at all since they cross established gender boundaries, assuming important financial roles and influencing decision-making processes in their families.[9] This is particularly striking because high levels of gender segregation and female seclusion are practiced in some parts of the country and among some groups.[10] Although woman have had ṭāblas in the market since the time of IFAC, their increasing numbers make their work potentially fraught since it is a visible marker of their male partners' inabilities to support their families; this constitutes a shifting social order in which women's roles and responsibilities are expanding and gender segregation is diminishing. Rumors that circulated during my research reflected women and men's anxiety about these changes. These accounts often focused on successful businesswomen from other towns, and included descriptions of how these rich women who had become "like men" were even paying men to marry them, thus upsetting typical bridewealth patterns. Such stories generally ended in disaster and thus indexed behavior women should avoid, not aspire to. Bīẓān women could face similar criticism. A Nouakchott Bīẓān woman who worked in a nongovernmental organization told me her husband followed her the first time she took a work trip to the interior of the country, believing she was actually having an affair.

In this fraught context, women struggle to justify their participation in income generating activities and their ability to maintain moral personhood while doing so. Their emphasis on adhering to elite feminine comportment does not simply reproduce Bīẓān ideals of femininity but rather helps suwāqāt to feminize their work and highlight its appropriateness, even as they transgress certain gender norms. Their emphasis on adhering to such comportment demonstrates they are behaving like proper women, even though they work outside of the home and in some cases surpass their husbands' incomes or do not need men's support at all. While such emphasis reflects elite conventions of femininity, it also challenges them; for Ḥarāṭīn, sitting in the market does not translate into an avoidance of labor but rather makes it possible to engage in it. This suggests that while ethnic pride in perceived bodily difference can in some cases help naturalize and reproduce structures of oppression (Holmes 2013, 173–74), here Ḥarāṭīn women's emphasis of their similar physical comportment to elite Bīẓān women helps them expand their possibilities to maneuver and cast their work as appropriate and admirable.

Furthermore, in this climate of shifting gender roles, the fact that women and men emphasize the gendered order of the market—men have boutiques, women have ṭāblas; men stand, women sit; men sell wholesale, women sell retail—indicates an attempt to maintain at least the illusion of clear gender boundaries despite the altering of these in practice. Women and men insist that failing to adhere to this order can have serious repercussions. One Ḥarāṭīn suwāqa, Lala, explained that ṭāblas are for women and that

> a man busy with this—it's not work. Go and do something, work. Go and find money to do a boutique. Or go and be a mechanic, or go and be a laborer, or work with cement, or build a house, or be a butcher. *But a man tying [spices] like women isn't a man. He's only a woman.* For us Mauritanians we say that this is women's work. A man who does this isn't a man. [emphasis mine]

Gender is not a passive identity; it has to be performed and continuously created, with men becoming and remaining men by conducting activities that are considered gender appropriate (Butler 1990; Grosz-Ngaté 1989; West and Zimmerman 1987). Behavior that violates gender norms risks punishment; a man who has a ṭābla may be accused of acting like a woman. Similar to Lala's assertion, other women contend that a man who performs women's work is a *goórjeegan*. This word combines the Wolof terms for man (*goór*) and woman (*jeegan*) and refers to men who display female qualities, particularly a class of musicians who are typically drummers. Goórjeegans are usually, though not always, Ḥarāṭīn and their positions in society are ambiguous; they are respected for their musical talents and dancing abilities, which are enjoyed at weddings and other celebrations, but they are also distrusted due to their ambiguous genders and because they are believed to be attracted to men.[11] Clearly, the stakes of transgressing appropriate gendered work are high. By emphasizing the feminine nature of their work, Ḥarāṭīn women are able to transgress certain gender norms while minimizing the risk of punishment. Furthermore, by framing their work as feminine, they attempt to make this transgression appear legitimate.

While other groups, including Bīẓān, may also emphasize that their work adheres to appropriate gender behavior for similar reasons, such acts have additional meaning for Ḥarāṭīn women. Suwāqāt's emphasis on the feminine nature of their work also distinguishes it from the less valued work slaves or lower-status people conducted. Since slave's work was often de-gendered with men and women conducting the same tasks (Coquery-Vidrovitch 2007, 57; Lydon 2005; Olivier de Sardan 1983; Ruf 1999; Webb 1995), Ḥarāṭīn women claim their femininity and distance themselves from slavery and its dehumanizing consequences by differentiating their work from men's.[12]

Women also dissociate their work from slavery by insisting market work is not work at all, thus associating themselves with elite values like abstention from labor. One Ḥarāṭīn suwāqa explained she likes her work because "It's *bārid* [cold], not heavy for me. It's cold, happy. I don't get tired." Conversely, men are supposed to conduct work that is *ḥāmi* (hot) and *mtīn* (difficult). Since cold work is thought to be less active and easier than hot work, it is considered an appropriate domain for women, thus corresponding to the notion of femininity that values stasis in women.[13] Some women did not classify ṭāblas as work at all, saying "real" work is with the government or abroad, which implies this activity is too easy and not profitable enough to be classified as actual work. Of course, women's work is not easy or static; suwāqāt work seven days a week, sitting for hours on concrete stoops in the desert heat, circulating in the market looking for produce, negotiating extensively with potential clients, and carefully calculating which products to invest in. Their insistence, however, that their work is easy helps ensure its classification as appropriate for women and distances it from the manual labor in which slaves participated.

As these examples illustrate, while ideologies that value stasis as a sign of femininity and assign low prestige work to certain groups in part reproduce gendered and racialized hierarchies, Ḥarāṭīn women also rework and expand their meanings. Their evocations of their own stasis and adherence to proper feminine comportment do not mean they are avoiding labor; rather it helps to justify their participation in work, feminize their labor, and signify their own free status. As anthropologist Rachel Newcomb has argued in the case of Moroccan women who assert new values, working "within the existing structures of power to gain acceptance for something new was often absolutely necessary" (2009, 5). Traders thus do not simply work with hidden transcripts to challenge the public order but rather shift the meaning of the public transcript altogether. As women draw on elite Bīẓān social values, they attempt to expand the boundaries of what is considered appropriate behavior for women in general by feminizing their work. They thus normalize activities that would have previously been unacceptable and, especially important for Ḥarāṭīn, connect their work with qualities associated with free people. In turn, they expand the underpinnings of what it means to be a woman and appropriate gendered activities. Redefining elite values is a powerful means for Ḥarāṭīn to expand their economic opportunities and claim their social worth; the fact that they also assert new values altogether further calls into question and challenges the underpinnings of hierarchy.

Revaluing the Importance of Independent Labor

When Ami critiques the static Bīẓān woman by comparing her to a waterlogged tree, she suggests the ideal of Bīẓān femininity is literally crippling since it leaves women immobile, voiceless, and powerless.[14] Her mocking tone when she imitates the Bīẓān woman's speech implies she does not consider such comportment to be worthy of emulation. Lakhsara later contrasted herself and other black women to Bīẓān women, noting, "We are in a hurry. We get up and run. We only run." Women "run" largely because they are working to support their families. Earlier in our conversation, Lakhsara explained the importance of doing so: "Rice is expensive, oil is expensive . . . A woman is not going to lie down if she does not have something to eat . . . A person can't always be sitting and waiting for something that is not there."

While suwāqāt employ and reinterpret elite understandings of femininity, Lakhsara's comments indicate that they also emphasize the value of activities elites historically rejected. Lakhsara and other suwāqāt assert the importance of their labor, not just as an economic necessity but also as an essential component of social worth under contemporary capitalism. They thus formulate new criteria that underpin social difference and hierarchy, suggesting that working hard no longer indexes low social status but instead indicates one's social value.

Such claims echo values Ḥarāṭīn activists have voiced since the 1970s when they framed their resilience and capacity for hard work as positive traits in their political tracts (Leservoisier 2012, 158).[15] While such national discourse does impact people's choices and possibilities, here I am interested in how women and men on the local level understand and assert these values. Such analysis speaks to the importance of exploring how such shifts play out in practice and of examining discourse as a tool through which local people assert and shift the underpinnings of social rank. Ignoring women's roles in these processes overlooks their essential contributions to social reproduction and how they create new constellations of social inequality and hierarchy on a daily basis.

Labor has long been an arena in which social difference is articulated, with elites avoiding manual labor, which they associate with slavery and lower-status individuals. Such understandings are not limited to Mauritania. Elsewhere in Africa, anthropologists have explored how conducting particular kinds of work have been important ways through which people assert valued status and personhood (Comaroff and Comaroff 2001; Guyer 1993).[16] Participating in certain kinds of work was a way to assert their value publically and was an important means of asserting personhood partly because not everyone was capable of conducting all kinds of work, nor were all types of work valued equally. In Mauritania, the work men and women conduct has also long been a way through which social difference and rank are constituted; however, the case of the Ḥarāṭīn illustrates that Ḥarāṭīn women and men do not only attempt to assert their value by participating in particular kinds of work but that they also try to redefine and reorder understandings of what constitutes respectable work and honored activities. In doing so, they expand the possible avenues for claiming social value and challenge the underpinnings of social status in general.

Like my interlocutor Lakhsara, many suwāqāt emphasize work as a necessity in this difficult economic climate. Fatima, an older suwāqa and a committed gardener, noted that if

> a person has a ṭābla that isn't successful, you go to another kind of work and do it. A person can't only be sitting and looking. If a ṭābla's goods don't sell, a person does something different. A lot of people only like to sit; that's not good. A person who doesn't find something here, do something there. If you don't get something there, do something elsewhere. That is what's good.

In Hassaniya, saying someone is "only looking" suggests she is inactive, a passive observer of the world (recall Ami's description of the seated Bīẓān woman staring vacantly into space). Fatima critiques those who behave in this way, noting that women should identify and pursue lucrative activities. Failing to do so, after all, has serious material consequences for women since it would mean they would drain resources themselves instead of contributing to their families. As Toutou, the trader who threatened to leave her husband for a Bīẓān, put it:

> It is necessary for a woman to always work. If not, children won't have what they need. [If I work] my children will eat good food. They will drink good drinks. They will wear shoes and nice clothes. So the woman must not sleep at her work. She must look after everything that she does so that children can continue their studies, continue their lives.

Toutou and other women contend that they should not resemble the Bīẓān woman who is stuck in the mud; rather, women should actively engage with work so that they better their children's lives. The value of work is reflected in a Hassaniya proverb: "Who works hard will find; who farms will harvest" (*man jada wajada, wa man zara'a ḥaṣada*). Women emphasize that part of the importance of earning income is how it ideally allows them to exercise more power in household decision-making processes. For example, when Toutou critiqued what she saw as her teenage daughter's excessive love of television, she warned her about the possible repercussions of neglecting her schoolwork. Toutou noted that a woman who studies can obtain lucrative, respected work and will not have any problems. She added, "If you don't have money, you will be just like a maid." Toutou suggests if her daughter marries without developing a means to earn a good living, she will be confined to domestic tasks like a servant, relinquishing both the increased role in social reproduction that can accompany an independent income and also financial security in case of divorce. In the Qur'an, women are permitted to maintain control over their own earnings, a prescription Kankossa women take seriously.[17] This mechanism helps protect their finances and allows them to exercise control over how they will spend their money, though this is not always the case in practice.

The importance of being able to support oneself became clearer to me as I tried to explain my own life to the suwāqāt. Women and men were often shocked and concerned when they learned that I remained unmarried and childless at thirty-three years old. This was over a decade older than the age of most of my interlocutors and friends at the time of their first marriages.[18] Early in my research, when discussing my marital status, I would emphasize how I had not yet met a partner who was right for me. This justification was generally met with skepticism and coaching on qualities that were desirable in husbands and ways I could improve my chances of landing one (e.g., "Wear makeup and carry a cute bag"). Eventually, I also started to emphasize how I wanted to finish my education before I married so I could adequately support myself. This explanation made more sense to women and many sympathized with me about the importance of being financially independent, especially in an unstable global economy where divorce remains common. Women's support of my decision to put work over marriage—though I doubt most would have done so themselves—signaled the importance they attribute to their own work.

Women emphasize, however, that their work is more than simply a means of survival; it can also help them foster other valued qualities. While conducting physical labor was historically a sign of being a dependent, women in contemporary Kankossa boast of their strength and energy that facilitates their participation in work.[19] Mama, one of the female vegetable wholesalers, told me her work keeps her healthy:

> We work for our lives. We here, we're not like you in America. You do sports. I've seen you at dawn wearing pants doing sports. We don't do sports. Haven't you seen some women here who get really big? They can't move. But that one goes to the market; she comes and goes, comes and goes. You see, I can pick up a big sack. That's good. I won't become bedridden quickly. I can always be a bit strong.

Mama rejects historic elite Bīẓān conceptions of femininity that favor sedentary women, arguing instead for the value of physical activity and the healthy lifestyle her work facilitates. The fact that she expressed these concerns about health to me may have been influenced by my own commitment to exercise (I ran several afternoons a week), but it also reflects larger campaigns by the government and NGOs, which in recent years have encouraged women to adopt more active lifestyles (LaFraniere 2007; Tauzin 2007). Mama's contention is an example of women revaluing work by drawing upon attributes that are highly regarded in the West—being fit, strong, and athletic—as well as contemporary global attention to obesity-related health problems. It therefore also indexes her connections to global discourse and concerns—a marker of modern, cosmopolitan citizenship.

Other women also highlighted the value of their strength. Khady, a Ḥarāṭīn woman in her twenties who helps her mother with her vegetable ṭābla, told me Bīẓān do not have ṭāblas because "they say it is hard. They can't do it . . . We are stronger than them [laughing]. We are healthier than them. They are weak. They don't support heat. They don't support work. Thanks be to God, we support heat and all of that." In the past, qualities like strength and an ability to withstand difficult conditions would have been attributed to slaves or dependents; here Khady claims them as valuable traits that equip Ḥarāṭīn for success in their economic endeavors. Her thanking god for such qualities further emphasizes their value. Claiming the value of hard work has special meaning for slave descendants since it distances them from the connotations of dependence associated with slavery and recasts characteristics that have been associated with slaves, such as an ability to withstand difficult labor, as valued attributes.

Mama also explained how participating in income generating activities enables women to conduct the pious acts required in Islam, drawing on this religion's long association with commerce (Hunwick 1999).[20] She noted that "a person must work. Get something, put something aside for the judgment day." Suwāqāt often give charity to beggars in the market, with many saving slightly damaged goods or vegetable pieces that are too small to sell expressly for this purpose. Their work thus facilitates their abilities to perform generous acts, and Mama's references to her charity infuse her work and earnings with morality (Stiansen and Guyer 1999, 8). By cultivating moral personas, Ḥarāṭīn women demonstrate their social worth since generosity and piety are valued qualities in this context. Mama's contention that one should "put something aside for the judgment day" refers to some women's belief that such gifts will literally be returned to them after their deaths; traders construct illustrious afterlives through their generous acts. By giving to beggars, women also display their wealth and power—demonstrating their capacities to support dependents themselves. Women's work, then, is not simply a survival strategy; it is also a productive pursuit that can lead to personal fulfillment and the nurturing of respected qualities such as health and piety. It thus serves as a signifier of their social worth.

That Ḥarāṭīn women value work, however, is not to say they value all forms of work equally. Women favor market work over other wage-earning possibilities for illiterate women in Kankossa, particularly being a domestic worker, or *shaqāla*. In Kankossa, Ḥarāṭīn and kwār women dominate domestic work, along with one woman who had migrated there from Liberia.[21] It is common for even middle-class families to employ domestic workers, partly because this work is poorly paid—salaries can be as low as 6,000 MRO (USD21) monthly along with meals and discarded clothing—which makes having a shaqāla affordable. A shaqāla's responsibilities vary; some primarily wash clothing and clean while others do more extensive work, including cooking. This work is often undesirable because of its resemblance to slavery; domestic workers labor for others and are responsible for tasks slave women would have conducted. That the word for female slave, *khādim*, also means servant in Arabic (Wehr 1994, 267), further indexes the connection between domestic labor and slavery.

Working as a shaqāla also has negative connotations because rumors circulate intimating that maids may have inappropriate relationships with male employers. A Nouakchott newspaper described a poor Bīẓān shaqāla, who worked in a town not far from the capital, whose employer convinced her to enter into a sexual relationship with him. The young woman became pregnant, a state considered shameful outside of marriage. Her story illustrates the coercive power relationships that can exist between employers and employees and also the fact that some Bīẓān experience intense poverty that can drive them into new forms of employment. The article reinforces the negative connotations of working as a maid, noting that "Bīẓān women will remember this scandal before thinking of looking for employment as a domestic worker" (Hebdomadaire Mauritanoix 2014).

For Ḥarāṭīn, then, part of market work's value comes from its independence, which helps them avoid working for others, a condition associated with slavery. In narrating their work histories to me, several Ḥarāṭīn women noted that they began their careers as domestic workers and saved their profits to eventually finance their own businesses. Many emphasized that they like working for themselves; Lala, the trader who argued that men should do appropriate male work, explained she is proud to have her ṭābla "because I become independent myself. Right? I have something myself. I benefit from it, not like working for people. I am open to a lot of opportunities." That some Ḥarāṭīn women do still work as maids despite the professions' undesirability speaks to the diverse economic positions of Ḥarāṭīn, and all groups, in Kankossa and beyond.

Despite the allure of independent incomes, as Lakhsara and Ami's depiction of the Bīẓān woman as fat and immobile suggests, many Bīẓān avoid manual labor. In Kankossa, Bīẓān women do not work as maids or have vegetable ṭāblas, while Bīẓān men generally do not participate in intense physical work, including construction and agriculture. Some Ḥarāṭīn and their black counterparts critique Bīẓān's avoidance of lowly regarded professions as impractical, warning such behavior can lead to poverty and immoral acts. As one Ḥarāṭīn man, Hamoud, put it, "A Bīẓān's mentality—he would prefer to steal than to be a laborer. He would prefer to steal than to be a mason. There are professions that you can't see them do. They'd rather die; they'd rather not eat than do them." When I asked another man, Kalilou, whose father is Soninke and whose mother is Ḥarāṭīn, why Bīẓān women don't sell vegetables, he echoed these sentiments, saying, "I am going to tell you the truth. Bīẓān are only going to go to something that has a lot of money in it. Some prefer being poor; there are some kinds of work that they won't do. Because that would diminish his *karāma* [dignity, respect, nobility, standing]. Not like us. Poor us, we don't care [laughing]." Kalilou contends that Bīẓān avoid work they feel decreases their social positions, even if the alternative is poverty. A friend of his who was sitting with him agreed and expanded upon Kalilou's comments saying that a Bīẓān man

> could come here to Kalilou's shop, sit here, spend an hour with Kalilou. Then he might steal shoes, putting them here [miming under his boubou] and fleeing. Kalilou could say to him, "Come here, I'll give you 2,000 MRO to make tea." [The Bīẓān] won't do it, but he could come and steal. If we say, "We'll give you 10,000 MRO to make tea," and we are all black [*noirs*, Fr.], he won't accept.

According to these men, a Bīẓān man would not make tea for black men even if they paid him an exorbitant sum (10,000 MRO is about USD35, the equivalent of one-third of a month's wages for the average Mauritanian) because performing such work could diminish his status and make him appear dependent upon Ḥarāṭīn or kwār men. Their comments suggest Ḥarāṭīn and kwār's shared racial heritage gives them some overlapping experiences in contemporary Mauritania.[22]

These men's remarks capture the tensions and prejudices that endure between Bīẓān and the Ḥarāṭīn and other black ethnic groups. Their insistence that such attitudes—that is, preferring to steal rather than work—are unwise again illustrates how Ḥarāṭīn and other groups are asserting the social value of work and rejecting elite Bīẓān understandings of labor. While Ḥarāṭīn respect some forms of work more than others, these men suggest that honestly earning an income and supporting oneself and one's family is more important than adhering to former conventions about valued labor. Of course, many Bīẓān men and women work hard and some do conduct manual labor, such as farming, but comments like these are common and promote particular understandings of social categories and values.

Like the women above, these men claim values such as honesty and hard work as essential to social worth. While in the past hard work was considered to be a marker of low social status, Urs Peter Ruf argues that, in the contemporary era, this was "turned into symbol of a new, modern attitude. Sūdān [slaves, ex-slaves] demonstrate pride when telling that they live from the work of their own hands, and portray these as being the sole source of wealth" (1999, 265). In the above men's opinions, Bīẓān's refusal to conduct manual labor neither makes them admirable nor does it pay off. One of Kalilou's friends noted that "a lot of people who know [Bīẓān] well will not agree to make them the directors of workplaces … for example, police. In the police there aren't many moors [Bīẓān]—only one or two—there are only Halpulaar, the Ḥarāṭīn, Soninke. Bīẓān are bandits. The person who is head of World Vision, he's black. They [blacks] do everything." According to him, Ḥarāṭīn and kwār begin reaping the benefits as they prove their morality and work ethic, earning increasingly powerful positions; conversely, Bīẓān dishonesty and avoidance of labor eliminates them from high-level posts. While in reality many Bīẓān do hold important positions throughout Mauritania (and are honest), this man's contentions illustrate how Ḥarāṭīn and others argue their work is an avenue to improved lives.

Women and men's insistence on the value of working hard corresponds to neoliberal policies' emphasis on the independent wage earner. As discussed in the previous chapter, the government adopted structural adjustment programs in the 1980s, and neoliberal reforms continued into the 1990s and up to the present. These reforms focused on expanding the private sector and diminishing the public sector. While such changes often occurred on an institutional level, an emphasis on the importance of independent labor and entrepreneurship has also been evident in government discourse and practice. For example, in 1995 the government adopted a national strategy for the promotion of women with, among other things, the goals of improving health, education, and self-employment,

The ṭābla of a woman who sells vegetables in bulk and by the piece. Photo by author.

including the profitability of women's work (Simard 1996, 89), suggesting that neoliberalism and women's rights may often be conflated. Even before this, in the mid-1980s, President Taya gave a speech in which he highlighted the importance of women to the nation and the significant roles they play in industrialization and democratization (Villasante-de Beauvais 1998, 195). Fatima, an older Ḥarāṭīn trader, remembered government officials visiting Kankossa who proclaimed, "Women must get up. Women must get up and work. The woman should support her house; the woman should do something for her children. If her man leaves, she can do something herself."

Ḥarāṭīn emphasis on the importance and value of independent labor parallels these neoliberal ideologies that encourage individuals to support themselves. Fatima, for example, noted that speeches like this from government officials made people "open their eyes" and accept women's participation in income generating activities. NGOs also reinforced such ideas, "calling for the participation and the commitment of the 'target groups', and no longer want[ing] to strengthen passivity and dependency" (Ruf 1999, 266). A focus on women's entrepreneurship continues, and in recent years NGOs have trained Kankossa women in dyeing cloth and sewing and have also financed women's cooperatives. This is further enforced by informal government policy; a representative at the mayor's office told me they do not collect taxes from female merchants in order to "encourage women's participation in work," as is also the case elsewhere in the country (Simard 1996, 125).

While neoliberal policies have had substantial negative effects on much of the continent and Mauritania, and in some cases have been most harmful to women and children (Osirim 2009, 46), this example illustrates that their effects, like those of colonialism, are "uneven" (Makhulu, Buggenhagen, and Jackson 2010, 13) and thus deserve deeper analysis. In Kankossa, the ideologies these reforms trumpeted helped to legitimize new possibilities for what it meant to be a valued person by highlighting the importance of participating in labor. This emphasis is especially important for groups such as the Ḥarāṭīn who were disenfranchised by earlier economic systems that were premised on dependents laboring to support elites and devalued engaging in physical labor. This suggests not just that local groups make new meanings of global products, as has been a recent focus in literature of globalization (Hansen 2000; Masquelier 2009; Smith 2006), but that women draw on ideologies of global capitalism in distinctly local ways that deserve greater attention. Ḥarāṭīn are not mindlessly adopting or ascribing to neoliberal ideologies; women and men frequently commented on the global economic crisis and very much felt the current economic system was perpetuating widespread poverty in their country. Rather, these ideas are powerful tools women draw upon that help distance their labor from associations with slavery and thus support their claims that participating in hard work is a means of cultivating valued personhood. While slave descendants have long drawn on new attributes to assert improved social rank (Fair 2001, 6–7), this example illustrates how they may validate their claims in surprising ways.

Although Mauritania is a special case because abolition is so recent, this example suggests people elsewhere may also draw on neoliberal rhetoric in ways that reshape social orders.[23] Conversely, their use of these ideologies in turn reinforces them, thus obfuscating, perhaps, the widespread negative effects of these policies (Makhulu 2010, 38). Despite this, it is important to analyze how different groups interpret and draw upon neoliberal ideologies to various ends; doing so can lead to insight on the complexity of the workings of contemporary global capitalism.

Polyvalence as an Asset in Difficult Economic Times

Ḥarāṭīn women use diverse and sometimes contrasting ideologies and ideals to frame their labor and assert the basis of social rank. But how far do their assertions penetrate? Do Bīẓān also accept participation in hard work as a modern attribute? Is Ḥarāṭīn discourse altering how others view the basis of social rank? When we return to the conversation about the Bīẓān woman, the Bīẓān shopkeeper Mohamed's views on these issues are ambiguous. For example, it is unclear what he thinks of the suwāqāt. On the one hand, the conversational tone of this interaction suggests a more equal relationship between Bīẓān and Ḥarāṭīn than might have occurred in the past. Similarly, his critique of the static Bīẓān woman may signal his agreement that participating in labor is an important pursuit and a sign of respectability. On the other hand, the very act of joking together may signal Mohammed's general lack of respect for the suwāqāt, since joking with respected people in Mauritania is a shameful act (see chapter three). His physical position above the women on a chair and his role as a proprietor of a boutique, albeit not one of the more lucrative ones, also reinforce Bīẓān and male power.

Such ambiguity characterizes this neoliberal moment in which social roles and responsibilities are rapidly changing. In such climates, "'Polyvalence'—becoming multipurpose—is a natural response, a subject in open stance toward the constraints and opportunities of a world turned upside down by protracted conflict, volatile politics, and economic turbulence" (Makhulu, Buggenhagen, and Jackson 2010, 8). In Kankossa, women's efforts to stress their adherence to multiple social ideals help them to maneuver in this climate. This can be an economic strategy in part: When women proudly affirm that they sit in the market like proper women, they justify the appropriateness of their labor, which is essential to their survival. When they emphasize the value of previously undervalued work, they expand their labor possibilities. But this is also a generative process through which women assert their social worth and attempt to alter the parameters of what constitutes valued personhood.[24]

Analyzing these attempts provides insight into what attributes equip women and men to navigate this volatile economic moment successfully. The Ḥarāṭīn social category itself is unique largely because of its own polyvalence, which provides slave descendants with a range of economic possibilities, as well as room to shape the meaning of social rank and gender. This is not to downplay other groups' advantages—for example, some elites (including elite Ḥarāṭīn) benefit from their wealth and connections—but Ḥarāṭīn have unique attributes to draw upon as they negotiate these social changes. This social category has long been characterized by its in-betweenness and its fluidity. Slave descendants are Ḥarāṭīn but may also be categorized as Bīẓān (and sometimes Khaẓarīn); they are Arab but black; they are free but retain a genealogy of slavery; they are gendered but have not historically been beholden to the same gendered prescriptions as their Bīẓān counterparts.

Such fluidity means Ḥarāṭīn often face disenfranchisement and discrimination, but it also means their polyvalent attributes allow them to draw on diverse ideologies more easily than their elite counterparts might. For example, while Lakhsara and Ami are women, because they are not Bīẓān women, they are not beholden to the same standards of comportment and thus can work outside of the home with fewer barriers than Bīẓān might face. However, since the category of Bīẓān can encompass slave descendants, suwāqāt can also argue they are adhering to the static comportment favored by Bīẓān social codes and can thus claim aspects of Bīẓān identity, including appropriate feminine behavior. Similarly, while their status as free people helps them to assert the value of their work since they no longer labor as dependents, their slave genealogy makes it more acceptable for them to conduct lower-status work than it would be for Bīẓān. This flexibility makes it possible for Ḥarāṭīn to act in sometimes contradictory ways, which gives them a wide palate of possibilities for making new social and economic configurations possible.

The fact that it is not as easy for all groups to maneuver is illustrated by a story Toutou shared about a Bīẓān woman who set up a vegetable ṭābla a few years ago. According to Toutou, the suwāqāt reacted negatively to the Bīẓān woman's choice, calling her crazy and stupid:

> We Ḥarāṭīn don't want the Bīẓān to set up tables. If a Bīẓānīyya was going to set up a table she should do only jewelry, bracelets, malaḥfas, and so on. In our tradition, a Bīẓānīyya must not do what a Ḥarṭānīyya does. Today they sell malaḥfas; we sell malaḥfas. Everything that they do, we do. But they say that [selling vegetables] is not good for them, this is the work of Ḥarāṭīn. In their culture they don't like this work.[25]

Rather than seeing the Bīẓān woman's choice to sell vegetables as a validation of Ḥarāṭīn work, Toutou views it as a threat. She complained that if Bīẓān have vegetable ṭāblas "they are not going to leave anything for the Ḥarāṭīn." If Bīẓān began conducting "dirty" work, it would cut into Ḥarāṭīn's profits; slave descendants' abilities to accept a wider range of employment than their Bīẓān counterparts is a distinct advantage in this market (c.f. Bouman 2003; Lecocq 2005). Toutou's narration of this event reinforces these distinctions by critiquing Bīẓān who infringe on Ḥarāṭīn work; she ended her story by relating how the Bīẓān woman's ṭābla ultimately failed, which serves as a warning to those who transgress these boundaries.

However, while Toutou depicts a dichotomy between Bīẓān and Ḥarāṭīn, in which Bīẓān must not do the work that Ḥarāṭīn do, she also emphasizes that Ḥarāṭīn can do the work of Bīẓān, thus drawing attention to their greater room to maneuver. Indeed, Toutou herself was already selling malaḥfas around holidays and aspired to open a clothing boutique. In her view, maintaining distinction from Bīẓān (i.e., Bīẓān should not sell vegetables) allows Ḥarāṭīn to continue to control part of the economic sector without encroachments and gives them flexibility in the type of work they can conduct; however, the similarity between these groups (i.e., Ḥarāṭīn are capable of performing Bīẓān work) is also crucial to Ḥarāṭīn success. Their ability to straddle both worlds can be a distinct economic advantage.

Maintaining their polyvalent identities helps Ḥarāṭīn to remain solvent in challenging times. However, as we have seen, this is not simply an economic strategy but also a way through which women suggest new social orderings and expand the meaning of particular social categories. This is not to say other groups do not also assert new social values and configurations. For example, one young Bīẓān woman who ran a clothing boutique with her sister told me, "We now have developed. We study, write, go, work in the market. The early women didn't do this. They only knew the home." This woman may be working because of her family's lower economic status, but her contentions about the value of work parallel Ḥarāṭīn claims. Ḥarāṭīn membership in an in-between category, however, helps them to avoid restrictions on behavior other groups face and makes it possible to draw upon various social values, allowing for a wide range of behavior. As they do so, Ḥarāṭīn women alter the underpinnings of social value, moving away from ascribed characteristics, such as genealogy, and asserting the importance of achieved attributes, such as participation in labor, piety, and respect.

These new versions of hierarchy, however, by no means privilege all Ḥarāṭīn equally. Men and women in Kankossa draw distinctions between Ḥarāṭīn and Khaẓarīn, defining Khaẓarīn as higher-status slave descendants whose families have been free for generations and who can claim other valued attributes, including education and wealth. This distinction is also delineated by the kind of work people perform. Khady, the young woman who helps her mother with her ṭābla, contended that "a Ḥarāṭīn is a person who still works for people." According to her, Khaẓarīn are distinct from the Ḥarāṭīn because they work for themselves instead of laboring for others as a slave would have. This means the stakes of working independently are incredibly high since doing so not only allows people to distance themselves from slavery but also enables them to claim new, more valued forms of group membership. Similarly, asserting the value of their work can legitimate women and men's claims to be Khaẓarīn. Through these processes, however, Khaẓarīn create new assemblages of hierarchy in which they assert their own social value partly by reaffirming the lower status of those who work for others, be it as maids or in other forms of dependent relationships.

While the reference to the Bīẓān woman as tree is a euphemism and thus a way of avoiding the repercussions that direct critiques could foster (Scott 1990, 152–53), the fact that the women explained its meaning to an ethnographer they knew was writing a book about women's lives indexes their power to voice critical material and their commitment to spreading these ideas. This is not an example of a hidden transcript; rather, it is one brought fully into view in front of a man whose social category they critique, with the knowledge that their words will reach distant readers. The polyvalent status of what it means to be Ḥarāṭīn and the subsequent complexity of women's maneuverings—sometimes drawing on elite Bīẓān values, sometimes rejecting them; sometimes celebrating their participation in hard work, sometimes claiming it is not work at all—in part accounts for why discourse is such a central part of asserting and redefining social rank as women work to control the meanings of their actions and others' understandings of social value. In the next chapter, I examine how women direct such discourse at others, considering how joking in the market is a way through which men and women challenge gendered and social hierarchies while also reproducing them.

Notes

1. The Assaba region is divided into departments, which are similar to counties in the United States. This market is the main market for the 63,000 inhabitants of the Kankossa department.

2. I use the term "black" in the way my interlocutors do: to encompass Ḥarāṭīn and groups that include the Halpulaar, Soninke, and Wolof. Note that in this setting, phenotype does not neatly equate with group membership; people in Kankossa give examples of "black" individuals who phenotypically appear to be white. Rather, blackness is linked to genealogy. For a more complete discussion, see chapter one.

3. James C. Scott's work explores relations between dominant and subordinate groups. While the "public transcript" refers to behavior these groups openly adhere to, the "hidden transcript" refers to ways through which subordinate groups resist the power structure out of view of the dominant groups. A hidden transcript "consists of those offstage speeches, gestures, and practices that confirm, contradict, or inflect what appears in the public transcript" (1990, 4). Scott argues that analysts often overlook offstage political action, which leads them to overemphasize hegemony and fail to see people's abilities to resist even in situations where they occupy severely subordinate roles. I am arguing that Ḥarāṭīn do not just rely on hidden transcripts for their resistance but, in actuality, also work to revalue ideologies that are part of the public transcript.

4. The valuing of female inactivity and its connections with social status are also found elsewhere in West Africa (Curtin 1975; Irvine 1989; 1990; Popenoe 2004) as are, conversely, the association of slaves and lower-status groups with manual labor (de Bruijn and Pelckmans 2005; Pelckmans 2011). For more details on Bīẓān bodily ideals, see Fortier (1998), Lesourd (2014), Simard (1996), and Tauzin (1986).

5. In Hassaniya, 'kwār' refers to sub-Saharan African groups whose first language is not Hassaniya. It thus encompasses the Halpulaar, Wolof, and Soninke (for a discussion, see Villasante Cervello 2004, 149 n4; Taine-Cheikh 1989, 100–103).

6. Note that men do have ṭāblas in other parts of Mauritania, such as some sellers of locally made jewelry and crafts in Nouakchott's *Marché Capital*. Understandings of appropriate men's and women's work vary throughout the country, and it is also likely these men are muʿallimīn and that their lower social status may give them different guidelines for comportment.

7. Such views are not uncommon elsewhere on the continent (Kapchan 1996, 36; Masquelier 1993, 19).

8. Historically, Ḥarāṭīn women similarly dominated the small-scale sale of vegetables in Nouakchott (McDougall 2015, 266).

9. Such shifts in gender roles also occur elsewhere. For example, Senegalese female migrants to the United States are often able to earn more income than their male counterparts and thus take on more power in their families (Babou 2008; see also, Osirim 2009, 85).

10. For example, among Bīẓān adherents to the Tijani order in the village of Maatamoulana (Hill 2012, 72).

11. Ghana provides a similar example to this in which men who perform women's work in feminine ways, such as by carrying food on their heads, are called *Kojo Besia*, a term that refers to a man who acts or behaves like a woman (Overå 2007, 558). Conducting sexual acts between consenting male same-sex partners is punishable by death in Mauritania, although this law has not been applied.

12. It is important to note that other groups in Mauritania, including the Halpulaar and Wolof, are also hierarchical. Future research might consider how these processes are playing out among these groups.

13. Erin Pettigrew notes that these ideas of hot and cold probably come from Islamic medicine, which is based on ideas in Greek medicine of the four kinds of bodily states (personal communication). Divisions between hot and cold have also been identified among Hassaniya speakers elsewhere. Azawagh Arabs in Niger, for example, try to maintain balance between "hot" and "cold" qualities since "heat is generally a quality of energy enclosed in the body, and cold a quality of the body being too open" (Popenoe 2004, 172). Rebecca Popenoe notes that people do this by monitoring what they eat, practicing particular bathing habits, and avoiding wind (2004, 172–74). Bīẓān and Ḥarāṭīn's understandings of hot and cold are similar to this in some ways; foods are often categorized as hot or cold (referring more to spice than temperature) and people caution others that eating too much hot food could make them overly active and unsettled. Notions of proper womanhood as being "cold" or "settled" are also found among the Chagga in Tanzania (Pietila 2007, 69).

14. Elsewhere in Africa, static comportment is also linked to avoiding work. In Ghana, the phrase "sitting in the house" is used to describe people who are unemployed (Overå 2007, 541). Claire Robertson also notes how a Mutira woman emphasized the importance of work, noting, "The one who just stays in one place is a fool" (1997, 148).

15. See Mahaman Tidjani Alou (2000) for a discussion of Timidria, an antislavery organization in Mali that also considers work to be liberating.

16. Anthropologist Jane Guyer (1993) discusses how becoming an important person in nineteenth-century Equatorial Africa was processual and could involve exhibiting skill in rhetoric, dance, military activities, and hunting. She argues, "Valued work was a means of endorsing personhood, validating a dimension of reality, singularizing the producer" and that people struggled to "value themselves in some publically demonstrable way" (1993, 256). Similarly, in the case of the Tswana in late colonial era South Africa, anthropologists Jean and John Comaroff (2001) argue that the production of personhood involved the idea of *tiro* (labor), which included activities like cultivation, cooking, nurturing a family, and participating in politics.

17. See Qur'an 4:32 for a discussion of women having the right to control their income; see Qur'an 4:34 for a discussion of how men are responsible for supporting women financially.

18. In 2000, the average age of first marriage in Mauritania was twenty-two years-old. See Quandl. *Age at First Marriage. Quandl*, Accessed March 11, 2016. https://www.quandl.com/collections/society/age-at-first-marriage-female-by-country.

19. Similar attention to the value of leisure and the revaluing of work occurred among slave descendants in post-emancipation Pemba, with former slaves both using their abilities

to participate in leisure activities as a sign of their improved status, but also revaluing working hard (McMahon 2013, 122–29). For similar processes in West Africa, see also de Bruijn and Pelckmans (2005), 74.

20. Hunwick (1999) notes how the Prophet Mohamed was a trader, as was his first wife, Khadija. Furthermore, Muslim traders played a large role in spreading Islam throughout Africa.

21. Villasante Cervello (2004), 136, notes how some muʿallimīn women in Nouakchott are working as maids. Their perceived lower social status makes engaging in domestic work more acceptable than it would be for their higher-status counterparts.

22. It is interesting to note that, as some of the people I write about in this chapter, including Kalilou, demonstrate, intermarriage between Ḥarāṭīn and kwār is not uncommon in Kankossa. Some young Ḥarāṭīn men told me that they hoped to marry Halpulaar or Wolof women. These mixed marriages may be due to the fact that, unlike many towns in Mauritania, Kankossa's population has fairly even amounts of the three major social groups (Ḥarāṭīn, kwār, and Bīẓān). Future research could examine these mixed marriages and how social roles and worth are negotiated within them. Intermarriage between Bīẓān and other social groups in Kankossa remained relatively rare at the time of my fieldwork. I did know one Soninke man who had married a Bīẓān woman, but he told me her family only agreed to the marriage because they were relatively impoverished. He explained that his position as a shopkeeper with a steady income made him a desirable match.

23. Hill's (2012) discussion of Maatamoulana, a Sufi village in Mauritania, also suggests such a practice where people use the resources of neoliberalism to support their own projects.

24. In chapter four, I explore how in Kankossa this polyvalence also characterizes women's economic activities since they conduct multiple kinds of work and build social and economic networks that help protect against economic loss.

25. Bīẓānīyya is the feminine singular form of Bīẓān. Similarly, Ḥarṭānīyya is the feminine singular form of Ḥarāṭīn.

3 Joking Market Women: Critiquing and Negotiating Gender Roles and Social Hierarchy

ONE MORNING I sat under a friend's tent waiting for her to bathe so we could walk to the market together. Several young women and children, including her twenty-something-year-old cousin Mariem, were gathered under the tent chatting in front of a dusty television that was playing Arabic music videos. Mariem has a round face, a loud voice, and a large smile she frequently employs. The topic of men came up and she asked me if I would like to marry Murād, the main character in a popular Turkish television series airing in Mauritania (the same character Toutou also planned to marry).[1] I told her I would not because I disliked the fact that Murād, although undeniably handsome, was always serious and rarely smiled or laughed. Mariem agreed about the importance of laughter, saying laughing is good. People no longer laugh after they die, she noted, so they should laugh while they are alive. When I asked her to explain, she told me if you laugh with people, you will get to know everyone and they will like you and want to be with you. Mariem's grandmother agreed, saying, "God does not like people who do not laugh."

Humor is not simply a way to pass the time for these women; it is an essential way through which people draw others to them and build communities. Much of the laughter in Kankossa is in response to women's joking, and their humor also gives voice to their viewpoints on a rapidly changing world. Women's jokes often comment on, and critique, the impact of social transformations on the Ḥarāṭīn and provide insight into their conceptions of shifting personhood and power. The previous chapter focused on how women draw on sometimes contradictory ideologies to make sense of changing gender relations and social rank and to revalue the basis of gender and hierarchy. Here I focus on joking as one way through which they make such ideas public.

Joking has long been a focus in anthropological studies of Africa, most famously by A. R. Radcliffe-Brown, who contended that joking between various categories of people, including relatives by marriage or members of different clans, helps to manage relationships that are characterized by "social conjunction and social disjunction" (1952, 91).[2] Recently, anthropologist Robert Launay (2006) has critiqued scholarship that overemphasizes joking relationships, arguing that it focuses on joking between particular people who are classified as joking partners (e.g., mother's brother and sister's son) at the exclusion of others who joke. He also argues that it wrongly portrays joking behavior between partners as mechanical and automatic, rather than constantly negotiated. He contends that "specific relationships do not in any mechanical way generate joking behavior: more frequently, it is the joking itself that creates, or at least reframes, a particular relationship" (2006, 805). I build upon this argument, analyzing the jokes of suwāqāt in a place where joking relationships are not formalized.[3] Examining two jokes in detail, I argue that women's joking does more than delineate their relationships with others; it also provides insights into their understandings of and hopes for their social worlds and provides an avenue to make these conceptions public.

The fact that women joke about topics, such as social status, which they may not be comfortable addressing directly due to their sensitive nature illustrates how joking can be a way to raise issues that may be challenging to bring up in other contexts. Furthermore, the settings in which jokes occur contribute to their significance; analysis of joking behavior must also consider the importance of place to these speech events—how it can both facilitate their occurrence and contribute to their meaning. In the Kankossa context, joking and the spaces in which it takes place mutually constitute each other. While the market, as women's space, makes it an acceptable place in which women can joke, their joking within it also delineates it as a space that is appropriate for women to inhabit and thus further affirms the suitability of their working within it. Furthermore, the spaces in which jokes are voiced affect their meanings; the joking incidents I discuss occurred *giddām an-nās* (in front of people) in a public space, which gave women's words weight they would not have had in other more private contexts. Through these public performances, women critique and challenge gender roles and ideas of social hierarchy that historically placed them in disadvantaged positions, and they simultaneously draw attention to alternative social configurations and testify to their own improved social positions in Mauritania.

What's in a Joke? Meanings of Joking in Mauritania

Joking is part of the daily rhythm of Kankossa's busy market. The market streets frequently ring with laughter as female ṭābla owners joke with each other and passersby. Joking content varies; topics include marital status, food preferences, or age. Some jokes are explicitly sexual. Women may draw attention to their vaginas, pointing to the lower parts of their bodies or even imitating them. For example, one woman acted out various states of genitalia; she pursed her lips firmly together to show what a vagina looked like in the heat, then waved her forearms back and forth, elbows at her sides, hands loosely clapping together to demonstrate what a "happy" vagina looked like in the cold. Some jokes take on an almost ritualized quality revolving around one topic and involving basically the same participants; others are more spontaneous, only occurring once in passing. Though not every woman jokes, many do, and I often left the market with my cheeks aching from laughter, reflecting on how these women contradicted US media stereotypes of Muslim women as somber and voiceless individuals whose only concern is their religion.

The positive view of laughter and joking (verb *ijawwaq*) that Mariem offered above is widely shared amongst market women. People who are always serious, like the television character Murād, are called *ka'ib* and *'abūs*, words that have negative connotations in Hassaniya, referring to people who do not laugh.[4] Conversely, being *mash'ūra*, an adjective describing a person who is funny and adept with language, is a desirable trait. When they discuss what characteristics make women attractive, people often mention not only their physical beauty but also their mastery of words and ability to make people laugh.[5]

Mariem's explanation of laughter indicates that people who laugh and joke are liked and will have many friends; other people are drawn to them. This has important material consequences in market settings where enticing shoppers is essential to making a living and also in a culture where cordial relations with others, and the subsequent exchange relationships that stem from them, are essential to getting by financially and garnering respect (see chapter five). Market women often cite laughing and joking as ways they attract and retain their customers. When I asked one market vendor who her clients were, she explained, "There are some of them who are my relatives. There are some who just like me, who are happy with me. I laugh with them, joke with them, and they buy from me." Similarly, suwāqāt also talk about their friends as people with whom they laugh. As I will later discuss, while wanting to laugh with friends is not surprising, it is significant because it sheds light on the contexts in which joking is acceptable in this setting.

Despite these positive connotations, joking is also characterized by its ambiguous nature (Bakhtin 1984; Crawford 2003) since it involves both friendliness and antagonism (Radcliffe-Brown 1952). This characteristic is captured in the Arabic word that means "to laugh," which can also mean to jeer, mock, or scorn (Wehr 1994, 626). Women acknowledge this ambiguity, sometimes explicitly pointing out that someone is joking to ensure the utterance is not misinterpreted. For example, when I was walking in the market with a friend, a butcher noted that he had not seen me for a long time. He then asked whether a man had shut me up inside, implying I might have been confined to my house and married. We assured him this was not the case and we all laughed. Later my friend explained the butcher was "only joking," assuring me that people do not seclude women in Kankossa. Her insistence that this was a joke highlights both her concern that I might have taken his words seriously and how jokers cannot control how the audience may interpret their utterances. My friend also might have been trying to soften a critique since his comments may have been reprimanding me for not being social enough, a valued behavior in Kankossa.

Throughout my research, I was often the target of women's jokes. Once, an older Halpulaar woman I barely knew stopped me in a busy market street and asked me when I was going to get married. She asked this question while vigorously rubbing one of my breasts—as though she were trying to unscrew it—to a chorus of howling laughter from the nearby suwāqāt and passersby. Similarly, several suwāqāt repeatedly teased me that I wanted to marry an older butcher from whom I frequently picked up meat for a friend. His wife soon got in on the act, miming slitting my throat and threatening me as I walked by her ṭābla, to the great amusement of the surrounding women. While my friend insisted the butcher's question about me being secluded by my husband was only a joke, he too was asking about my marital status. These examples show joking as one way people in Mauritania publically discuss and ask about important topics.

As these examples suggest, jokes that focused on me illustrate the ambiguity of jokes themselves, as well as the ambiguity of my position in Mauritania.[6] Women's teasing in the market was often unnerving, largely because I was never sure whether the joking that involved me was a means of including me and displaying closeness or of singling me out and showing difference. After all, many of these jokes clearly offered a dimension of critique. During her fieldwork, Susan J. Rasmussen observed that "joking was an ethnographic analysis by local residents of field researcher" (1993, 219). In my case, women's joking was one way through which Kankossa residents both tried to understand my peculiar marital status and also critiqued it. Indeed, some women disapproved of my being single because it was unnatural for a woman to remain unmarried and childless at my age of thirty-three. Furthermore, as a single woman from a country that is a desirable destination among Mauritanian men, I posed a threat to women's marriages. As I will explore, my presence also affected the sorts of jokes and concerns women voiced since they knew speaking to me meant their words might reach an imagined audience beyond Mauritania.

I draw upon Judith T. Irvine's (1992) discussion of insult in a rural Wolof village as a way to understand joking in the Mauritanian context. While joking and insult are different speech genres, they are closely related; a joke gone badly may be taken as an insult and an insult may be masked as "only a joke." The colorful newspaper article I mentioned in chapter two, for example, documented how two female shoppers in one of Nouakchott's largest markets fought following a joke, "beating each other like boxers, disfiguring each other like tigers" (Aliou 2012). A joke can rapidly turn laughter into something else.

Insults and jokes must be understood based upon more than simply their content. Insults are "constructed in interaction"; they emerge in particular social settings and under particular cultural frameworks of moral assumptions (Irvine 1992, 109). Wolof speakers got away with insults by voicing them in certain contexts (e.g., ritual settings), diffusing the responsibility for utterances (e.g., nobles having others speak for them), and performing metacommunicative acts, such as laughing and smiling. Determining whether an utterance is meant to be a joke involves paying attention to the interactions and cues speakers provide to accompany the content (Kotthoff 2006; Robinson and Smith-Lovin 2001). Mauritanians rely upon a variety of signals to indicate that they are joking: the setting in which jokes occur and who is present, the metacommunicative keys that accompany their speech (laughing, smiling, exaggerated tone or gestures on the part of the performer), and explicitly stating they are joking are all ways utterances become classified as jokes instead of something more serious. The example below illustrates how one woman marks a speech act as a joke.

Shaping Reputations and Gender in the Market

Toutou is a middle-aged Ḥarāṭīn market woman. She is one of my closest friends in Kankossa and is a fairly successful trader. As described earlier, she frequently laughs and jokes with her husband and female friends, including myself. Toutou arrives at the market early each morning, setting up her vegetable ṭābla along one of the main thoroughfares and roaming the side-streets in search of the best deals on fresh produce, spices, and other cooking necessities she sells. Despite the fact that Brahime, her husband of over a decade, boasts one of the rare salaried positions in Kankossa, Toutou often speaks of how his earnings are not enough for their family to make ends meet, and she contributes to her family by using her earnings to purchase food, clothing, and other household items. She also uses her income for her own projects—investing in land and business ventures, giving cash and gifts at ceremonies, and helping friends and family members in need—that attest to her relatively secure financial status and help reinforce her respected social position within her community. Her financial responsibilities do not prevent her from frequently joking with her customers and friends, tilting her head back and leaning into her hearty laugh.

One day I stopped by Toutou's vegetable ṭābla in the late morning. She told me there was not any money in the market, a common refrain—particularly during the hot season when produce is scarce—and that, with no business, the suwāqāt were all just sleeping. She laughed as she demonstrated, drooping her head toward her chest and closing her eyes. If there was money, she said, they would be more alert, pantomiming an active vendor by opening her eyes widely, swaying her hands back and forth in front of her chest in a little dance, and grinning. We laughed. She continued her discussion of finances, saying that having work as a woman was important because men like to marry women who have money themselves. And, she added, if women have their own money, they do not have to worry about husbands at all. Laughing, she said if she had been wealthier at the time, she would not have married her current husband; rather, she would have chosen someone who was good looking and rich, a joke similar to her critique of him in the Introduction. A tall friend of her husband's happened to walk by her ṭābla as she said this and she called to him, saying if she had had money, she would not have paid attention to people like him and her husband. He laughed and responded they were not interested in people like her, that it was now young women her teenage daughter's age who liked them. She retorted that he was a liar and we all laughed.

Toutou's joke makes visible unraveling gender relations and suggests ways in which they may be shifting—or have already shifted. Marking her commentary on marriage as a joke with her exaggerated gestures and laughter, Toutou juxtaposes her husband and his passing friend with men who are good looking and rich—implying that they are not. Her words call into question men's reputations and their abilities to support their families, concerns shared by most of the suwāqāt. Women often connected their own participation in work to poverty, absent men, and divorce. One day, after watching a friend imitate both a sad and a happy vagina to much laughter from her friends, a young woman solemnly said to me, "Vagina *mā 'andha* penis *lā buda tishtqal* [A vagina that does not have a penis must work]." Although her saying "vagina" and "penis" in English—words she had laughingly asked me to teach her and never forgot—continued her friend's joking, her statement also voiced the serious concerns many young divorced women or women with absent husbands face and highlighted women's important roles in productive activities.

In her joke, Toutou proposes an alternative life path in which she would have married a wealthy man. Going further, she suggests a world in which women would replace husbands with money. Her words suggest that women's increasing access to income will provide them—or perhaps has already provided some of them—with expanded choices; they will not be dependent upon men for financial support. That her commentary occurs in the market is significant since women's work there can be a major source of income for them, as it certainly is for her.

But while Toutou's joke contains elements of critique, the accompanying interaction with her husband's friend illustrates the ambiguity of joking and social relations. She suggests that, due to their increasing economic power, women will take more control over who they marry. But the man's response contradicts this, implying that men—at least those who are relatively powerful and independent—will select who they wed. He also contradicts Toutou's earlier assertion that men want to marry women with money (like herself) by suggesting men will choose young, attractive women over older women. Younger women, like Toutou's teenage daughters, generally have less access to resources than older women. While marked as a joke by his laughter, his words bite since many

Mauritanian men do leave their wives, often for much younger women, and a high divorce rate is a major factor that propels women to work for money. Thirty-one percent of first marriages in Mauritania end in divorce (BESCAD 2011), and this percentage may be even higher among Ḥarāṭīn (Brhane 1997). While Ḥarāṭīn emphasize that few of them practice polygyny, the permissibility of this practice within Islam further contributes to the potential for marital instability, particularly if a woman disagrees with her husband's wish to marry a second wife.[7] So does the practice of secret marriage in which, unbeknownst to their wives, men marry other women and support them financially, thus draining resources away from their other families (Fortier 2011).

Women's anxiety about these practices was heightened by the fact that both occurred in Kankossa. During my time there, a man entered a polygynous marriage with the daughter of a friend of Toutou's. Women could also point to examples of secret marriage in their own community, including one man who, unbeknownst to his wife in Nouakchott, frequently visited Kankossa for work and was also married to a Kankossa woman.

While Toutou's joke suggests a social order in which women have more control over who they wed, the man's response implies this vision has not been achieved. The fact that he references Toutou's young daughters as examples of the kind of women men his age are interested in also implies his potential power over her and her family. Furthermore, his immediate laughter at Toutou's words marks them as a joke and thus dismisses their seriousness.

Despite the ambiguity of this exchange, Toutou's implied critique of men is significant; reputations in Mauritania are fragile and can be considerably damaged with words. This power of language is illustrated by the *iggāwen*—a caste of poets, singers, and musicians who are often referred to as griots in the West African literature. As they have elsewhere in West Africa (Hale 1998), iggāwen have long occupied ambiguous positions in Mauritania (Deubel 2012; Nikiprowetzky 1962; Tauzin 2001). While they play an important role at ceremonies, praising notable people and entertaining the audience with their songs and dances, they are also feared because their public praise or critique of others can have an effect on people's reputations (Diawara 1990; Shoup 2007).

Ḥarāṭīn women and men told me they were afraid of iggāwen. Although people in Kankossa often complained about iggāwen, particularly those who asked for things in the market or came to family ceremonies to collect money, they generally met these requests. When I asked why, they told me they were afraid that, if provoked, iggāwen would say negative things about them in front of others, thus jeopardizing their social standing. One woman explained that

> a person buys his *'arḍu* [reputation] from the griot. If you now find a griot and he says 'Give me that now, that bag,' if you don't give it to him, he could

> say something about you that is not good. Also he could say [something bad] about your father, about your mother, about all people. That's not good. It will shame you, hurt your *karāma* [dignity, respect, social standing]. That is why we give money to griots. A person buys his reputation from them.

In this woman's view, people literally purchase their reputations by giving money to iggāwen, thus trying to ensure they say positive things about them and their families in the future. Similar to the Wolof griots that Irvine (1992, 1989) discusses, their ability to insult people in front of others gives the iggāwen significant power despite their low social rank.

The idea that talk could affect how people viewed others was not limited to griots. When women taught me about the importance of giving, they emphasized that I should tell others what I was given and by whom. Sharing the news of gifts received and testifying to the giver's generosity is an essential part of exchange processes. Talk could also damage one's reputation. A young man told me it was not good to talk on the phone too much because others might overhear you saying something bad; even worse, the phone company might have a record of this transgression. Similarly, wedding hosts are anxious that guests will feel they have not been given enough food and drink and will subsequently complain about their hosts' stinginess. People who can only afford a small wedding celebration may not invite others, hoping to avoid criticism for the lack of refreshments. Words both build and destroy people's reputations, which are important for women's abilities to garner clients in the market and for affecting how others perceive their social positions. Women's jokes in the market are thus utterances through which others are evaluated, critiqued, and brought into being. Toutou's joke voices a public critique of men's failure to uphold their obligations to their families, which can potentially tarnish their reputations.

As speech act theorists have argued, speech can be performative—not just communicating something but actually having an effect on the world—and have real material consequences (Austin [1955] 1962; Searle 1972). Mauritanians use the phrase "having a word" to signify people who are important and who garner attention when they speak.[8] Someone who can speak for and about others is a significant person. Toutou's ability to speak in ways that called others' reputations into question and potentially destabilized their social standings serves as a testament to her own power. Her joke not only questions her husband's and other men's abilities to carry out particular roles; her voicing of it also indexes her authority since she is someone who "has a word," or at least acts like she does. This is further reinforced by the fact that she has the final word in this interaction, ending it by calling her husband's friend a liar, which shows her willingness to contradict and speak back to him. The fact that Toutou voices her joke aloud in front of others and invites one of the targets to listen attests to her agency and suggests the power her economic and social positions can offer. While women in less secure social positions than Toutou (e.g., younger women or poorer women) might joke in the market, it is likely they would be seen as disrespectful or acting inappropriately if they uttered a joke like hers.

Getting Away with It: Joking in the Market

A speech act's meaning is not solely delineated by its content and the identity of the person who voices it; the spaces and settings in which they occur also add meaning to what is being communicated (Irvine 1992).[9] In Toutou's case, the market setting both facilitates her joking and intensifies her words' weight. In Mauritania, proper comportment varies, depending on the setting and who is present. This is connected to the idea of *iḥtirām*, the codes of behavior, etiquette, and honor that are also found elsewhere in the Muslim world (Abu-Lughod 1986; Buggenhagen 2012). Bīẓān children and adults follow a code of politeness (*saḥwa*) that regulates their relations with others and prescribes behavior, including accepted positions for sitting and the content and volume of speech. My Ḥarāṭīn interlocutors frequently instructed children—and me—in proper conduct, which they often explained with references to the Qur'an. These guidelines include showing respect and deference to women and men of higher age and rank, thus marking them as valued people. Having the ability to garner respect can have real repercussions; for example, the powerful religious leader Shaykh Sidiyya's claim to respect in colonial Mauritania enabled him to influence negotiations between groups (Stewart and Stewart 1973). Social identities are, of course, not fixed but are shifting and relational (Buggenhagen 2012) and proper comportment varies depending upon the setting and the gender, social status, relationship, and relative age of those present (Tauzin 1989; van Til 2006).

These models for comportment are not always rigidly followed and some women spoke to me nostalgically about times when they felt respect was more valued. But conducting oneself respectfully today continues to be an important marker of status. For example, one man told me it was easy to identify a particular man as znāga, a low-status group, because his children did not treat him with respect, allowing him to travel at his advanced age when they should have kept him home and taken care of him themselves.

Transgressing notions of respect can lead people to feel *ḥishma* (shame, embarrassment), and avoiding ḥishma was a commonly cited reason when people explained their actions to me. A bride does not dance at her wedding ceremony, a woman told me, because she would feel shame in doing so in front of elders. A sense of shame, therefore, can be entwined not just with the idea of doing something wrong but of doing something wrong as observed by particular others (Abu-Lughod 1986; Irvine 1990; Myers 1979, 361–62). Ḥishma was generated by acting inappropriately—or by being aware of the potential to act inappropriately—*giddām an-nās* (in front of people) of higher status. The ability to feel shame is connected to social rank; in some places in West Africa, slaves were thought to have no shame and thus could not be full, social people (Grosz-Ngaté 1989). Lower-status individuals' abilities to engage in shameful acts before others gave them increased possibilities for action, since their behavior was less regulated than people of free status, and also marked them as members of lower social categories (Irvine 1989; 1992; Heath 1994). Conversely, the elite's adherence to saḥwa differentiated the group from slaves or lower-status people (Klein 1998; Ruf 1999). Avoiding shame, therefore, can be a way of making one's social rank visible.

People in Mauritania consider joking with or in front of older, more respected people to be a shameful act. When describing Mauritania in the 1930s, French traveler Odette du Puigaudeau described how a man told her people should not drink, eat, smoke, sing, laugh, or joke in front of their older brothers; doing so would show they were not ashamed ([1937] 2010, 39). In Kankossa, people who joke, especially vulgarly, in the presence of elders are called *'aīn matīn* (strong eyed), an expression that can mean impolite but that many people say especially refers to people who speak rudely or bawdily. Accepted behavior differs among peers, those who are *intāj* (of the same age, of the same generation), and conversations that I observed between age-mates often involved bawdy teasing. At one gathering of female age-mates, the women asked me to teach them the English words for "penis" and "vagina," enacted sexual gestures (one woman lay on her back undulating her body as if she were having sex while making satisfied "ohs"), and discussed whether men preferred small or large vaginas. All this was accompanied by raucous laughter.[10] Interactions like these would have been unacceptable if elders or in-laws had been present, but women among their peers could confide in one another and speak freely. Such exchanges also illustrate how Muslim women are more nuanced and much funnier than their somber portrayal in Western media.

Toutou's public critique of men seems to ignore concepts like iḥtirām and ḥishma and the kind of comportment they advocate. After all, people from all walks of life visit the market: children during morning school break, men on their way to friends' shops, women of all ages shopping for the midday meal. Since markets are often unbounded spaces that anyone can enter (Masquelier 1993), the large volume of people who visit Kankossa's market each day means joking women may have audiences—speaking, in effect, in front of people. This means they have the possibility of acting shamefully; the audience could contain older or more respected people than themselves. Women acknowledge the potential for spectators by making their performances more or less public. While they may loudly berate customers who fail to pay debts in the hearing of others to encourage payment, suwāqāt also avoid having audiences, whispering when discussing something particularly private. That Toutou performed her joke in a loud voice with exaggerated gestures meant it might be heard by shoppers who were older or of a higher social status than her and it was, of course, directed at a man. So how did she get away with joking giddām an-nās?

In part, Toutou's ability to voice jokes in this way relates to her bold, confident personality; there were plenty of other women who would not act as she did. But understanding this seemingly blatant rejection of these codes of comportment also requires taking into account the particular space in which it occurred. While, in highly stratified societies, markets can be places in which people are able to speak in ways they cannot in others (Bakhtin 1984; Kapchan 1996), the gendered nature of Kankossa's market streets also facilitates joking. Though the shops themselves are run by men and women, women's ṭāblas compose the majority of small businesses that line the streets. Likewise, the shoppers at these ṭāblas are primarily, though not exclusively, women and many of the goods they stock target female customers. Women frequently joke that men do not understand how to shop for food, maintaining that a man shopping in the market will end up buying much more than he needs. One day, a local *gendarme* (military policeman) garnered loud laughter by acting this out. He asked a woman for a kilo of onions and then, laughing, scooped up large handfuls of onions himself, piling them on her balance until it was overflowing with what was obviously much more than a kilo. The saleswoman laughed and poured them out and he proceeded to repeat the process to the laughter of nearby suwāqāt and observers. Part of the reason his actions were funny was because, as a male shopper, he was not expected to understand market transactions as well as women. That he was a frequent shopper who everyone knew was aware of the approximate number of onions in a kilo only enhanced the joke.

The gendered space of the market makes it a place of peers, where women can feel comfortable joking together in a way they might not in mixed company. This is heightened by the fact that Ḥarāṭīn traders often sit near friends and family, meaning the market also reflects women's social circles. Outside of the market, joking often occurs in places that are segregated by gender and age, such as at naming ceremonies where women tend to sit with their age-mates and men are generally absent. While I also observed women joking with men in their homes, they usually did so with relatives or close family friends. While it is true that a man might come around a corner at any time in the market, women create and claim the market for themselves by lining its streets with their ṭāblas and calling to each other, thus making it a de facto female space where women can get away with joking in a way they might not within more male-dominated areas. Furthermore, the act of joking itself, in which women's

Ṭāblas lining the market streets in front of boutiques. Photo by author.

laughter rings out from both sides of the street, helps constitute the market as a space where women can speak freely. The large presence of women also visually reinforces women's claims from chapter two that their work in this sphere is appropriate.

But that men or other targets of jokes are potential audience members gives women's joking added weight it would not have in spaces where they primarily joke with age-mates, such as naming ceremonies. The effectiveness of insults or praise depends not just on the utterances' content but on having people to hear them and on how hearers interpret them (Irvine 1992, 113). While it is true that "the advantage of communication by voice (including gestures, clothes, dance, and so on) is that the communicator retains control over the manner of its dissemination—the audience, the place, the circumstances, the rendition" (Scott 1990, 161), in this case, the fact that the speaker cannot completely control who hears them is an important aspect of these jokes. This is because the existence of an audience, which can sometimes be composed of the very people at whom their jokes poke fun, gives women's words a significance they would not have in a setting only occupied by peers or close friends. It is also important because the fact that women cannot know who will pass by at any given time allows them a reasonable deniability they would not have in other settings.

Aspects of women's identities also make it possible to joke before others. Many suwāqāt are middle-aged, which makes them a de facto peer group that can joke together. But Ḥarāṭīn women's joking in public also speaks to their ambiguous status. Since slaves' or lower-status people's behavior was historically less regulated than those of free status (Grosz-Ngaté 1989; Heath 1994; Irvine 1992; Launay 2006), the fact that Ḥarāṭīn joke in ways that clash with proper social comportment is befitting of low social rank and thus reinforces their historically lower social positions. Bīẓān women do joke in the market, but their jokes usually occur quietly within their shops. Conversely, this kind of speech also suggests a sort of authority: the authority to speak before others. In this sense, women's joking is an assertion of status and power, especially because others may witness it. Stallybrass and White have argued that "the history of political struggle has been the history of the attempts to control significant sites of assembly and spaces of discourse" (quoted in Scott 1990, 122). The fact that women claim this market space as their own and raise public critiques within it demonstrates their authority and their commitment to challenging the status quo.

Joking and Hierarchy

Joking, or the absence of joking, is also a way through which hierarchy is constituted since the ability to joke in Kankossa depends in part on one's own social rank in relation to that of others.[11] One day, for example, two older market women teased a younger unmarried woman, Mona, about her interest in men. They said Mona's eyes were constantly focused on the street watching for men and that her ears were white—a phrase that can mean someone is a good listener—since she was always listening for men to walk by. The older women laughed as one of them imitated Mona, turning her head from side to side with her eyes bugged out as if she were following a passing man. The other one took over, adding that even if Mona heard a man cough she would look up. She demonstrated, giving the tiniest cough and then quickly snapping her head up and grinning. Finally, they mimicked how Mona—and all women who wanted a man—greeted men, with one woman giggling, covering her mouth with her hand as she said hello excitedly to an imaginary man. Mona did not respond, looking down and seeming to be embarrassed.

This interaction, in which older women teased a teenage girl, reinforced dynamics of age, social status, and family. Mona's shameful response—averting her eyes, not speaking—was appropriate in this context since she was teased by women who, due to their more advanced age, had the power to shame her. The younger woman could not respectfully contest the words of the older women, one of whom was her mother, and their ability to make her the butt of their joke emphasized their more powerful social positions—as women also did with me when they made me the target of their jokes.

The older women were also exerting a measure of social control. People denounced premarital pregnancy in Kankossa, and their joke warned Mona that too much interest in men could have severe consequences. It cautioned her against entering into relationships outside of their oversight; many parents in Kankossa influence who their children marry to ensure they make good matches, though this does not always work out in practice. But jokes like this also illustrate the anxiety people feel about their social worlds. While the women attempt to exert control over Mona through their joke, that they voiced it at all suggests Mona's potential for transgression and their unease over this possibility. This example shows that jokes in Mauritania have a purpose beyond the people directly involved, and can be a way of reinforcing power dynamics and important cultural values.

Unlike this example, which reinscribes the authority of elders by their shaming of a young woman, other jokes challenge the social hierarchy. Late one afternoon, I sat with Lala, a middle-aged Ḥarāṭīn woman with a deep voice and a quick wit. Lala has a ṭābla down the street from Toutou and, like her, Lala is married and beyond childbearing years. Her husband has a fairly successful shop in the market and her vegetable ṭābla is better stocked than most. I was interviewing her about women's work, and I asked her why so few Bīẓān women sell vegetables in the market. She told me, "Bīẓān women, they say that they are not like us [Ḥarāṭīn]. You see Soninke, Pulaar, us, we are the same [pointing to her skin, indicating its dark color]. Those who have white skin, who are like that..." Lala trailed off, pointing to a Bīẓān woman who was walking down the street. She began an exaggerated imitation of a Bīẓān, pulling her veil over the lower part of her face and swaying gingerly from side to side, her arms bent at the elbows, hips swinging back and forth, nose in the air. I laughed and she continued, saying Bīẓān women "don't like our work... That's the reason a [non-Bīẓān] woman does a ṭābla—she leaves them. Understand? Leaves them there." This claim could indicate that Ḥarāṭīn leave Bīẓān behind economically since Bīẓān refuse to conduct this kind of work. It also has deeper implications, suggesting that Ḥarāṭīn literally leave (or have left) Bīẓān they might have worked for or been enslaved by, and that their economic autonomy facilitates such departures.

Lala continued to discuss these dynamics, noting that "some [Bīẓān] now they say, 'Did you see a maid for me?' Like that one there." Lala again indicated the Bīẓān woman who was passing and then, in her own voice, responded to the question of whether she had seen a maid: "There isn't one. There isn't one." She laughed as she broke from her impersonation, as did I and other nearby suwāqāt who had been listening. When mimicking the Bīẓān woman's voice, Lala adopted a high-pitched tone; her laughing, smiling, and exaggerated movements helped mark her utterance as a joke. Lala's gestures and high-pitched voicing also suggest Bīẓān women are lazy prima donnas, a popular stereotype shared by many Ḥarāṭīn.

Lala's commentary on the Bīẓān provides insight into her vision of the social order, ultimately suggesting that Ḥarāṭīn have made gains within it. She begins by referencing the persistence of social hierarchy by noting that Bīẓān "say that they are not like us." Lala also emphasizes that Bīẓān do not like to engage in Ḥarāṭīn work, which both indicates the enduring connection between work and social rank and also implies that Bīẓān think they are above Ḥarāṭīn. But Lala's words and performance also call this hierarchy into question. By asking for a maid, the imagined Bīẓān woman is indirectly asking Lala if she will work for her, or she is at the very least implying that Lala associates with lower-status people who might take such work. Lala lowers her voice in her own response and speaks gravely, not merely saying she cannot work for the woman but that there is no one at all who can. This bold statement suggests Ḥarāṭīn no longer need to be dependent on Bīẓān, a contention that is reinforced by her insistence that Ḥarāṭīn leave Bīẓān to begin working in the market. Since free status has been marked by an ability to work for oneself, while slave status is linked to working for others, Lala's statement emphasizes Ḥarāṭīn autonomy and suggests the importance independent labor and wealth play for her in defining what constitutes a valued person.

Humor can shift the status quo since it provides new perspectives and thus "communicates sovereignty, creative power, and the freedom to intervene in the world" (Kotthoff 2006, 5). Lala's joke illustrates her agency and her ability to assert a higher social position. By making fun of Bīẓān women, Lala challenges a social order that historically placed her beneath this group. Her words suggest that Ḥarāṭīn have already earned valued positions and do not have to work for others. Going even further, her joke in front of a Bīẓān woman implies that she does not have to respect members of this social category, suggesting a revision of proper comportment and social rank.

Lala's life reflects this change. She grew up in the countryside, farming with her family. As a young woman, she started coming to Kankossa seasonally, supporting herself by working for others. While she was not clear with me about the kind of work she was doing at this time—she only pantomimed it by wiping imaginary sweat from her brow—it is likely that she worked as a maid. Women are often reticent to discuss such past employment due to its low status, but such labor was an historically common first profession for Ḥarāṭīn who moved to Kankossa. Lala described how she used her earnings to start a small table in the countryside. After marrying and permanently relocating to Kankossa, she began to expand her ṭābla, eventually moving it to the market and dealing in larger quantities of goods. Lala emphasized that she prefers this work over working for others "because I am independent myself. Right? I have something myself. I benefit from it, not like working for people. I have the possibility of a lot of opportunities." The sacks of bulk goods—dried corn, beans, etc.—she sets out in front of her ṭābla are visible markers of her success and the fact that she has no need to be a maid.

That Lala's performance occurred in front of others further emphasizes her challenge to the social hierarchy, as she even directly references a Bīẓān woman by pointing at her as she passed. While I could not tell if this woman overheard, Lala did not do anything to prevent her from hearing; she spoke in an audible voice. If the woman did hear, she ignored it rather than confronting Lala, which suggests Lala's power in this context. The presence of other suwāqāt also helped ensure it was safe to voice this joke since they made this section of the market a predominately Ḥarāṭīn space. Since this interview occurred late in my research when I had become close with many members of Lala's community, it was clear that I would also be a sympathetic listener given my place in the larger Ḥarāṭīn community. This example again illustrates how the market is a female space populated not just by women but by women who will generally be on the side of suwāqāt jokers, which helps facilitate the utterance of jokes like Lala's without risking shame. Furthermore, the Bīẓān woman Lala singled out was young and alone. She might not have criticized her so openly if the woman was accompanied by others or was closer to Lala's age.

Lala was not just asserting her power and authority in front of a Bīẓān woman and other suwāqāt; she was also doing so on tape in front of a foreigner who she knew was writing about women's work. When speaking about the high status of Ḥarāṭīn, Lala may very well have had an imagined audience of readers in the United States and beyond in mind to whom she wished to send a particular message about her community. My own interest in women's work and changing social relations and my commitment to working for myself may have also influenced the content of her jokes.

While she acts out rejecting Bīẓān requests for work, Lala still utters these requests, thus indicating the positionality of status. Even while she seems to consider Ḥarāṭīn rank to be much improved, Lala admits in her joke that many Bīẓān may not recognize it, voicing the imagined Bīẓān woman's request for a, presumably, Ḥarāṭīn maid. But later in our interview, she suggested that Bīẓān also acknowledge the shifting social hierarchy. Lala noted that a Bīẓān might indeed come to her and ask her if she could find her a maid, but Lala then added that if she responded that she was a maid and was willing to work, the Bīẓān would reply, "'That's not true.' She knows that you will not come and work. 'That's not true.'" Again employing a high pitch when voicing the Bīẓān's part,

Lala emphasizes that it is not only Ḥarāṭīn who believe the social hierarchy has shifted; the fictional Bīẓān woman also recognizes that Lala will not work for her. The fact that this imagined conversation likely occurs in the market while Lala sits behind her well-stocked table demonstrates the role wealth plays in social configurations. Lala thus testifies to a less significant difference between Ḥarāṭīn and Bīẓān status than in the past when many Ḥarāṭīn would have worked for Bīẓān or been their dependents. In her mind, her own improved social position is recognized by others, but this does not mean, of course, that all Ḥarāṭīn occupy similar places in society.

Lala's joke occurred in a fluctuating social hierarchy, since, as we have seen, many Ḥarāṭīn over the past decades are new to participating in the paid work force. Their increasing access to income may be shifting how social rank is configured, basing it more on economic status than ascribed attributes, such as genealogy, as it was in the past. In her joke, Lala testifies to and makes visible her own economic success; presumably, the imagined Bīẓān's insistence that Lala would not work for her is due to her successful ṭābla. Her joke thus also reinforces her own positive reputation and testifies to the possibility that independent labor can transform an individual's opportunities and social rank. The fact that both Toutou and Lala have successful market businesses has certainly contributed to their power to speak and joke before others. But while the Bīẓān woman Lala voices rejects her contention that Lala could work for her, the fact that she asks her at all suggests other Ḥarāṭīn continue to occupy lower social positions.

Joking and Personal Concerns

Ultimately, Toutou and Lala's jokes are somewhat ambiguous. While they propose alternatives to the social order, they also reproduce it. Toutou indicates that she has more control over wealth and marriage than past women, but the man counters that wealthy men prefer younger women. While Lala implies that status is shifting, her example suggests many Ḥarāṭīn continue to occupy disadvantaged positions by acknowledging that Bīẓān women would come to her looking for a maid.

Despite this ambiguity, Toutou's testimony that she would have married differently also emphasizes her ability to mock men who do not treat women well and draws attention to men's failure to fulfill expected gender roles. Similarly, Lala's assertion that Bīẓān cannot and do not command her labor demonstrates her economic independence and her ability to criticize this category of persons before others. Both of these incidents also emphasize these women's understandings of themselves as agents who can shape their worlds. Toutou says if she had been wealthier she would have chosen her husband differently; given her business, she now might have the power to do so. Likewise,

Lala says a Bīẓān would not believe a successful businesswoman like Lala would work for her; her economic success has altered the way others view her. Since their joking occurred in a space occupied by a variety of people, these women also worked to influence others' understandings of the social order. That they did so in the presence of a researcher, who they knew might write about these happenings elsewhere, suggests an aspiration to extend their words in space and time.

There was more behind this joking than simply "getting away with it." Toutou and Lala's comments had real bite and critiqued gender relations and the social hierarchy—subjects of deeply personal concern for them. As demonstrated in chapter one, Toutou frequently emphasizes the challenges she faces to help support her family and pay for the kind of life she wishes to live. She explained:

> A man doesn't give anything. So a woman always has problems at home, providing for the family is left to her. If a guest arrives, the woman will go and take care of him. If tea is finished, she will buy it. If the goat and *zwreig* [milk beverage] are finished, she will buy them. If clothes are finished, she will buy them. She will give the parting gift [to the guest]. Meaning that the family is a problem for the woman. Always the woman is not patient. Like me, she always has a problem with the man. We fight.

Toutou's joking voices real concerns with men's lack of financial stability and the strain that lack puts on women to provide for their families. Kankossa's market women were not trying to radically alter the established gender order; rather, they were trying to improve their positions within it.[12] Toutou noted, for example, that one reason to have money is because it helps to attract men. Nevertheless, Toutou's joke captures and makes public some of the difficulties women grapple with during these challenging economic times, and it simultaneously emphasizes women's growing potential to wield economic power.

Likewise, Lala's suggestion that the Ḥarāṭīn not only no longer need to work for the Bīẓān but that the two groups also share a more equal status is reflected in the fact that she defines herself as Khaẓarīn, not Ḥarāṭīn. She employs the term in the sense that refers to black Hassaniya speakers whose families have been freed for generations and who claim wealth and respect. When used in this way, it suggests a separation from Ḥarāṭīn, creating a hierarchy of "black" Hassaniya speakers in which Khaẓarīn come above Ḥarāṭīn with slaves falling at the bottom. The fact that Lala defined herself in this way suggests she was giving voice to a world in which the social hierarchy was already reconfigured.

There is a saying in Mauritania that you should listen to the words that make you cry, not those that make you laugh (*isma' gūl imbakīnak, lā tasma' gūl imẓaḥkīnak*).[13] My research assistant explained that this proverb is helpful because the truth makes you cry, but people who make you laugh are "only joking." But Toutou and Lala's jokes highlight the importance of taking joking seriously, particularly when it occurs in spaces that a variety of people occupy—in these cases, an audience that extended beyond the Kankossa context. The public space of the market gave their jokes more weight than they would have had in other places with more limited potential audiences. Furthermore, women did not only joke in the market because women occupy it; rather, they actually created the market as a women's space where they could speak and act freely. Their joking contributed to this construction.

Through their joking, women critiqued others—a powerful act that could tarnish reputations. They asserted their economic power, value, and agency. They called into question gender roles and the social hierarchy, and they envisioned and expressed alternative social orders. Joking, then, did not simply make people laugh but was also a way through which women voiced their hopes for altered and improved social configurations and helped bring them into being. In the following chapter, I analyze how women's actions in the market reinforce and rework relations of hierarchy.

Notes

1. See http://www.kurtlarvadisi.com/ and http://middleeast.about.com/od/turkey/qt/valley-of-the-wolves.htm for information about this television series, "Kurtlar Vadisi: Pusu" (Turkish); "Valley of the Wolves: Ambush" (English).
2. Scholars have also examined how joking relations can diffuse social tensions and aid in conflict resolution (Davidheiser 2006; de Jong 2005; Mitchell 1956).
3. While Halpulaar have particular joking relationships in Mauritania, joking between Hassaniya speakers is much less formalized. There may be some joking between particular qabīla or social categories, but the practice is not institutionalized or widespread (personal communication E. Ann McDougall, Erin Pettigrew).
4. In Arabic, ka'ib means dispirited, downcast, sad, and melancholy, and 'abūs means frowning, scowling, gloomy, and melancholy (Wehr 1994, 688, 944).
5. This is different from notions of proper comportment elsewhere in this region where higher-status people are expected to act reserved, talk quietly, and have others speak for them (Buggenhagen 2012; Irvine 1989).
6. The ambiguity of other researchers' positions has also been highlighted through jokes. Susan J. Rassumseen, for example, discusses how the Kel Ewey Tuareg in Niger's jokes highlighted her position as both an outsider to nobles and as someone who was identified with them (1993, 212). See also Launay (2006).
7. While polygyny is allowed in Islam, marriage contracts in Mauritania often stipulate monogamy (McDougall 2016); however, women in Kankossa noted that men can threaten divorce if their wives do not allow them to take a second wife.
8. This use is also found elsewhere in the Arabic-speaking world (Abu-Lughod 1986, 108).

9. A good example of this elsewhere in Africa is in twentieth-century Pemba, an island off the coast of Tanzania. The fact that courts had no walls meant accusations could easily be overheard (McMahon 2013, 107).

10. I started to understand these age groups better when some women incorporated me into their own. Most of these women were in their twenties and married with one or two children (with the exception of one member who so far had not been able to get pregnant). While my unmarried and childless status meant that I differed from them in some significant ways, women seemed comfortable making me part of their group.

11. Social rank can be an integral part of joking; one's status can facilitate his ability to "allow him to make temporary play things of other people" (Basso 1979, 9).

12. Rasmussen (2003) makes a similar claim when discussing Tuareg smith (griot) women who criticize men.

13. This proverb is similar to others elsewhere in the Arabic speaking world (e.g., Kassis 1999, 136).

4 Women's Market Strategies: Building Social Networks, Protecting Resources, and Managing Credit

Fatimetou's ṭābla is located on one of the market's busy streets. Each morning she sweeps the area around her ṭābla with a short broom, kicking up dust that mingles with the smells of rotting cabbage, freshly fried beignets, and the ever-present mint tea that market vendors and visitors drink throughout the day. Fatimetou then carefully sets up her ṭābla, laying out vegetables and spices in neat rows and positioning herself on stuffed rice sacks that cushion the concrete stoop she sits upon. While it is quiet when she arrives, during the busy mid- to late-morning the noise swells: bullhorns rigged to the roofs of boutiques call out (on repeat) the latest discounts on prepaid cell phone cards ("Buy 1,000 MRO, get 2,000 in credit!"), blare taped Muslim sermons, or blast rap music from Mauritania and abroad. Cars honk as they navigate the few unpaved, sandy streets that are wide enough to accommodate vehicles, and boys driving donkey carts pass through the narrower ones, calling out to shoppers to let them by while thumping their animals' backs with wooden batons. Similar thumps come from the butchers hacking their meat into kilo-sized portions, and millet and wheat grinders are so loud that conversation near them becomes impossible. Over all of these sounds, Fatimetou and other female traders call out to friends, greeting them ("How is your family?" "How is your health?"), asking others where they got various goods ("Who has tomatoes today?" "How much are they?"), directing children ("Go buy mint for me. Make sure it's fresh!"), trying to attract customers ("My cousin, why have I not seen you lately?"), and shouting to scare away hungry goats.

Such dialogue represents the many relationships—with fellow traders, clients, family members, and friends—suwāqāt nurture in the market. The affective dimension of these networks is central to their importance, but creating and maintaining relationships with a broad range of women can also be a real advantage in traders' abilities to get by in a volatile economy. Women cultivate such connections in many ways: through involvement in *ʿaṣr* (social groups composed of women of similar ages), participation in group savings associations, and constructing complex relations of credit and debt. I examine such processes here, focusing on Fatimetou to provide an in-depth look at one trader's experiences while also exploring ways they converge and diverge from those of other traders.

Although Ḥarāṭīn traders revalue their work and mark it as independent in ways that resonate with neoliberal values, which favor individual workers, an examination of what female traders do in the market illustrates that women's work increasingly relies on social connections. This resonates with anthropologist Anne-Maria Makhulu's (2010) contention that while neoliberalism emphasizes the independent worker, nurturing relationships can be essential to survival under austerity programs. The Kankossa example challenges ideas about how global capitalism reorganizes labor, particularly the notion that it undermines collective groups and furthers individuality.

Such strategies are not unique to Ḥarāṭīn women; in fact, lower-status (and sometimes elite) Bīẓān may also cultivate broad social networks, partly by participating in group savings associations and elaborate gift exchanges. However, suwāqāt's status as slave descendants affects the importance and meaning these connections have for them. Cultivating social networks not only helps suwāqāt achieve economic security; the ties they form with other women are also an essential means through which they assert and create social worth. Such connections help women claim and make visible important signifiers of status, including wealth, generosity, and an ability to garner dependents. Through these processes, Ḥarāṭīn distance themselves from slavery and affirm the value of labor, thus challenging and reconfiguring the social hierarchy as they assert the centrality of achieved attributes to social value. Exploring how hierarchy intersects with economic practices illustrates how similar strategies can have very different meanings for those who employ them.

The kind of people who can access these avenues, however, is limited. While these processes provide important opportunities for Ḥarāṭīn to garner resources and assert social worth, they also reproduce social hierarchy between Ḥarāṭīn women of different socioeconomic classes and junior and senior women as well as more broadly between social groups. The fact that such networks in Kankossa are often segregated—Fatimetou's network is composed primarily of Ḥarāṭīn and kwār women—also illustrates enduring divisions between Ḥarāṭīn and Bīẓān and demonstrates how such processes reinforce hierarchy and social difference.

Making a Living: The Importance of Relationships in the Market

Though she is not wealthy, Fatimetou is an example of a successful suwāqāt. Like many other market traders, she has trouble estimating her daily earnings since she quickly reinvests her money in produce, but the contents of her ṭābla attest to the success of her business. It is well stocked with vegetables and spices and, unlike many of the other less well-appointed ṭāblas, almost always has a pile of onions and potatoes she sells by the kilo, weighing them in her battered balance. This contrasts with some other suwāqāt whose offerings are sparse and who rarely have the cash on hand to take advantage of new shipments of vegetables that will sell quickly. Many of Fatimetou's customers come from surrounding villages to stock up on goods that are not available at home, while others are friends, family members, and neighbors from Kankossa. In-between shoppers, Fatimetou catches up on news with neighboring suwāqāt, negotiates with rural farmers over bulk produce, and discusses how to best run her ṭābla with her daughter, Khady, who helps her with her business. Khady and her two-year-old son are living with Fatimetou since Khady's husband is working in a shop abroad.

Fatimetou works hard at her business and fights for good deals, unafraid to speak her mind freely. It is not uncommon to hear her arguing with a customer over the price of dried fish or loudly accusing another woman of skimping on the quantity of tomatoes she sold her. She is also generous with her time, often pulling me aside to ask if I understood a concept or phrase in Hassaniya and then patiently explaining it. She is a deeply faithful woman, and during quiet times she prays, running her plastic prayer beads through her fingers one by one.

Fatimetou's compound reflects the success of her business and family; her twenty-something son has one of the rare salaried positions in Kankossa working for a local government agency. Her compound is located close to the lake and features a concrete *limbar* (permanent tent) under which friends and family gather in the late afternoon to watch television and drink tea. These tents are reminiscent of Mauritania's nomadic past and provide shade in the desert heat. Although expensive, the concrete versions have become popular in recent years, and many families have gradually been replacing their wooden limbars when they can afford it.[1] Fatimetou's concrete limbar signifies her wealth, as does the fact that she owns her land, which she purchased herself while married. Now divorced, she lives there with her son and two daughters. Her eldest daughter lives nearby with her husband and children. Fatimetou also has a garden on the edge of town, and she sells its produce during the growing season. She earns enough money to save, so she sets a portion of her income aside each day in two *kīṣ* (group savings associations). When it is her turn to collect the pot, she augments her ṭābla's offerings, purchasing bulk products, including dried corn, peanuts, and millet that she then sells in the market.

Fatimetou did not always have so many resources. She moved to Kankossa from her nearby natal village over twenty years ago, and first worked as a maid. She then transitioned to making couscous, a staple for the evening meal among Bīẓān and Ḥarāṭīn families. This is a time-consuming task since women form the tiny grains by hand. The process involves slowly adding water to a pile of flour and rubbing it in a circular motion in a bowl and on a flat woven basket until small balls of couscous start to take shape. Women pause throughout this

Limbars (of the older wood variety) with sand dune in background. Photo by author.

process to shift the mixture to separate out grains that have reached the correct size. Fatimetou would make couscous early in the morning before selling vegetables in the market; in the evening, she would return to the market to sell the couscous by generous scoopfuls. When describing her business, Fatimetou noted that she was the first woman to sell couscous in Kankossa—a distinction at least one other woman also claimed: "All people would come wanting my couscous . . . I wore a nice malaḥfa. I wore good shoes. I wore a nice shirt. If you saw me sitting at my ṭābla above the couscous, you'd say I was rich." Fatimetou's emphasis of her respectable dress and ostensible wealth may be connected to the fact that making couscous was formerly an activity conducted by slaves that Bīẓān women would have supervised (McDougall 2015, 266); her descriptions illustrate how women may creatively remake the meaning of a formerly servile activity, as historian E. Ann McDougall (2015) also demonstrates in her study of Ḥarāṭīn in Mauritania's capital, Nouakchott.

Fatimetou's business thrived. A few years ago, on the cusp of old age, she gave up it up at the urging of her children since making couscous is physically demanding and many women complain that inhaling the flour makes them sick. Now Fatimetou focuses on her ṭābla.

Like many other suwāqāt, Fatimetou has dense social networks that she cultivates inside and outside of the market. Beyond her clients, she has an active social life; she attends the naming ceremonies and weddings that occur almost weekly. Her economic success is displayed at these events as she tucks monetary contributions into the hands of brides' mothers or presents them with *matériels* (household goods, Fr.)—including plates, cups, and bowls—which their daughters will take with them when they move to their husbands' compounds. Fatimetou also provides credit in the market, allowing some customers to take vegetables and other items from her table without paying. She records the cost of these items in a notebook so she can collect what they owe days or even months later. Through such exchanges, Fatimetou creates relations of credit and debt that help ensure her economic security. She also rents a boutique with two other women and one man where they store their ṭāblas and produce overnight. This allows them to protect their goods and their physical positions in the market since they control the stoop in front of their shop. Women who do not rent their own boutiques depend on the generosity of shopkeepers who may allow them to use their stoops, sometimes for a small fee. This situation is precarious, however, as the arrangements can be changed without warning. Fatimetou is quite close to the women who share the shop with her, and she often manages their ṭāblas if they step away.

Fatima's story illustrates the range of social ties she cultivates in the market and beyond. Along with the important connections with customers, she is part of a group savings association, works closely with her daughter, invests in family ceremonies, and provides credit to shoppers. These social networks are almost exclusively composed of women. In Kankossa, suwāqāt do benefit from men's assistance: some receive money from husbands, brothers, or grown sons to help them start and maintain their businesses; literate men help illiterate suwāqāt keep track of credit given and debts owed; and, in at least one case, a woman sold vegetables wholesale for a man and turned the profits over to him. This help, however, is often limited.

Suwāqāt told me their husbands generally support their working and that they appreciate women's contributions to household expenses, but as Fatimetou's example suggests, it is suwāqāt's associations with other women that are essential to their success at a time when men often cannot fully provide for their families and state social services are limited.[2] While Fatimetou and her son are close and help each other financially, she has no other notable male supporters; like her, many other suwāqāt also rely on social networks of women. Similarly, the erosion of the qabīla—political groups loosely structured around genealogy that help organize Bīẓān political and social life—means women and men cannot depend on these kinship-based institutions' support. Historically, the qabīla played an important role in assisting members when they were sick or facing economic hardship, but some qabīla members today worry that the growth of the state threatens the strength of these institutions (Villasante-de Beauvais 1998, 235). Even if the qabīla does provide some support, Ḥarāṭīn (especially women) have long been marginalized in these organizations, rarely holding positions of power. Forming networks outside of the immediate family and qabīla, then, is essential to women's economic security especially when money does not go far—a condition Fatimetou pantomimed by blowing on her outstretched palm as if scattering bills.

Kankossa residents take caring for each other seriously, a fact emphasized by Toutou's shock over learning there are homeless people in the United States. She wondered why I did not shelter people in my own home or why the government—"The richest government in the world!"—did not provide housing for them. She asked, "Why don't they just build a new city?" Toutou turned this neglect into a kind of joke, urging me to tell others about homeless people in my home country; then, driven by her disbelief and what she saw as the ridiculousness of this situation, she would laugh hysterically about my descriptions of life there. Beyond her concern with US citizens' values and morality, her surprise is connected to the fact that the few individuals who do not have places to live in Kankossa are cared for by community members who take turns feeding them and giving them a place to sleep. While such care is shifting in urban areas where people may be more concerned about personal safety, Toutou's reaction illustrates how informal safety nets in Mauritania may in many ways be more empathetic and advanced than ours.

Fatimetou's reliance on a variety of social networks is not uncommon, and even married suwāqāt depend on female friends and relatives in the market. Women teach each other business skills, with more experienced suwāqāt instructing younger women on the proper size to cut vegetables or the current prices. Neighboring suwāqāt share market implements such as knives or balances, and they direct shoppers to friends' ṭāblas if they do not have the sought-after products themselves. They impart information about the fluctuating prices and availability of goods, reporting to each other when a new shipment of produce arrives from the countryside or capital.[3] Of course, not all women help each other and women become angry when a friend fails to share important information with them; not learning, for example, that a farmer is selling tomatoes at a good price can make a suwāqa lose out on a profitable deal.

Generation and Socioeconomic Status in Social Networks

Such connections are essential to women's economic security and can be at least partly formalized. Many Ḥarāṭīn women who are *intāj* (of the same age, generation) are parts of *groupes* (group, Fr.) or *ʿaṣr*, social organizations of women who are born at roughly the same time and generally in the same neighborhood—and who, as we saw in the previous chapter, often joke together. These groups are similar to age sets elsewhere in Africa (Evans-Pritchard [1940] 1969; Piot 1999), though the members do not undergo initiation ceremonies together. Most groups are composed of women of the same ethnicity, though there are a few kwār in some Ḥarāṭīn-dominated groups. Some members are related, but many are not. Women of the same 'aṣr often remain close friends throughout their lives and frequently socialize together—spending Friday afternoons drinking tea and eating snacks at each other's homes. Some groups have small businesses, investing in household goods such as plates, cups, and cooking pots, which they then use at group members' events and rent out to others for profit. 'Aṣr members also play important roles at each other's family ceremonies, providing money, gifts, and labor, such as help with cooking. They return each other's contributions at future events or during times of need, such as when a member's relative falls ill; ideally, return gifts should consist of a greater amount than what was initially given. Such exchanges thus create debt, which helps propel the giving into the future and provides a sense of security in times of hardship (Buggenhagen 2012). Beyond assisting with family ceremonies, 'aṣr members may also support each other's economic endeavors, sitting near each other in the market and helping with various tasks. 'Aṣr members, then, are an essential part of women's economic security and emotional well-being.

Cultivating social networks like these has special importance for Ḥarāṭīn, given the links between relationships and social status. Historically, after all, slave status was defined in part by a lack of connections with others. While elites—such as Bīẓān who could claim descent from the Prophet—had dense social networks, slaves had few relatives (Scheele 2012, 36). This was partly because they were taken away from their families but also because slave owners exercised some control over slaves' relationships; slaves could only marry with their permission, and owners retained rights over the children from these unions. Of course, slaves did form relationships with other slaves, but these could always be disrupted if the slave was sold or moved. Conversely, garnering dependents and distributing resources reinforced elite status.

Today the extensive social networks suwāqāt create and maintain attest to their social worth and prestige by demonstrating their ability to draw others to them and thus indexing their wealth, generosity, and respectability—attributes that are important markers of social worth. That many of these relationships are frequently made visible to others (e.g., women sit near their friends in the market, help close friends with cooking and logistics at family ceremonies, and socialize together outside of their homes where passersby can see them) reinforces the importance of these connections and ensures that others know about them. Elites, therefore, no longer monopolize power and prestige.[4] However, it is also the case that not everyone is equally capable of cultivating such connections, which leaves some women at a distinct economic and social disadvantage.

Being the same age helps women to establish social networks, but their economic status affects their ability to take full advantage of them. Women may be friends with poorer women who cannot equally participate in exchanges, but a lack of access to financial resources can make it challenging to act as a proper friend. For example, a poorer suwāqa told me she would not attend a naming ceremony for her friend's grandchild because she had nothing to give. Giving at such ceremonies is not required, but hosts and others take note of, and often record, women's contributions, so this woman wanted to avoid the embarrassment of failing to give. This is not to say women consider their own potential financial gain as the basis of friendship, but the fact that social connections among Ḥarāṭīn are cultivated and made visible through exchange processes makes it challenging for poorer women to develop the broad social networks of their wealthier peers (Buggenhagen 2012; Cooper 1997; Masquelier 2004; Piot 1999). Women do help their poorer counterparts in times of hardship, but their gifts have a different meaning; while they may index ongoing relationships, they are considered akin to charity and thus reproduce social difference.

Generational position also affects the extent to which women can cultivate and utilize their social networks. Unlike some settings where women may occupy weaker positions after moving out of their child-bearing years (McMahon 2013, 234), some senior women in Kankossa exercise great power, becoming, as Fatimetou suggests, important and respected individuals. Fatimetou's decades of work helped her garner the funds needed to support a lucrative ṭābla and her grown son can also assist her financially. By expanding their social networks and establishing their reputations as trustworthy, older women have also had the time to develop the social and symbolic capital that help them garner clients and credit. Such symbolic capital can be turned into material wealth (Pietila 2007, 59); it helps women to attract customers and obtain credit. With 43 percent of Mauritanian women marrying by age eighteen (UNIFEM 2010, 7), single women rarely have the time or the resources to start businesses before marriage. Likewise, few young wives have ṭāblas, since many have significant household duties, including childcare, and they do not yet have older children to assist them. Fatimetou's oldest daughter, for example, stayed home to care for her young children. While she sometimes sold dried couscous off of her mother's table, she did not have the time or the resources to start a table herself. This is consistent with anthropologist Gisèle Simard's findings in Nouakchott, where the average age of veil merchants she worked with was thirty-nine (1996, 143).[5]

Women's ages and marital statuses also influence their abilities to maneuver in the market. Fatimetou, for example, had decided not to marry again. Recently divorced, she explained, "I'm no longer with men at all. It's finished. I'm a *shaybanīyya* [old woman]. I have children. I'm not going to bring a man to my children. That's not good. I've become a *mra kbīrra* [older woman]. I must not want a man. Thanks be to God. I only pray to God and bring up my children. That's enough." Fatimetou suggests that part of the reason she does not remarry is her belief that such behavior would be inappropriate for a woman her age. Her use of the adjective "kbīrra" signifies age, but this term can also signify someone who is influential and important.[6] This suggests that being single also allows Fatimetou to maintain her influence in her household. She is able to keep her position as the head of her family and avoid the risk of a husband trying to limit or control her work or profits. A younger woman might hope her husband would contribute to her business; Fatimetou's position is such that she no longer needs such aid.

Senior women's success is also due to their abilities to access junior labor in the form of daughters or daughters-in-law who perform domestic chores in their absence. While older women are still responsible for overseeing housework, it is junior women who primarily carry it out. This means older women can spend the entire day in the market, arriving early in the morning and leaving shortly before sunset, as Fatimetou often does. Working these long hours gives them an advantage over other women who return home to conduct domestic labor since they do not miss new shipments of produce and clients can depend on their presence. Similarly, being freed from domestic labor allows senior women to attend family ceremonies and garner social and symbolic capital, which is essential to success in the market. For example, women's generosity at such events helps to portray them as credit-worthy and also allows them to attract clients.

To ensure they have adequate access to junior labor, Kankossa women may encourage their sons to marry locally. Marriage in the region remains virilocal, meaning married couples often live with the groom's parents. If women's sons marry elsewhere, which is not uncommon due to high out-migration rates, older women risk missing out on daughters-in-law's contributions of labor to their households since couples may set up house alone. Having daughters-in-law living with them also helps senior women to benefit from young men's contributions, as it is often men's mothers, not the young wives, who control remittances.

Women who do not have access to junior female labor have to take care of domestic tasks themselves. Such women sometimes benefit from other women in their neighborhoods who do not work—either older women or young women who remain at home with small children. While these women are generally busy with their own household tasks, they may keep an eye on others' young children while they play throughout the neighborhood. For example, the neighborhood where I lived had a small band of three- to six-year-old girls who entertained themselves outside for much of the day. The fact that there are few cars in Kankossa and that many people spend their time outdoors under tents meant these girls were not at great risk and were usually in at least one person's sight. Women without access to junior labor may also invest in consumer goods that reduce household tasks (e.g., buying couscous in the market rather than preparing it themselves). Doing so frees up time, but expenses like these also cut into women's profits.

Junior women thus form important parts of women's networks, and drawing on their labor can free up senior women's time. Many Ḥarāṭīn women told me they hoped their girls would have better lives than they did since their education would expand their employment possibilities. Schooling is compulsory up to age fifteen, so most of the suwāqāt's daughters attend, helping their mothers with their ṭāblas after school or on weekends. Ironically, suwāqāt's businesses sometimes detract from their daughters' focus on education, since suwāqāt expect junior females to complete extensive household tasks after school, such as helping them prepare items for the ṭāblas—roasting peanuts or packaging spices. Likewise, when senior women attend family ceremonies, they sometimes have their daughters miss school to watch their ṭāblas. Young women do exercise agency in such matters, complaining about absences from school or noting that they cannot help with a task because they are ill, but, despite their efforts, the demands placed on them generally outweigh those placed on their male counterparts. The fact that men have fewer household responsibilities allows them to concentrate on their studies or economic pursuits and thus reinforces gender disparities.

Social networks, therefore, can greatly benefit women in the market both economically and socially. Suwāqāt work together to help ensure economic success, and the networks they form illustrate women's abilities to build and maintain relationships, a sign of free status and social worth. However, not everyone has equal access to such support or is able to harness it in the same way. Senior women's dependence on junior female labor reinforces a hierarchy in which older women have more social and economic power than their younger counterparts. Senior women's control of junior labor is nothing new in this setting, but men's postponement of marriage due to the difficulty of collecting the resources needed to wed means younger women may remain under their mothers' control for longer periods. Once they marry and move in with their in-laws, they may have similar responsibilities in the household, but young married women are much more likely to have ṭāblas than their single counterparts because their husbands may support their start-up costs.

Similarly, women's socioeconomic status also has an effect on their abilities to engage in these networks. Class disparities are reinforced in the market; not only it is more difficult for poorer women to participate in the exchanges that are central to forming social networks but wealthier women also have the ability to hire household help. This allows them to devote time to their businesses and thus expand their potential for profit while better supporting their daughters' educations. Social networks, then, are essential to women's well-being and economic success, but not all women have equal opportunities of forming them.

Rendering Resources Invisible

Social networks play an important role in women's personal and professional success in Kankossa, but maintaining such networks is no easy task. To do so, women must balance opposing demands, such as putting money toward maintaining and possibly expanding their businesses while also contributing to their social communities. Women's group savings associations, known as kīṣ or *purrī*, serve as powerful tools to help women manage these demands and retain control over their money. Participants in such associations contribute fixed amounts of money in a predetermined cycle (i.e., daily, every other day) to a woman who manages it and receives a small sum for her efforts. The pot is then allocated to members on a rotating basis. For example, members of large associations might each collect the proceeds once every two months. The size of purrīs varies, with some operating on small payments like 100 MRO (USD0.35) daily, and others requiring larger contributions of up to 2,000 MRO (USD7). Sociologist Bilal O. Hamzetta's study in the early 2000s found that savings organizations were concentrated in urban areas, and he speculated that they developed as a response to city dwellers' increasing needs that were provoked by urbanization (2003, 172). The fact that these practices are now common in semirural areas like Kankossa speaks to widespread economic insecurity, while also illustrating how women adopt new practices to help sustain their financial well-being.

Savings organizations like these were first used in Mauritania by Halpulaar women, and by the 1980s, Ḥarāṭīn were also participating (Hamzetta 2003, 165). The spread of these practices from kwār to Ḥarāṭīn illustrates how Ḥarāṭīn are often connected to members of these ethnic groups as neighbors, friends, or marriage partners. Such links give Ḥarāṭīn increased possibilities to create expanded economic repertoires that help them to be flexible and respond to economic insecurity.[7] Bīẓān women in Nouakchott largely avoided these methods of savings in the 1990s due to saving associations' connotations with black African groups and concerns that such practices were prohibited in Islam (Simard 1996, 151). During my research, Bīẓān women continued to avoid them in Kankossa where mainly Ḥarāṭīn and kwār women participate in such organizations, along with a few men. Men generally do not take part in these organizations because of purrīs' association with women and because men can more easily access larger sums of money (i.e., by securing loans from financial institutions). However, since only wealthier men are able to do so, men's avoidance of these savings opportunities disadvantages poorer men.

In my discussions with Ḥarāṭīn women about these saving practices many maintained that Bīẓān women did not participate in them in Kankossa. Whether or not they did—and poorer Bīẓān women certainly do save in these ways elsewhere—women's insistence that this is a Ḥarāṭīn (and kwār) activity emphasizes their own innovative practices. It also differentiates them from Bīẓān, particularly poorer Bīẓān women. It is common in Kankossa for Ḥarāṭīn to critique lower-status Bīẓān, especially muʿallimīn, such as by suggesting that they are dishonest. Contrasting themselves with Bīẓān thus enables Ḥarāṭīn to highlight their own morality and, in this case, economic acumen. One Bīẓān woman did echo the above concerns saying she did not participate in such practices because Islam forbid them and also because they could lead to fighting. This demonstrates how Ḥarāṭīn's lower status can give them more room to maneuver than elite Bīẓān, which can help them capitalize on economic opportunities in the market. Since status is relational, however, the Bīẓān woman's comments suggest she sees such practices as fostering immoral behavior and thus as a sign of lower social rank.

Ḥarāṭīn use purrī funds for a variety of purposes, including purchasing merchandise and assisting their children. Fatimetou, for example, gave half of the 100,000 MRO she collected from a kīṣ to her son to help finance the construction of a home for him on her property. She hoped having his own dwelling would help him to marry since it would allow him to house a wife and would also make him an attractive marriage partner by indexing his financial success. Fatimetou's ability to support her son's construction project and his future marriage indicates how women's contributions play a significant role in social reproduction. While her son had a salaried position, her support allowed him to marry more quickly, which he eventually did with the daughter of one of the suwāqāt with whom Fatimetou worked closely. The marriage formalized her relationship with this woman, making them kin on top of close business associates. It also meant the arrival of another junior woman into Fatimetou's home who would contribute to household labor and Fatimetou's economic pursuits.

In Kankossa, wealthier suwāqāt, like Fatimetou, participate in purrīs that require more significant contributions; since these purrīs guarantee larger returns than others, they reproduce socioeconomic status, as does the fact that the poorest suwāqāt have difficulty joining such organizations at all since the required daily payments can be prohibitive. However, Fatimetou's management of her purrī demonstrates that women employ their funds in strategic ways that may improve their livelihoods. In her case, she used her earnings to invest in human capital, helping to both facilitate her son's entry into adulthood and also to secure the benefits she would garner from his marriage in the form of additional labor and his continued financial contributions to her household. This was a strategic investment; Fatimetou's choices gave her the possibility of improving her financial standing and cementing and expanding her social networks.[8]

Beyond helping women to expand their businesses, investing in purrīs also protects their money, rendering it invisible and "redirecting consumer desire," since such funds restrict the withdrawal of deposits (Makhulu 2010, 36). Joining a purrī makes it difficult for suwāqāt to access their money, since they are not supposed to take their shares out of turn. This restriction helps them avoid spending and makes it more acceptable for them to refuse requests for aid since they can honestly say they do not have money in hand. While women's social networks are essential to their economic, social, and emotional well-being, the accompanying high expectations for giving mean they can also drain women's resources; succeeding in the market requires balancing individual needs with the collective needs of women's communities (Guérin 2006). The people who depend on suwāqāt for support can extend beyond their own children to foster children, domestic workers, their husbands, and poorer community members.

Such large numbers of semi-dependents can strain women's resources. Fatimetou explained she puts her money in a purrī because "we can't put it in our bags. Because when you put it in your purse, you won't be able to use it. We couldn't buy our products. We couldn't buy something . . . You see, tomorrow the children could say, 'Give me.' I could open my bag. I could take out that money. I'd no longer be saving." Depositing the money in a purrī protects it from the demands of others, allowing women to invest in their businesses or other pursuits when they collect their shares. Women can sometimes withdraw their contributions early in case of an emergency, but most try to avoid doing so as it can risk damaging their reputations as trustworthy and make it difficult for them to garner future credit or join another purrī. Some women consider this to be an advantage of savings associations over the local bank since clients can withdraw money from the bank at any time without penalty, thus making it more difficult to resist demands for assistance.[9] Depositing their money in a saving association allows women to refuse requests for aid in a way that helps them to avoid looking stingy since they honestly do not have the money. My own experience was similar during my research. Although I did not participate in a purrī, I could only access money in Nouakchott since I relied on ATMs, which were not available in Kankossa. This meant it was easier for me to avoid requests for money at the end of several months in Kankossa because I literally did not have enough left to give.[10]

Women protect their money in other ways as well. Some suwāqāt select the goods they stock based upon the ease with which they can or cannot be liquidated or consumed; one woman told me she sells clothing instead of vegetables, since the latter can be used to feed her family, which can deplete stock daily. Others invest in livestock or land they sometimes inhabit. Several divorced women, including Fatimetou, told me they bought land while they were married that they now live on, and others invested in land they hoped to one day build on themselves, perhaps to provide their children with housing. Kankossa's history with IFAC and settlement outside of qabīla control means slave descendants can own land there, unlike in some more rural areas where they continue to cultivate land owned by Bīẓān and therefore do not control all of the profits themselves (Ruf 1999, 247). Fatimetou also aspired to purchase a cow:

> When you leave a cow in the *bādīya* [countryside], it gives birth. It will give birth. When its calf gets big, she will also give birth. They give birth, give birth, give birth until I have many. When I die, then my children have this. If I'm also living we have something. If we have nothing, we'll go to the cow, capture it, tie it with rope, find a butcher, and sell it to get money.

Fatimetou's cow would ideally multiply, helping to provide for her family's future. Such investments can provide economic security, but they are also risky; Fatimetou had formerly invested in several sheep and goats that were killed by a predator.

Despite their precariousness, investments like these are especially important for women given the instability of marriage. While men also invest in livestock and housing, in the case of divorce they are not required to give their wives a share of their assets. Women can inherit property, but they only receive a portion of what men do.[11] Accumulating their own wealth helps women to ensure their financial security, no matter their marital status. Similar to purrīs, investing in land or livestock also makes their money harder to access and thus can serve as a form of protection against requests for aid.

The most extreme example I saw of protecting financial resources was near the end of my research when a young man disappeared. When I asked one of his friends about him after I had not seen him for several weeks, his friend told me that the man had left Kankossa two months ago. Even the man's wife did not know where he was and his cell phone had been turned off. When I expressed distress about this situation and wondered if we should report him as missing to the authorities, his friend remained calm, saying he was probably having money problems and that he would return when he found a solution. In this way, the man rendered himself and his scant resources completely invisible, removing them from exchange cycles and from the demands of others. Choosing to disappear rather than struggle in Kankossa with limited resources helped him to protect his relationships; he did not have to reject requests for aid. His sudden and extended disappearance also illustrates how even married women cannot depend solely on their husbands to support them; my friend's calmness in light of this event suggests such disappearances are not uncommon.

Many men in Kankossa and Nouakchott disappear, in a less extreme way, through migration. Men told me one of the major benefits of migration was the chance it provided to save money since it helped free them from the financial demands of friends and relatives. While most migrants do aim to send money home, both the lack of daily in-person demands and their families' limited direct knowledge about their income give them greater control over their finances.

Movement, then, is a way to render oneself and one's resources invisible. However, new forms of connectivity, especially cell phones, make it harder to escape people's demands unless, of course, one turns his off.

In other settings, anthropologists have analyzed the importance of keeping-while-giving (Buggenhagen 2012; Foster 1993; Weiner 1992), exploring people's strategies for holding objects back for themselves and their families, despite high pressure to give to others in the community. This often involves inalienable goods, items families try to keep across generations that serve as repositories of value and help to authenticate men's and women's social positions and histories (Weiner 1992). In Kankossa, however, due to their recent change in status and their historically weaker economic positions, Ḥarāṭīn have not had the ability to collect inalienable objects over the *longue durée*. Instead, they move their money into domains that are harder for children, friends, or husbands to access, including purrīs, land, and livestock. The Ḥarāṭīn example demonstrates that keeping can be an essential part of giving even if it is not heirloom items that are withheld. Making their money difficult to access helps women manage balancing requests for aid with attempts to hold onto the resources they need to successfully run their businesses and improve the lives of their family members. Since generosity remains a key aspect of social worth, women's abilities to render income invisible or make it difficult to liquidate allows them to at least partially protect their resources while still participating in the exchange networks that are so important for cultivating women's social worth.

Credit, Debt, and Social Inequality

While the market is a place where social ties are formed and reinforced, it is also a place where difference is reproduced. Senior women exercise authority over junior women in this space, and women with greater economic capital have clear advantages in terms of cultivating their businesses and participating in the gift exchanges that are central to relationships. Given these differences, the relationships suwāqāt form are not always equal. This is particularly true of relations of credit and debt. Such practices are common today in part because, with the ongoing diminishment of wage labor under neoliberalism, "another kind of labor is invested in the forging of relations of borrowing, lending, and the extension of credit" (Makhulu 2010, 37). Giving and taking *dayn* (credit) is an essential part of Ḥarāṭīn women's attempts to not only get by but also get ahead.[12]

Kankossa has one bank. It began providing loans in 2011, but these opportunities were quite limited, so most men and women who needed smaller loans generally obtained them from individuals rather than institutions.[13] Almost all suwāqāt frequently buy larger items—kilos of carrots, sacks of potatoes—on credit and pay them off when they can. This is the case for household goods and items they will sell in the market. It is common for a woman to buy vegetables on credit from a wholesaler in the morning and to repay this debt from her ṭābla's profits in the afternoon. Fatimetou described such processes:

> I can go to a boutique, I say to the boutique owner, "you see, I don't have anything. I have only a purrī. I'm saving with a purrī with that woman there. Give me rice, give me oil, and when she gives me my purrī, I will come and bring you your money." He will say to me, "Of course." I take a sack of rice. I take five liters or ten liters of oil. I go with it. When I get that purrī, I will take it and go to that boutique owner, I'll tell him, "Look at that notebook [where he keeps track of credit]. How much?" He wrote it. He'll say, "At that time it was this or that much money." I will say, "Ok, take this. Thank you." I pay.

As this example illustrates, purrīs can serve as important collateral for women who may not have many assets. Relationships are also central to these processes, and suwāqāt like Fatimetou cultivate ties with particular wholesalers, hoping to build the trust over time that will grant them access to increasing amounts of credit. Being able to access credit is important economically and also because it serves as a marker of women's and men's respectability, which, in turn, is an essential part of garnering such support (McMahon 2013). Ḥarāṭīn women's abilities to take on and repay debt demonstrate their reputations as honest, respectable people and make this visible to others. In her description of how she accessed credit, Fatimetou highlights her own trustworthiness; the shopkeeper unquestionably accepts her claims and she promptly repays him as promised.

Such trustworthiness is especially important in this context where the risk of granting credit is high because most shopkeepers and suwāqāt abide by Islamic principles that forbid collecting interest. This raises the stakes of lending; if a person does not repay his or her loan, the lender cannot cover the loss with interest from other loans. Despite these challenges, most traders do grant credit. Doing so is often necessary to making sales at all. This is partly because many of the region's residents are farmers who earn the bulk of their income during a few months of the year, at which time they pay off the debts they have accumulated throughout the lean season. Refusing to sell to them before the harvest would mean missing out on significant potential earnings.

The importance of having a good reputation for accessing credit makes it challenging for new sellers to start businesses; one young man who aspired to do so complained he could not find a wholesaler in the regional capital who would give him credit because he was not known there. Men's desire to deal in large quantities of goods can be a barrier to beginning to trade since garnering extensive credit is challenging. Conversely, women's willingness to deal in smaller quantities of goods can make it easier for them to access credit; it is possible to start a ṭābla with only a small amount of goods and, thus, minimal credit.

Malaḥfas for sale in the market. Photo by author.

Suwāqāt also grant credit themselves and their decisions about such processes involve complex calculations that take into account a variety of factors, including the relationship a trader has with the potential credit seeker, the trader's current financial situation, the shopper's reputation, and how likely the trader thinks it is that the shopper will repay her. Traders are more likely to provide credit to regular customers who they call *kliyān* (clients, Fr.). The word kliyān is used to refer to both suwāqāt and their customers; a suwāqa's frequent customers are her kliyān and the suwāqa from whom a woman frequently buys or takes credit is also her kliyān. That this term is used to refer to both shopper and seller suggests the mutual dependence between the two.[14] Similarly, suwāqāt also call suppliers from whom they regularly purchase their ṭābla goods "kliyān." Ḥarāṭīn women attract and keep kliyān by creating a positive shopping experience, laughing and joking with them, and ensuring that they receive high quality goods.

Merchants also frame the practice of giving credit in terms of Islamic principles and the importance of caring for their neighbors. As one man put it, giving credit "releases people from their problems." He thus suggests it is a pious act that can help improve his neighbors' futures. Fatimetou explained, "If you come to me now and you don't have money, I could give you a kilo of potatoes. I could give you half a kilo of onions; you take some vegetables with you. You cook. You and your children eat. If you find money tomorrow, bring it to me. If you don't, it is in God's hands." Giving credit thus indexes sellers' generosity and piety, qualities that are important aspects of social worth.

Shoppers expect the suwāqāt they frequently buy from to treat them well; for example, one woman complained when a suwāqa gave her niece beets and squash with the vegetables for their daily meal, noting that she had been buying from that woman for a long time and that the trader should remember that she dislikes those vegetables. Traders sometimes give kliyān an extra onion or bag of spices at the end of a transaction, a gift that aims to continue the relationship (Kapchan 1996, 176; Pietila 2007, 59). Such acts blur the line between commodities and gifts, bringing these transactions into the realm of exchange, which is an important way through which relationships are constituted in this setting.

Courting and maintaining relationships with kliyān is an important part of suwāqāt's economic success, especially since there are dozens of suwāqāt in the market who sell many of the same items, often for the same prices. Giving credit, then, is an investment in a woman's own business because she hopes that the debtor will shop from her in the future, not just because she owes money but also to repay the suwāqa's generosity. Building expansive webs of credit and debt can also help serve as guarantees for women's economic futures (Guérin 2006, 555), giving them the possibility of collecting money owed to them if they encounter times of hardship. Suwāqāt often tried to collect debts at particular times of the year, such as before holidays for which families often spend significant funds on food and clothing. Men and women joked that these were bad times for some people to be in the market, as they risked having attention called to their debts.

The importance of the relationships suwāqāt form with their customers is evidenced by women's contentions that their ṭāblas do not do as well when they leave someone else in charge. Toutou noted, "When I send someone else to my ṭābla, my daughters or even my niece, things don't sell. Shoppers will ask them where I am. Then they will say they will come back later, but they won't." I experienced this myself when I managed women's ṭāblas (including Toutou's and Fatimetou's) while they did other errands. While people would make small purchases from me and many seemed curious about or amused by the white foreigner selling in the market, most people who approached the table simply asked me when the proprietor would return. This was partly because they rightly doubted my knowledge of the latest prices or my business skills; however, customers are also hesitant to buy from someone other than the proprietor because such transactions do not enhance their relationship, a connection that can help customers obtain better prices and service, as well as credit. Buying from me was especially risky since, because I was a foreigner and new to the community, I might not be able to accurately report the transaction and the identity of the purchaser to the suwāqa upon her return. Suwāqāt sometimes remind shoppers of these special relationships, calling out "kliyān" as they pass and asking why they are not visiting their ṭāblas.

While relations of indebtedness help women to expand their businesses as they increase their own borrowing and clients, credit also serves as a means of marking and reproducing inequality (Clark 1994, 173). Informal financial practices perpetuate socioeconomic difference since credit is most often given to people who have a history of paying off debts, which disadvantages the poorest members of the community who have difficulty doing so. Conversely, people who are better off financially can give credit, which enables them to enhance their power and control over others (Guérin 2006, 564). Such practices are nothing new in this context. Historically, elite groups throughout Mauritania reinforced their social positions by garnering dependents who would pay them tribute in return for protection (Ould Saleck 2003). The interdependence the term kliyān suggests between seller and shopper calls to mind these older patron-client relationships.

What is new here is not just that Ḥarāṭīn are constructing patron-client relations but also that women take part in these processes, which would have formerly been dominated by men.[15] When Ḥarāṭīn women give credit, they make visible and enhance their power and control over others by expanding their social networks and claiming dependents themselves. The more customers a woman can attract, the more prestige she garners (Simard 1996, 215). For someone like Fatimetou who started working in Kankossa as a maid, a position that is reminiscent of a slave, the ability to support others is a powerful symbol of her improved social position. Such power is tentative, however, since debtors may always default on their loans. While slave descendants in some cases maintain dependent positions in order to survive conditions of extreme poverty (Rossi 2015, 310), the Kankossa case illustrates that they may also have the possibility of entering such arrangements with other Ḥarāṭīn. This does not necessarily index increased liberation per say, but it does suggest a reworking of social positions among Ḥarāṭīn themselves, which, while it still reproduces inequality, can provide additional avenues for support.

Granting credit thus provides people the possibility of making their generosity, and subsequently their social worth, visible and also facilitates the reproduction of social difference. For example, one Ḥarāṭīn male merchant noted that he gives credit to those who are *mawthūqa* (reliable, trustworthy) and, "If we didn't give credit, we would now be Bill Gates." His assertion that he, and his father who he works for, would be rich if he avoided giving credit speaks to the risks of this practice. Furthermore, by claiming that if he refused to give credit he would be as rich as one of the richest men in the world, this merchant implies that he gives massive amounts of loans. Shoppers share information about which merchants grant credit and merchants themselves often make this visible by complaining about the loans they have given or recording shoppers' debt in notebooks in front of others. This man's claim is an example of such processes, demonstrating how granting credit is an important way through which people display their generosity and wealth and thus attest to their social worth.

Generosity has long been a valued social quality in the region. Noble social codes historically valued this trait, while lower status was associated with having to ask for support rather than provide it to others. These opposing forms of comportment reinforced each other since "the beggar gives the noble the opportunity to prove his nobility" (Klein 2005, 843). These values continue to be meaningful in Kankossa, with men and women critiquing those who ask. For example, when one young man was discussing various social categories with me, he noted that iggāwen, muʿallimīn, and znāga occupy low social positions in the Bīẓān hierarchy, partly because they are always "asking." He explained that "people who ask, they are nothing." Given the negative connotations that come with asking, it makes sense that women justify their work by the fact that it keeps them from having to ask others for support.

Negative associations with asking continue to resonate in the market. For example, Toutou's husband, Brahime, told me he stopped frequenting a particular shop when the proprietor suggested Brahime owed him money. Brahime's insistence that he was not in debt at all since he always pays his bills at the end of each month illustrates the enduring negative connotations associated with taking credit. So while practicing generous acts in the market indexes social worth, asking for credit can do the opposite.

Women sometimes take advantage of these negative connotations to avoid giving credit, and to justify such decisions. One day, an old Halpulaar woman in worn clothing bent over Fatimetou's table and asked about the price of the peanuts Fatimetou was selling out of an old rice sack that leaned against the table.

The woman was unhappy with the price Khady, Fatimetou's daughter, offered and asked her to lower it. Khady justified her refusal to do so by explaining that the requested price was less than their wholesale cost. After the woman left, Khady complained, "Kwār only ask. They always want gifts." She laughed as she said this, but her implication that this woman is like a beggar helped to justify her refusal to lower her price. The social networks women form help them to avoid asking for help, which is part of their appeal due to asking's connotations with low social rank. Women should ideally be generous with friends and family in need, giving before they have to ask.

Shifting Hierarchy in the Market

While suwāqāt work to revalue their labor as independent and as an integral part of the modern economy, their comportment in the market makes it clear that this work is not independent at all. For Kankossa's suwāqāt, like Fatimetou, social relations are increasingly essential to their success in this volatile economic climate. While women's relationships with others provide important friendship and emotional support, the range of social networks they cultivate—be they 'aṣr, group savings associations, or new forms of patron-client relationships—give them flexibility to maneuver in difficult economic times. Women have also shifted networks, such as 'aṣr that would have formerly been part of domestic spheres into the economic realm. This example calls into question the workings of contemporary capitalism and the centrality of the individual worker to it and shows how relying on others is essential for many suwāqāt in this particular economic context.

That many of the people who are central to these networks are not relatives also illustrates how Ḥarāṭīn are remaking the underpinnings of social hierarchy by emphasizing the importance of ties outside of genealogy and their abilities to cultivate them. Historian Elisabeth McMahon has argued that scholars often overemphasize the importance of blood and marriage in forming kinship and relationships among slaves and ex-slaves (2013, 194). It is, of course, a fact that slave descendants lack the depth of known genealogy of their elite counterparts, some of whom can trace their genealogy back to the prophet Mohamed (Scheele 2012). However, Ḥarāṭīn women's ability to form relationships with a broad range of women, essentially building their own social networks that act similarly to other groups' kin networks, helps ensure their economic security. It is also a means through which they assert free and valued status by displaying qualities that elites would have formerly publically monopolized. Cultivating social networks allows traders to assert their social worth as generous, respectable people who now garner semi-dependents themselves. Since their economic strategies help women to assert their social worth, they also reinforce women's verbal claims about the value of their work.

In this climate, women's socioeconomic class affects their abilities to exercise power over others, with wealthier suwāqāt being able to grant and take more credit than their poorer counterparts. This example illustrates scholars' contentions that economic class and wealth are impacting the way social status is understood and manifest in Mauritania—with ascribed attributes like birth being superseded by achieved ones like wealth. This is not a new phenomenon. In 1943, a French colonial administrator wrote that a Ḥarāṭīn "working class" was forming, saying that "a new social hierarchy, founded uniquely on wealth, is being established. Politically, it is difficult to predict the consequences of this evolution which consecrates the importance of work and which destroys the ancient *seigneurs* [masters]" (quoted in McDougall 2005, 960). In the context of increasing wage labor, understandings of the value of work also shifted. While in the past hard work was considered a marker of low social status, in the contemporary era this was a symbol of "a new, a modern attitude" (Ruf 1999, 265). Ḥarāṭīn's labor ensured their financial independence and helped mark their status as free people. But while French administrators might have respected Ḥarāṭīn's economic success, Bīẓān elites did not necessarily feel the same way (McDougall 1988), again illustrating how cultural values are contested.

Ascribed attributes do still have meaning in contemporary Kankossa, especially when people are contracting marriage, but wealth also serves as an important avenue to negotiating status. This is true not only because of wealthier individuals' abilities to acquire material goods, such as real estate and livestock, that make their wealth visible but also because of the possibilities greater economic resources in the market offer. Fatimetou's successful table, along with the security that having a son with a salaried position provides her, makes it easier for her to expand her social networks by offering credit and participating in gift exchanges than it is for her less well-off counterparts. Her access to resources and wealth thus also helps her make visible other valued qualities such as respect, generosity, and piety.

An ability to claim and cultivate such attributes is especially important to slave descendants. Not only does this give women like Fatimetou the possibility of being associated with higher-status categories like Khaẓarīn, but women's emphasis on and valuing of such qualities reinforces the centrality of these achieved attributes to hierarchy in general, thus making it easier for them to claim spaces within it. While Bīẓān may use similar strategies and value these attributes as well, the entrenched hierarchy among Bīẓān themselves can limit the kinds of people they can draw into their networks. This is especially true in a place like Kankossa, where the Bīẓān population is relatively small. Ḥarāṭīn have more flexibility, then, in who can become part of their networks (including kwār). This ability expands their possibilities for cultivating these markers of social worth, though inequality between Ḥarāṭīn themselves is also increasingly visible.[16]

Since not all suwāqāt have the financial means to provide credit or the respected reputations needed to obtain it, the practice of giving credit also engenders inequality between traders. Traders' lending practices thus inscribe difference and contribute to the formation of new hierarchies, with poorer Ḥarāṭīn occupying lower positions than their wealthier Ḥarāṭīn counterparts. Poorer suwāqāt, for example, may not be able to grant credit if they need money to purchase their own daily necessities. This fact reproduces their disadvantaged status and makes it difficult for them to garner kliyān. Similarly, since most suwāqāt take credit from male wholesalers, these relationships also reinforce the enduring differential power relationships between men and women in the market. Of course, inequality is also reproduced and made visible in other ways. For example, some wealthier shoppers purposefully buy from poorer individuals, especially relatives; in this way, they turn the client relationship on its head as they deliberately support others through their purchases. Likewise, giving credit to someone a woman knows likely cannot repay her becomes charity and indexes the trader's morality and her power and privileged position.

The importance given to these social networks also means an inability to nurture them can have serious consequences. After all, not all women are successful in the market. Some suwāqāt have small ṭāblas with tiny piles of dusty bags of spices that rarely attract customers, even during the mid-morning rush. Some of these women do not have access to adequate start-up funds, others may have made poor business decisions, and still others do not have the broad social networks that help facilitate success. One malaḥfa seller complained she had a hard time attracting clients since she had recently moved to Kankossa with her husband and had limited social contacts. Women who are not successful businesswomen and who do not have other family members to support them risk becoming dependent on others or, perhaps worse, becoming isolated. Someone without friends is seen as lacking personhood in Mauritania, as was made clear when women criticized a local man who liked to spend excessive time alone.

The market, then, is a place where some suwāqāt successfully assert their social worth, but it is also a place where the lower status of others is reproduced. It is important not to assume all Ḥarāṭīn women are the same but rather to take into consideration their intersecting attributes, including generation and socioeconomic class, and how these contribute to the shaping of their opportunities and experiences (Collins 1998; Crenshaw 1991). Doing so can help illuminate the diverse experiences of Ḥarāṭīn and better identify attributes that contribute to women's well-being. This is important given reports in the international media surrounding slavery in Mauritania that imply all Ḥarāṭīn are equally oppressed and downtrodden. Acknowledging diverse experiences among Ḥarāṭīn themselves paints a fuller picture of this social category and helps identify factors that contribute to women's success. After all, the increasing centrality of diverse configurations of women's social networks—business partners, clients, group savings association members, junior women, friends—to women's operations in the market reinforces new kinds of hierarchies and thus leaves some women behind. Such difference is further reinforced by the fact that women who are successful in the market can more easily invest in exchange relationships, which, as I analyze in the following chapter, are an important way through which women not only assert their own social status but literally remake others' social standing as well.

Notes

1. Wooden limbars consist of wooden posts that hold up the tent-like covering. One advantage of the cement versions is that they have elevated concrete floors (often covered with carpets). Since wooden versions' floors are generally the desert's surface covered with mats, the concrete versions are easier to keep clean.

2. During my research, the state did provide people with subsidized staple goods throughout the country: flour, sugar, oil, and rice. However, lines for these items were long, which made it difficult for many Kankossa residents to regularly access them, and these "solidarity boutiques" experienced frequent shortages. Women depending on other women is not unique to Mauritania but can be found in other parts of Africa as well (Ilahiane and Sherry 2008; Osirim 2009; Overå 2007; Robertson 1997).

3. Anthropologist Clifford Geertz has emphasized the importance of one's ability to access and control information to success in markets: "The search for information—laborious, uncertain, complex, and irregular—is the central experience of life in the bazaar, an enfolding reality its institutions at once create and respond to" (1979, 125).

4. Historian Elisabeth McMahon provides an in-depth analysis of similar processes in post-abolition Pemba where honor shifted from being controlled by elites to being a "network of relationships defined by respectability" that former slaves and slave descendants could cultivate (2013, 18).

5. In 2011, life expectancy in Mauritania was sixty-two years old, meaning thirty-nine was middle-age. "Mauritania." *The World Bank*. Accessed May 19, 2016. http://data.worldbank.org/country/mauritania.

6. See chapter five for a more complete discussion of this term.

7. Such positive connections are not always present in Mauritania. Leservoisier (2000) examines relationships between the Halpulaar and Ḥarāṭīn in the Senegal Valley from the mid-1800s to the present, noting how Ḥarāṭīn often worked as laborers for the Halpulaar and faced discrimination and prejudice. The relationships between these groups in a variety of settings merits further research.

8. Fatimetou's example thus contradicts Hamzetta's contention that group savings associations fail to undermine structural poverty and thus reproduce inequality because it is difficult for women to increase their levels of contributions (2003, 172). It also contradicts William Lawrence's contention that such money is rarely used to invest in productive activities (1999, 13).

9. The overall banking rate in Mauritania is generally low and was 5 percent in 2010 (Victor Muisyo, "Mauritania records low banking rate despite growth in financial sector."

Africanews.com, July 6. Accessed July 8, 2016. http://www.africanews.com/2016/06/07/mauritania-records-low-banking-rate-despite-growth-in-financial-sector/).

10. Learning how to fit into exchange networks is a challenge many anthropologists share. I relied heavily on Kankossa friends to guide my participation in exchange processes and they provided helpful advice on how much to give, in what circumstances, and to whom. While I aimed to be generous with my interlocutors and friends, I did appreciate the time at the end of a stint in Kankossa when I could honestly say I did not have the ability to fulfill requests. I think my feelings stemmed less from being able to save money and more from a brief relief of the stress of navigating such complicated networks. Of course, my experience of giving differed in key ways from that of my interlocutors due to a variety of factors, including my position as a US citizen, my relative wealth in comparison to many of them, and people's assumptions about the economic means of foreigners, which are heavily influenced by television.

11. This is based on the Qur'an (4:11).

12. While in Arabic dayn refers to debt, in Hassaniya this term is also used to mean credit (Wehr 1994, 353).

13. Some men told me they received loans to construct their houses or to fund other projects from financial institutions elsewhere in the country, but I heard of no women who did so.

14. Reciprocal terms like this are also used in Ghana where market traders call both buyers and suppliers "customer" (Clark 1994, 228–34).

15. Anthropologist Rachel Newcomb describes a similar process in Fes, Morocco, in which women are coming to construct patron-client relations, which men would have monopolized in the past (2009, 6).

16. This is not to say there has not been hierarchy among Ḥarāṭīn and even slaves. Slaves who were born into the master's household were more highly valued than those who had been captured. Likewise, how a slave became freed impacted how others viewed them, with slaves who had been freed by French colonial law, as opposed to those who had been freed by Islamic law, seen as not being properly freed (McDougall 2015). Historically some Ḥarāṭīn were also able to cultivate great wealth and powerful social positions (McDougall 2005). However, such hierarchy was not as formally entrenched as it was among Bīẓān, giving Ḥarāṭīn more flexibility in constructing social networks.

5 Making People Bigger: Wedding Exchange and the Creation of Social Value

HASSAN WAS MARRYING his cousin Meimouna at the end of the cold season. I piled into the back of a pickup truck with his Kankossa friends and relatives, and we traveled for close to an hour over the sandy track that led to his village where the wedding would take place. Located near the border with Mali, Hassan's village is populated by a few hundred residents who make their livings primarily by farming and herding. Hassan had left his home close to a decade earlier to attend high school in Kankossa where I had met and become close with him and his extended family while teaching English in the Peace Corps. Upon graduating, he enrolled in the university in Mauritania's capital, Nouakchott. His educational success is impressive, partly because it was rare for anyone from Kankossa to study at the university and because Hassan, like his family and Meimouna's, is Ḥarāṭīn, who continue to be underrepresented in higher education. Meimouna lived with her immediate family in a nearby village and was in her mid-teens, a common age for women to marry there (Hassan was in his mid-twenties). It is also common for cousins to marry (Stewart 1992); a 1991 study found 22 percent of Ḥarāṭīn married first cousins, though the percentage of marriages that were consanguineous has declined over time (Hammami et al. 2005, 40).

Along the journey, we shouted out the praise name of Hassan's qabīla and held tight to the thick rope netting that secured the luggage as the driver honked to anyone we passed. As we pulled up to Hassan's family compound, a large open space surrounded by several small buildings, the driver—one of Hassan's best friends—drove in tighter and tighter circles to make an impressive entrance as the women in the back shrieked. Upon disembarking, we piled our dusty plastic bags of clothes into a room that had been reserved for out-of-town female guests. The most important pieces of luggage were part of the *ṣaḍāq*, the bridewealth or money and gifts the groom's family would give the bride's after the contraction of the marriage. Throughout the day, the women in our party, as well as friends and relatives from Hassan's village, rooted through the two *valises* (suitcases, Fr.) that were part of the ṣaḍāq, pulling out the veils, dresses, shoes, and beauty products and exclaiming over their quality and value.[1] These items and the rest of the ṣaḍāq were essential parts of Hassan's wedding. The exchanges that revolved around these gifts would help bind the couple and their families together, delineate their broader social networks, and display their wealth.

In this chapter, I concentrate on exchanges at a single wedding to explore how a family's particular history and social position affect these processes. Since Hassan's family members are better off financially than many other Ḥarāṭīn families in the region, this wedding provided extensive exchanges to analyze; these gift exchanges also reflected practices that occurred at other Ḥarāṭīn weddings that I heard about and attended during my research, if on a different scale. Since the bride's and groom's families are generally separated throughout the wedding celebration, my observations largely focused on Hassan's family, although I did spend several hours at the bride's home the day after the marriage was contracted when Meimouna's bridal henna was being applied. This attention to the experiences of the groom's family compliments other literature that has primarily examined the wedding practices and exchanges of the bride's family and also demonstrates the innovative practices that women and men employ to generate social and economic value in the neoliberal moment.[2] While this chapter focuses on the groom's side of the exchanges, I attended several other Kankossa weddings as a guest of the bride's family, which allowed me to gain a sense of both sides' experiences.

Recently, copious exchanges at family ceremonies in Mauritania have come under attack by Muslim clerics and others who claim they are an unproductive waste of resources; similar critiques have also been raised elsewhere in West Africa (Buggenhagen 2012; Masquelier 2009b). Hassan's wedding contradicts this contention by demonstrating that exchange can be a productive act. While in the past slaves did not have as much control over contracting marriages or generating bridewealth as their free counterparts, today marriage exchange is an important way through which Ḥarāṭīn generate social worth. These processes reinforce social networks, display wealth, and bestow value on others.

The effects of exchange were amplified at Hassan and Meimouna's wedding because, while the ṣaḍāq was ostensibly intended for the bride's family, Meimouna's relatives returned a large portion of it to the groom's family the day after the marriage was contracted. By doing so, they associated both families with the gift and helped heighten the display of wealth and generosity. This example complicates the binary between dowry-based marriage systems and those relying on bridewealth, showing not only that both systems are employed here, but also that the meaning of gifts shift as they pass back and forth between the involved parties.[3] It also illustrates how the return of gifts can be an integral part of exchange processes and a vital way through which people strive to bestow others with value and position themselves and others socially. There is, however, no guarantee that such value will endure; women and men employ discourse to try to ensure the effects of exchange continue well into the future. Ultimately, slave descendants assert higher social rank and attempt to reconfigure the basis of status through their engagement in exchange, which suggests social rank is coming to be based upon achieved attributes, such as economic standing and generosity, and not ascribed factors, like genealogy, as it was in the past.

Meanings of Marriage in Times of Slavery

Marriage and wealth have long been connected to the production of social hierarchy in Mauritania since slave status was partly based upon exclusion from kinship relations (Coquery-Vidrovitch 2007; Ruf 1999). While slaves' links with their biological kin were severed when they were sold or captured in raids, slave owners' regulation of marriage practices was also an important means of controlling slaves and their descendants. Slaves in Mauritania and elsewhere in the region could marry, but they needed their owners' consent to do so. Masters retained rights over their married slaves; they could dissolve their marriages and also maintained the right to restrict slaves' movements, determine their domicile, and control their domestic labor (Ali 2010). In Islam, freeborn women are forbidden from engaging in sexual relations before marriage, so slave owners also reinforced distinctions between freeborn and slave women by taking slaves as concubines (McDougall 2008). Becoming a concubine could allow women to claim increased agency and rights; if a master acknowledged paternity of a concubine's children, she was to be freed upon his death, though this was not always carried out in practice (McDougall 1998, 290).[4] In some cases, slave owners also pushed their slaves to marry Ḥarāṭīn men in order to increase their slave holdings because the children from these unions would be considered the property of the masters (McDougall 2014). The freeborn also generally avoided contracting marriages with people who had slave ancestry. This practice continues today to some extent; when I asked a Kankossa woman why a friend was having trouble contracting a marriage, she implied that he was of recent slave descent or was perhaps still a slave himself.

Similarly, slaves were prevented from accumulating excessive wealth; slave owners controlled slaves' possessions. Elite status was associated with an ability to accumulate wealth, and high-status groups often increased their wealth by garnering dependents who paid them tribute in exchange for protection. This meant that beyond their slaves, elites had freeborn dependents, including Bīẓān. Slaves and other dependents' experiences thus overlapped in some ways but diverged in others, including the level of control elites exercised over the various groups. Masters controlled slaves' possessions and could arbitrarily claim their goods (Ould Cheikh 1994; Ruf 1999, 90). Wealth that slaves had accumulated over the course of their lives was also inherited by their masters upon their deaths (Brhane 1997, 68), though in some places slaves may have been able to keep assets that they earned during their spare time, including dowries (Hall 2011, 76). Slave status, then, was partially defined by an inability to accumulate—or distribute—wealth.

What former slaves' marriage ceremonies and the surrounding exchanges were like after they gained their freedom has not been extensively documented, but their bridewealth would have been much lower than their elite Bīẓān counterparts (McDougall 2014; Tauzin 2001, 161n). While she does not discuss the composition of Ḥarāṭīn bridewealth, French traveler and ethnologist Odette du Puigaudeau (2002) noted—through observations during her travels in Mauritania from the 1930s to 1960—that ṣaḍāqs varied based upon the wealth and occupations of the wedding participants. Fishermen gave dry fish, while rich merchants gave up to fifty camels (2002, 195–96). Despite little available data, it seems clear many newly freed slaves asserted their independence by attempting to control their work and family lives, for example, by negotiating their own marriages and collecting bridewealth (Klein 2005, 844).[5] Changes in former slaves' wedding practices reflected and engendered their changing positions in the polity, with collecting bridewealth being a way to signify freeborn status and differentiate freeborn men and women from slaves (Cooper 1997; Grosz-Ngaté 1988; Strobel 1979).

Today, bridewealth remains an important part of weddings for all social groups in Mauritania, and escalating expectations for the amount of such gifts have put pressure on young men and their families. During my research, in Kankossa and the surrounding region, the cash given as part of bridewealth for most first marriages was at least 100,000 MRO (USD351), but it often far exceeded this amount. This represents an immense increase in rural ṣaḍāqs, which were approximately 30,000 MRO (USD105) in the early 1990s (de la Brosse 1991, 118). In the 1800s and early 1900s, ṣaḍāqs would have largely consisted of gifts of animals and locally produced goods; cash, cloth, and other merchandise were also acceptable items of marriage exchange, which illustrates how the region has long been integrated into the global economy (du Puigaudeau 2002, 195). The bulk of ṣaḍāqs today are composed of cash and consumer goods. The contemporary escalation of the quantity of goods and the amount of cash that compose the ṣaḍāq, along with the ever-increasing variety of imported goods that can be used as wedding prestations puts growing pressure on men and women to participate in the cash economy to be able to fund such ceremonies.[6]

High expectations for what constitutes a reasonable ṣaḍāq and the kinds of goods that should be included make it difficult for young men to gather the resources needed to wed. Young men's inabilities to fund weddings themselves are also exacerbated by the country's high unemployment rate. These challenges result in the delay of marriages and put increasing pressure on young men's wider social networks to fund such ceremonies. Such costs are not limited to financing bridewealth. Older women also complain that while weddings used to take place over the course of one night, today it is common for them to last several days, with evening events—including live music and dancing—and a great deal of food, all of which are expensive. Similarly, the expenditures of the bride's family have also increased. These challenges are not unique to Ḥarāṭīn and may put pressure on even wealthy individuals' finances, though poorer individuals of all social groups feel them most acutely. Despite these overlapping experiences, I am interested here in how Ḥarāṭīn specifically deal with such challenges and how their participation in wedding exchanges articulates with their larger social positioning.

Growing expectations for bridewealth are not uncontested. Some men and women draw on Muslim teachings to challenge what they see as inflated ṣaḍāqs as well as the lavish spending that occurs at weddings in general. They insist that, in Islam, only a small sum is required to marry, so even a token gift like a *miswāk* (a stick that is used for cleaning teeth) can be sufficient. These critics contend that copious exchanges at weddings conflict with Islam's teachings, and they suggest the size of ṣaḍāqs be drastically limited. Some groups have already reduced expenditures at family ceremonies; leaders of one qabīla, for example, decided that the size of the ṣaḍāq for their members should be limited to between 60,000 and 100,000 MRO (USD211 and $351) (L'Authentique 2012). This ruling was intended to make it easier for young men to marry and came in tandem with a decision to allow polygynous marriages, which leaders said would help the group cope with the high numbers of single women. Despite such challenges, many Ḥarāṭīn women and men continue to support and produce large amounts of bridewealth, in part because of the essential role it plays in asserting social worth.

Reinforcing Relationships Through Wedding Exchange

After our arrival in Hassan's village, the suitcases—one large, one small—that contained part of the ṣaḍāq remained the center of attention. Aminetou, a relative of Hassan's, had brought them from the capital, where she had purchased them and their contents with money Hassan's family had provided. In her early twenties, Aminetou always seemed to be impeccably adorned in the latest fashions. Her veils were made of high-quality fabric that matched what she wore beneath them: glittering costume jewelry, stylish platform shoes, and dresses that were embellished with details that marked them as expensive—shoulder straps braided in intricate patterns or necklines decorated with rhinestones. Aminetou also spoke with great authority about fashion. She insisted, for example, that three-quarter length sleeves were en vogue, noting that popular singers wore them on television and in performances in the capital. While items for the ṣaḍāq can be purchased in Kankossa, bringing them from Nouakchott ensured that the valise contained the latest goods and signified the family's connections to elsewhere.[7]

The larger suitcase that is part of the ṣaḍāq. Photo by author.

As is common in this part of the country, the larger suitcase was filled with gifts—dresses, shoes, lotions, soap, and mirrors—that were all in the same quantity, in this case twelve. The quantity of marriage prestations creates an image of prosperity, illustrating families' productive capacities and their social networks that help purchase these items (Cooper 1997; Masquelier 2009b, 190). These items were funded collectively by contributions from friends and relatives throughout the country, so the bridewealth helped reinforce and delineate the participants' broader social networks.[8] These ties were reiterated after the wedding. For example, when I was visiting her one afternoon, Hassan's sister recited the amount of money each of his siblings had provided for the bridewealth. While exchange processes can engender and strengthen relations for other groups in Mauritania, including Bīẓān, this aspect of exchange has special resonance for Ḥarāṭīn given that barring people from forming enduring relations with others reinforced one's slave status historically. These exchanges demonstrate women's and men's abilities to create, nurture, and display social ties, thus distancing them from lower-status individuals.

Beyond helping to fund the ṣaḍāq, Hassan's parents also worked to influence the timing of his wedding. Hassan framed his marriage to Meimouna in terms of love, frequently speaking to her on the phone in the months leading up to the wedding and visiting her when he returned to his village. But his family had pushed for the wedding to happen quickly, even having it take place several months earlier than originally scheduled. Hassan said he was unsure of why they were in such a hurry, but he suspected they wanted to tie him more firmly to them and his natal village. Since marriage is typically virilocal in this region, Meimouna would move in with Hassan's parents after the wedding—meaning his family would enjoy Hassan's visits and economic contributions to her. In part, his marriage to Meimouna helped prevent him from marrying a stranger in Nouakchott, which would risk diminishing his affective and economic ties with his family. Their hurry to contract the marriage reflects the anxieties many Kankossa residents feel about how to maintain family ties when men migrate elsewhere for work. Hassan's lack of significant income provided his family members with greater control over this process than they would have had if he had been able to fund his wedding himself.

The smaller suitcase held four sets of high-quality costume jewelry, as well as lotion, spray deodorant, perfume, face powder, and nail polish, which would later be used to adorn the bride. In addition to these items, Aminetou had brought six high-quality dresses and malaḥfas (Mauritanian veils) that were reserved exclusively for Meimouna. The women added some jewelry from the smaller valise to this pile, noting that if they did not it would "walk away," since the contents of the suitcases would later be distributed to others. The ṣadāq also included an expensive blanket, a boom box, and a cellphone.

On the afternoon of our arrival, the valises took center stage as female relatives and friends of Hassan's stopped by the room to examine them, pulling out their contents and asking about their value, trying on jewelry, and unfolding malaḥfas to scrutinize the colorful fabrics and patterns. In the late afternoon, as the sun was beginning to drop toward the horizon, women brought the valises into the courtyard. A crowd of women gathered around them, trying to see their contents. Some women clapped and danced, while the two muʿallimīn who would later do the bride's henna removed the items one by one, holding them up and commenting on their quality and value. They counted the contents, verifying that the larger valise contained twelve of each item, and examined the black malaḥfa, dress, and headdress the bride would wear the next day when she would first appear in public as a married woman.

The groom's family then loaded the valises onto the top of a truck that took them, along with the sacks of rice, flour, sugar, and other food items that were part of the ṣadāq, to the bride's family's compound. Most of us followed on foot. Upon arrival, the women sat on cushions along the edges of bright plastic mats that now held the ṣadāq and would later become the dance floor. As is typical in Mauritanian weddings, neither the bride nor the groom was present at this point. The older men gathered in one corner, preparing for their role in the ceremony. After the *ʿaqd*, during which men recite from the Qur'an and officially contract the marriage, an older man shot off a gun several times in celebration. This action marks the signing of the contract and makes the marriage public (Tauzin 2001, 160) and, historically, was also meant to help protect the bride from spirits (Fortier 2001). Older women from both families then examined the ṣadāq, opening the valises and counting the contents. The bride's mother would later redistribute some of these items to her friends and relatives, a practice that delineates her social networks and reaffirms virtues like generosity.

As is typically the case, the ṣadāq included a sum of money; 500,000 MRO (USD1,754) was presented at this time. This was high for a rural wedding, especially because the average per capita income in Mauritania in 2011 was USD1,140.[9] The size of Hassan's ṣadāq demonstrates growing expectations for what constitutes a reasonable ṣadāq and suggests some Ḥarāṭīn are making significant gains financially. It also reflects his family's connections in Nouakchott, where several of his relatives had well-paying jobs at private companies. By asserting their wealth and generosity through these exchanges, Hassan's family members displayed their productive capacity and social value. I heard people call low ṣadāqs "ṣadāq Ḥarāṭīn," but the amount of wealth circulated at Hassan's wedding disassociated Ḥarāṭīn, at least these Ḥarāṭīn, from poverty and low social rank. The quality and quantity of the gifts and cash that constitute the ṣadāq thus contribute to displaying and creating social difference and hierarchy since not everyone is capable of producing equally sizable ṣadāqs.

Hassan's family's display of wealth was heightened by the fact that the ṣadāq was just part of the exchanges that would continue over the next several days. Wedding exchanges also include the *'āda* (customs), which refers to gifts given to women in the bride's family by the groom, although it may also indicate other exchanges at weddings (Tauzin 2001, 183–85). In determining the ʿāda, men are expected to follow the bride's family's customs, and women told me that a marriage could be ruined if they did not. While they might vary slightly between families, Ḥarāṭīn women in Kankossa in 2011 noted that their ʿāda included: approximately twenty-five veils for the bride; ten veils and 10,000 MRO (USD35) for the bride's mother; money to pay for the bride's henna and hair braiding; money for her friends who had collected the mats and other furnishings that would be used in the ceremony; and money that would fund a small party for the bride and her friends held at her parents' home. The veils are generally redistributed among the social networks of the bride and her mother and thus help reinforce and make visible these ties, as do the small celebrations that such funds support.

In the past, ʿāda were determined largely by qabīla, and each qabīla's ʿāda differed (de la Brosse 1991; du Puigaudeau 2002; Fortier 2001). Today, Ḥarāṭīn in Kankossa insist that their ʿāda are "ʿāda Kankossa," which vary slightly based upon the neighborhood in which women live. The fact that wedding customs seem to be becoming disentangled from those of the qabīla suggests the weakening of these institutions and the opening of other avenues for defining social worth and value. Drawing on their locality as an important part of identity provides an alternative way for Ḥarāṭīn to define themselves (Ruf 1999, 270), and the fact that they have long been marginalized in qabīla helps facilitate such processes. Kankossa's unique history, in which early settlers secured economic opportunities outside of the qabīla system, further opens the possibility for the creation of new forms of belonging for Ḥarāṭīn that center around geography rather than genealogy.

Additional gifts from the man's family help to mark the end of the ceremony and the bride's movement to her new home with her in-laws. Two sums of money—*jamal itbrīka* (stooping camel) and *isbū'* (the week; marks the end of wedding week)—are given either at the end of the celebration or once his family is able to gather them.[10] Women noted that the amount of these gifts is not fixed; it varies proportionally with the groom's family's wealth. Furthermore, the contents and quantities of goods demanded in the ʿāda may shift and increase over time. For example, by the time I left Kankossa, the number of veils expected for the bride's friends had increased to thirty.

The bride's family also gives a variety of items to the man's family; the amount they spend on them varies based upon the size of the ṣaḍāq. As is the case elsewhere (Cooper 1997, 94; de la Brosse 1991, 108), women and men agree that, ultimately, the bride's family spends more than the groom's despite being given the bridewealth payment. Their expenditures include two gifts of money or household items that are sent to their in-laws, called *ḥenna* and *qaṣṣa*.[11] The largest expense, however, is the bride's *rahīl*, the household items and furnishings that accompany her to her new home and remain her property in the case of divorce (du Puigaudeau 2002; Tauzin 2001), thus serving as a form of economic security.[12] There are high expectations for the bride's family's gifts, which can put a great deal of financial strain on them.

Together these exchanges help delineate the participants' social networks and assert their generosity and wealth. Social connections are cultivated and reinforced through the financial contributions friends and relatives make to help fund these gifts. Likewise, networks are delineated by the distribution of the wedding gifts to friends and relatives, often the same people who contributed in the first place. The fact that Meimouna's mother gave me a malaḥfa at this wedding helped to incorporate me into their social network. Hassan's family urged me to wear it at one of the evening celebrations, which made these ties visible to anyone who had seen the ṣaḍāq's contents (that is until I had to change after a wedding guest threw up on me due to eating too much meat—a sure sign of a successful wedding).

For the Ḥarāṭīn, then, exchange is not unproductive but is rather a generative process. It makes visible Ḥarāṭīn's abilities to cultivate and nurture strong relationships—along with valued attributes like generosity—and thus indexes their free status and social worth. Such wedding exchanges also serve as one step in many exchanges that may bind the two families together in a long-term relationship that ideally will be characterized by later reciprocity at holidays and other family ceremonies (de la Brosse 1991).

Bestowing Value Through the Return of the Ṣaḍāq

The giving (and accepting) of the ṣaḍāq helped to delineate Hassan and Meimouna's families' social networks, as well as their wealth and generosity. But what about its return? The day after the contraction of the marriage, Meimouna's family divided the gifts and money that comprised the ṣaḍāq and returned half of them to Hassan's family, sending them back to his compound on a donkey cart. This practice surprised me because it appeared to be a rejection of the gift, and it occurred so quickly. Theorists have emphasized that both of these elements are important parts of exchange processes; returning the exact gift one has been given risks signaling its rejection, while a temporal gap between exchanges helps propel the relationship between both parties into the future since one is in debt to the other.[13] Meimouna's family members violated both of these tenets by giving back a significant portion of the items that had been presented to them and returning the gift quickly. Why did they do this, and was it intended to be a refusal of the bridewealth? I was especially surprised about this act because of the many gifts the bride's family would be responsible for presenting to the groom's family and their daughter over the next few days and weeks. The money that came with the ṣaḍāq could help finance these purchases.

A few weeks after Hassan's marriage, I asked Nahna, one of the women who had attended it with us, to explain the gift exchanges that had occurred there, particularly the return of the ṣaḍāq. I explore her analysis here because she spoke in such detail about the events and because her explanation reflects how many other people discuss the significance of exchange in this context. Her comments provide insight into how, rather than being a rejection of the gift, the return of the ṣaḍāq is an integral way through which exchange participants bestow themselves and others with social value.

Such processes help both parties display their wealth and generosity. As Nahna explained, "Not every person returns it. A person who returns it is only a person who is a rich person, who has something. He also likes you. He knows that you also like him. He likes you a lot, his heart likes you." Nahna emphasizes how only a family who is well-off can afford to return the bridewealth, an act that then signifies their economic status. In the case of a marriage between poor people, or a second marriage, the ṣaḍāq is often smaller and the bride's family is not expected to return a portion of it or to conduct the many other exchanges that typically occur around weddings. The fact that not everyone returns the ṣaḍāq further highlights the wealth of those who do so. Nahna also insists on an affective dimension to exchanges like these, demonstrating how love and material exchanges may be intertwined (Cole 2009; Ferguson 1999; Masquelier 2009a; Thomas and Cole 2009).

Some grooms' families do not accept the bride's family's return of the ṣaḍāq but rather urge them to keep it. As it is with the bride's family, this is no small act considering the many gifts they must purchase in addition to the ṣaḍāq. Beyond the gifts they are responsible for, the groom's family also hosts a large evening celebration and a luncheon for the newlyweds and their friends, while also feeding out-of-town guests for several days. Nahna explained that refusing to accept the return makes visible the groom's family's wealth, generosity, and productive capacity, indicating that they do not need these funds to offset the cost of their additional wedding expenditures. She voiced a groom's family's explanation of why they had refused the return: "We won't take it, we—praise be to God—have a lot of wealth. We are *mqadārīn* [capable, powerful], full [of money]. We don't want it: you take it."

The back-and-forth movement of the ṣaḍāq also has the potential to strengthen the social and economic ties between the two families. In West Africa and elsewhere, gifts are often expected to be returned, ideally with increment, thus creating debt and binding people together in ever-growing displays of generosity (Buggenhagen 2012; Malinowski [1922] 1984; Mauss [1950] 1990; Strobel 1979). Inequality is central to the continuity of these relationships (Strathern 1988; Weiner 1992). By returning the ṣaḍāq to the groom's family, the bride's family effectively puts the groom's family in its debt, an act that works to extend their relationship into the future since the groom's family effectively "owes" the bride's family an equivalent gift. It thus helps participants ensure their economic security; they can assume a gift of equal worth (or more) will be returned in the future. Similarly, these exchanges help givers enhance and display their social worth and reputations by exhibiting their generosity, which has long been a sign of nobility and prestige in the region (Tauzin 2001) and is central to religious merit (Buggenhagen 2012, 154). As one person explained, failing to return the ṣaḍāq would make a bride's family look stingy; a groom's family's full acceptance of this return could do the same to them. Nurturing generous reputations through exchanges like these also helps men and women secure their economic positions by helping them to acquire credit both in the market and among social acquaintances (McMahon 2013). Such exchanges make one set of gifts count for both families in the marriage union, which is quite clever economically.

Men and women are creative in how they attempt to display their virtue through these exchanges. For example, Hassan told me his family returned the portion of the ṣaḍāq Meimouna's family had given back to them, but instead of directly returning it, they used it to purchase gifts for her family. This suggests

Contents of the smaller suitcase that is part of the ṣaḍāq; all items purchased by groom's family. Photo by author.

that he, and perhaps his family members, tried to claim credit for giving away the complete ṣaḍāq while actually keeping part of what was returned to them and using it to fund purchases they would have had to make anyway. This illustrates how people do not always follow expectations without question but rather try to maneuver within them creatively.

While these dimensions of the return gift are important, Nahna emphasized that its meaning extends beyond indexing wealth and binding the families together. She argued that the bride's family's return of the ṣaḍāq also allows them to bestow value on the groom's family. Here, "value" is a rough translation of the word *maqdār*, which can also mean rank or social standing. According to Nahna, the return is not required, but if it occurs, it will please the groom's family because by doing this "someone is going to give a person a maqdār; he will *kabbara* [make bigger] a person." In other words, by returning the ṣaḍāq and making a person "bigger," the giver helps increase the recipient's social standing or value. The root of the verb *kabbara* (*kibīr*) is related to the Arabic word for "big" or "large" (*kbīr*) and can literally be translated "to make someone bigger."[14] Beyond indicating size, the adjective kbīr can be used to describe someone who is powerful, influential, and important. For example, people in Kankossa often describe the president as kbīr. Women and men consider being "big" a valued quality; when I asked women about their aspirations for the future, they sometimes listed becoming bigger as one of their goals. One woman told me she would like to expand her business and "become a big person and have a lot, to always sell." Used in this sense, being "big" refers not to physical size but rather to one's importance, power, and, relatedly, wealth.

The verb kabbara, then, can literally mean to make someone bigger and also suggests that doing so contributes to her importance, influence, and reputation. Acts that kabbara others mark them as important people and signal this importance to others. Hassan explained that people whom you respect might not be well-known, but if others see that you kabbara them by honoring them with good, generous acts, they too will come to think highly of them. This kind of treatment is not limited to weddings; the notion of kabbara is essential to Mauritanian hospitality, which involves serving guests copious amounts of food and drink. Such treatment signifies that the recipients are *bāriz* (prominent, known, important) and can influence others' opinions of them.

As Nahna suggests, in this context, the return of the gift not only makes recipients' social worth visible, but it magnifies it; it bestows them with additional social value. As Hassan later explained, acts that kabbara someone are those that "put someone in a higher place." These acts have real outcomes in the world as they literally enlarge people and their importance and thus help them improve their social positions. The rapid back-and-forth movement of the ṣaḍāq is essential to these processes; it permits both the bride and groom's families to associate the other with this copious gift and to garner the social prestige connected to being the recipient of such a sizeable gift. Nahna's contention that exchange processes are a way through which people bestow value on others demonstrates the essential role that the material realm plays in constituting prestige and social worth.

The idea of becoming bigger has special resonance for lower-status groups, as this state also connotes freedom and autonomy. In narrating her life history, one Ḥarāṭīn woman told me that decades ago her mother and father moved to Kankossa from the countryside, leaving the Bīẓān they were working for without pay, presumably in a form of slavery or extreme dependence. She described how, when her parents came to town, they made a living in a variety of ways, such as by making couscous and selling firewood, and that "the man got bigger. They stayed here. People gave them money." As her father gained income and respect, he became bigger, exercising increasing power and influence in his own life and those of others and leaving his dependent status behind.

Conversely, remaining "small" can signify enduring dependence on others. One man pointed out that the former owners of a Ḥarāṭīn may sometimes still refer to him as their slave. He explained, "It could be that it is not true, but it's an insult for him [the Ḥarāṭīn]. He feels small, below people. He doesn't feel equal to others." Implying that someone is "small" can have serious psychological consequences and can contribute to the reproduction of the status quo in terms of hierarchy. Such use resonates in English-speaking countries. For example, after a strong showing by Republicans in the midterm elections, political scientist David Legee wrote in the New York Times, "Bi-election year 2014 was the final chapter in making the president small." He characterized President Obama as weak and lacking influence and thus the opposite of "big."

While it is the case that one of exchange's fundamental attributes is the "authentication of difference" (Weiner 1992, 40), the passing back and forth of the ṣaḍāq here asserts and magnifies the social worth of both sides. Since it was difficult for slaves to accumulate wealth, slave descendants often cannot lay claim to the kind of inalienable objects, like heirlooms, that can authenticate people's social positions or family histories in some exchange contexts (Weiner 1992).[15] The gifts given by Hassan and his family, therefore, are cash and alienable goods that were recently purchased and have little direct association with his kin. While these items are not heirlooms, the rapid exchanges increase the potential value these items can bestow upon exchange recipients since they associate them with both parties, making each side bigger. This example illustrates how women and men make meaning and generate value using alienable goods and that these practices may vary according to individuals' personal backgrounds and histories. The practice of returning part of the ṣaḍāq was not discussed in early descriptions of weddings in Mauritania (du Puigaudeau 2002), which suggests it is a contemporary innovation.[16] Its current popularity in Kankossa also illustrates how exchange practices shift in times of economic volatility (Guyer 2004). This practice demonstrates how people create new ways of making value when other avenues are unavailable to them. It also shows how, contrary to what critics of these practices suggest, excessive consumption is not necessarily wasteful but can play an important role in social reproduction.

As Nahna illustrates, giving can create—and augment—the status of the giver *and* the receiver; participants in exchanges actively enhance the social standing of others. Anthropologist Marilyn Strathern's (1988) discussion of agency is helpful here. Strathern rejects Western notions of people as autonomous agents who act with their own self-interest in mind; instead, she argues that, in Melanesia, people come into being in relation to other persons, and it is their relationships with others that motivate them to act. She uses the term "agent" to mean someone who "*from his or her own vantage point acts with another's [interests] in mind.* An agent appears as the turning point of relations, able to metamorphose one kind of person into another, a transformer" (1988, 272, emphasis in original). As she suggests, the Mauritanians involved in the exchanges and counter-exchanges of the ṣaḍāq are in part acting with others in mind as they kabbara them. However, this example expands upon Strathern's claims that gift exchange "involves a process in which human value *is* made apparent" (1988, 167, emphasis in original) since givers attempt to make recipients' social worth visible to others. In Mauritania, exchange participants are not simply considering the recipients' present value; rather, they are thinking about the recipients' *potential* social worth and are working to help them realize it.

The immediate return, then, is not a rejection of the gift but rather a way to extend and amplify its effects by bolstering or magnifying a person's value. Such practices have special meaning for slave descendants, since they help them secure and project their improved social rank. Rather than counteracting the outcomes of exchange, the rapid return of a portion of the ṣaḍāq helps to multiply them, enabling both parties to display their own generosity and social value and to magnify and enlarge that of others. The back-and-forth exchange of the ṣaḍāq is a sort of "tournament of value," exchange events that are distinct from mundane, everyday exchange processes; the kula is one example. The rapid movement of the ṣaḍāq qualifies as such a tournament since the context (wedding) and the quantity of the gifts (large) differ from everyday exchange. Participation in such events is often monopolized by privileged individuals and serves as a way to negotiate and display status. Arjun Appadurai contends that "though such tournaments of value occur in special times and places, their forms and outcomes are always consequential for the more mundane realities of power and value in ordinary life" (1986, 21). This aspect of wedding exchanges is essential for slave descendants since these exchanges have the potential to alter participants' social worth long after the ceremony has ended. Furthermore, the fact that people can potentially improve each other's social positions through exchange suggests that Ḥarāṭīn are conceptualizing status as something that is created, not simply something one is born into. Value here is dissociated from genealogy and tied instead to achieved characteristics, like generosity and wealth.

Making Exchange Work

Despite some Mauritanians' contentions that wedding exchanges are unproductive and wasteful, many Ḥarāṭīn continue to not just partake in these displays but to increase the amount of money and goods they contribute to them. Exchange, as the example of Hassan's wedding illustrates, contributes to women's and men's attempts to build meaningful lives in difficult circumstances. Ḥarāṭīn might formerly have received handouts at Bīẓān weddings, but at Hassan's wedding they displayed their own wealth and productive capacity, as well as their dense webs of social connections. Furthermore, as women and men kabbara exchange partners by bestowing them with large gifts, they do not simply make visible their social value; they actively enhance it by "making them bigger." Such processes demonstrate the agency people exercise in this social context and, thus, how social rank is created and altered, not simply ascribed.

The back-and-forth movement of the ṣaḍāq multiplies these effects of exchange, but lavish exchanges do not guarantee the prestige they generate will endure over the *longue durée*. Participants work to ensure that others are aware of the prosperity and social value their exchanges generate. The display of objects that are part of exchanges can be an essential part of such processes.[17] At Hassan's wedding, the display of the generous ṣaḍāq at his family's compound and then at Meimouna's made visible his family's economic status, suggesting members' productive capacity and extensive social connections. However, the viewing of the ṣaḍāq is generally relatively brief, and many of the wedding exchanges are seen by only a small group of people. For example, when the bride's family returned half of the ṣaḍāq, it arrived by donkey cart in Hassan's family's compound, where only a few friends and relatives were gathered. It was talk about these gifts after the wedding that helped to extend their reach, allowing others to "see" them. While the discourse surrounding exchange is often insufficiently analyzed (Buggenhagen 2012, 207), it plays an essential role in Kankossa to ensure that the social value exchanges generate is sustained—that it remains visible to others and extends people's reputations in space and time (Munn 1986). Much of the work of exchange, then, is verbal work. Conversely, exchanges can fail to have their intended effects if discourse about them does not adequately circulate or if the discourse that does circulate is negative.

Language is powerful in Mauritania, and everyday talk is central to creating and maintaining the positive reputations that are important forms of social value in this region (Wiley 2014; 2016). Discourse is an essential part of exchange processes, as language is an important way of assigning meaning to persons and things and trying to sustain particular meanings (Keane 2001; 2005). When Toutou instructed me on proper exchange etiquette, she told me it was important not only to give gifts to close friends and relatives, but also to tell others about what people had given me. She warned that if I did not speak of givers' generosity, they might be perceived as stingy. Talk thus helps make visible the reputations that exchange engenders. People took this quite seriously, and it was common to hear women reciting long lists of gifts others had given them. One woman, when describing her daughter's baptism, named all the relatives who had presented her with goats and sheep to slaughter for the occasion.

The circulation of talk about wedding exchanges helps ensure the value they generate is not confined to the event itself. In our discussion of weddings, Nahna noted that when the man's family returns the ṣaḍāq to the bride's family, "All people will say 'That is good, that is good.'" People in Kankossa openly discuss and comment on ṣaḍāqs, including the amount of cash given and the quantity and quality of the contents of the wedding valises. Often, when a woman told me she had attended a wedding, she would immediately, and without prompting, list the gifts that had been given as well as her evaluation of the quality of musicians and refreshment. Videos and photographs also help preserve and extend the value created at weddings, since they circulate well after the event (Fortier 2001, 60–61). Hassan asked me to photograph his wedding, and he carefully crafted the content of the photos, explaining that having Meimouna's jewelry visible in them was "very important." Her expensive adornment symbolized his family's largess and thus needed to be seen to extend knowledge of their wealth beyond the confines of the event itself.

Conversely, failing to provide a wedding that garnered positive talk could damage reputations. One woman noted that if someone does not give "we don't say anything." On the one hand, this comment can be interpreted as meaning that someone who fails to give will not be critiqued, but, on the other hand, it suggests that such a person will not be praised. Exchanges can fail to enhance the reputations of giver and recipient if discourse about them does not adequately circulate or if such discourse is negative.

Since being known as generous and wealthy is an important form of cultural and symbolic capital in this small community, giving a small ṣaḍāq or not adequately participating in wedding exchanges risks damaging a family's reputation. Once Toutou and her husband, Brahime, were complaining about how it is often the bride's family who ultimately spends more on weddings. Brahime claimed that, when it came time for their teenage daughters to marry, he would like to avoid the wedding and its surrounding costs altogether, instead giving his daughters to their future husbands for a token sum. Though he was likely joking, knowing that statements like this irritate his wife, his comments reflect the view held by many West African reformist Muslims who suggest such wedding expenses are extravagant, wasteful, and contrary to Islam's teachings (Buggenhagen 2012; Masquelier 2009b). Toutou insisted this plan was unacceptable, saying people would call him *mḥaylī* (stingy, cheap). "Would I be stingy if I gave you my daughter?" he asked, implying that the "gift" of his child was enough and did not need to be supplemented by material items. Toutou, ignoring Brahime's question, listed the extensive expenditures she had made for one of her other daughter's weddings, including purchasing many sheep and paying for popular musicians to come from the regional capital. Toutou's insistence on the importance of providing lavish weddings for her daughters indicates the significant work these ceremonies do in producing reputations. Failing to provide the goods and money needed to express a family's worth is dangerous "because it lodges permanently in the social memory to mark a woman's reputation" (Masquelier 2009b, 190). In this conversation, Toutou also works to regenerate her own reputation by recounting her earlier expenditures for her daughter's wedding.

People who cannot afford elaborate exchanges at their weddings often try to limit damage to their reputations. Some people who cannot fund lavish ceremonies do not tell many people that they are marrying, hoping to reduce any resulting negative talk that could circulate about an inadequate ṣaḍāq or the absence of copious amounts of meat. Some weddings in Nouakchott are by invitation only, but weddings in Kankossa and surrounding areas are open to anyone. In the case of rural weddings like Hassan's, much of the village's population attends the evening celebrations and the number of people who are present can further demonstrate the prestige and size of a family's social circle. By limiting the number of people who hear about a wedding, families try to control the damage inadequate expenditures or exchanges might do to their reputations and social positions.

Some people take this even further, getting married in secret with only a few witnesses in attendance. This practice, *sirrīyya* (secret marriage), generates anxiety in Mauritania because some men use it to take a second wife, unbeknownst to their first wife, and thus threaten that union and potentially drain resources away from their families (Fortier 2011). For elite groups, secret marriage can be a way to circumvent certain marital conventions, including monogamy and the relative ages and social statuses of the future spouse (Villasante-de Beauvais 2000, 298–99). It may also be a continuation in a slightly different form of historic practices of concubinage.[18] Though bridewealth is paid in these unions, this practice may also be a way to avoid the costs of a wedding and the accompanying critique of inadequate expenditures, since by the time such marriages become known, often the wedding is far in the past. While these practices may often involve Bīẓān men marrying Ḥarāṭīn women (Fortier 2011; McDougall 2016), my interlocutors in Kankossa worried that their own (Ḥarāṭīn) husbands might participate in such practices. They reported that some do so because the husband travels for work and secretly takes a second wife in a place of business dealings far from his family. But secret marriages also take place between Ḥarāṭīn who live near each other. One suwāqa told me her marriage to her husband had initially been secret and only became public after she became pregnant.[19]

Unlike this clandestine version of marriage, Hassan's wedding and the accompanying exchanges occurred in public view. Discourse about Hassan's wedding circulated after it was over, with attendees discussing the sizeable ṣaḍāq, the copious amounts of food and drink served, and the popular musicians who had played and danced. When we spoke about this event later with some of Nahna's friends and family members, Nahna proclaimed she had eaten so much at his wedding that "my stomach will be full for forty years!" She said she would long remember this celebration, testifying to how events like this, and the meaning they bestow on participants, can endure. Similarly, Hassan's sister told me that his wedding had been an *'urs Murād* (wedding of Murād), referring to the ever-popular Turkish television character. In her eyes, her brother's wedding was fit for a star. Their descriptions of the event emphasized its opulence and reminded listeners of the family's wealth and generosity; they thus attempted to make the effects of these exchanges extend into the future.

Illusions of Exchange

The importance of talk and guests' testimonials to the value of goods exchanged at weddings is heightened in this economic moment when the proliferation of credit is destabilizing wealth as a marker of status; since women and men may purchase items on credit, displays of riches may not reflect actual wealth (cf. Makhulu, Buggenhagen, and Jackson 2010; Masquelier 2013; Newell 2012). I once admired a particularly beautiful malaḥfa that hung in a boutique, commenting to the shopkeeper that only a wealthy person would be able to afford such a high-quality veil. He shook his head, sighing, and said poor people are more likely to purchase the most expensive clothing. Pressure on merchants to give credit to keep clients and garner income means people can obtain goods beyond their means. Similarly, some Kankossa men financed the construction of elaborate homes with large loans. They were then saddled with high loan payments, which diminished their abilities to support their families even while their large, partially finished homes testified to their supposed wealth. Such acts are not so different from recent events in the US, such as rapper Curtis Jackson (50 Cent) admitting he had been renting or borrowing expensive items to display a socioeconomic status he did not have the resources to maintain or the events leading up to the recent housing crisis in which people purchased homes that were vastly beyond their financial means.[20]

In this economic climate, the size of the ṣaḍāq does not necessarily reflect the groom's family's actual wealth. Increasing difficulty in garnering the resources needed to wed has led some groom's families to borrow half the total ṣaḍāq from friends or wealthy relatives, hoping the bride's family will return it quickly and allow them to settle these debts almost immediately. They thus try to garner the prestige and aura of wealth that comes from bestowing a high ṣaḍāq without actually having the resources to back it up. Even if they must depend on credit to fund the ṣaḍāq, the ability to garner a large amount of credit speaks to a family's reputation, trustworthiness, and standing in the community. However, the groom's family's inability to return the full ṣaḍāq to the bride's family risks labeling them as stingy and fails to further elevate her families' prestige. In this economic climate, then, in which former markers of status such as wealth are increasingly destabilized and are potential illusions, women and men must work harder than ever if they aim to make their social worth and rank visible and believable. Talk can therefore also be important as a way of assuring others that displays of wealth are, in fact, genuine.

It is also worth asking whose productive capacity such events are demonstrating. As young men face increasing difficulty in marrying because of the high unemployment rate and the rising expectations for wedding expenditures, Hassan depended on his family to fund his wedding. He was close to finishing his bachelor's degree at the university and had a temporary government job, but he worried about his future employment prospects. The discourse that circulated—which sought to praise his wedding, himself, and his family as valued people—as well as his own attempts to circulate images and talk of his wedding through photos, were not backed by wealth he held himself; rather, they created an illusion of wealth, which might help propel him into a more profitable social position in the future, though this was far from guaranteed in a country where 31.2 percent of the active population in 2008 was unemployed (ONS 2011, 44).

I am not trying to imply that Hassan's marriage was self-serving. He often spoke of his love for Meimouna and after the wedding he traveled to his village from Kankossa, where he was working, almost daily to see her. But his example illustrates how marriage in Mauritania is not only about love between two people; it is also a way for the involved families to assert social rank through exchange. It also illuminates the risk of such exchange: while it can bind people together and assert economic and social status, the future is always precarious. That, in turn, raises the question of how enduring the social value generated at these ceremonies can be if the young people who participate in them are unable to generate wealth as their parents did. Perhaps, in a volatile economy, it is possible that the value exchanges generate will not extend into the future that makes the rapid return of gifts and the discourse surrounding them more important than ever, since these practices attempt to enhance people's social worth and ensure the value exchange generates endures. In the following chapter, I examine how women's participation in the production and consumption of malaḥfas is another way through which they generate economic capital and shape the meaning of social rank.

Notes

1. These suitcases are sometimes also referred to as "*Samsonite*."

2. Marriage and the accompanying exchanges have long been of interest for anthropologists and historians of Africa (Radcliffe-Brown and Forde 1950). Many of these works have largely focused on the bride's family's experiences (Buggenhagen 2012; Cooper 1995; Kapchan 1996; Masquelier 2004).

3. For an overview of these classifications see Bunting, Lawrance, and Roberts (2016).

4. Note the relationships that emerged between slave women and their masters were often ambiguous, with some women being the concubine of one man and the slave of another (McDougall 2014). Freeborn women did not always accept their husbands' engagements in such relationships passively. One way some Bīẓān women tried to keep their husbands faithful and protect bloodlines was by accusing the potential concubine of bloodsucking (a form of witchcraft), a serious offense (Pettigrew 2016, 431). Children born from concubine relationships technically inherited the father's free status (El Hamel 1999; McDougall 2014; Ruf 1999; Strobel 1979), although this did not always occur in practice.

5. In her life history, one Moroccan freed slave woman noted that after being liberated she arranged to have her son married and conducted the preparations for the wedding, receiving some support from her former master's family, including a horse to carry the bride to the groom's home (McDougall 1998, 289). Her story illustrates how some freed slaves maintained ties with their former owners. I want to thank E. Ann McDougall for reminding me of the difference in meaning of Ḥarāṭīn between Mauritania and Morocco. While meanings of Ḥarāṭīn vary throughout Morocco, people who self-identify as Ḥarāṭīn often claim an imagined lineage of indigeneity to southern Morocco; in other contexts, the term may be used to refer to slave or slave descendants (personal communication, Addison Bradford). For more on social and racial categories in Morocco, see El Hamel (2013).

6. Anthropologists have shown how similar processes also occurred throughout West Africa. Adeline Masquelier (2004), for example, illustrates how brides in Niger now hope their *kayan 'daki* (things for room, purchased by the bride's mother at the time of her marriage) will include expensive Formica beds, rather than less expensive versions that were common in the past. She argues that such expenditures are not unproductive but rather demonstrate the bride's value, make visible women's participation in the cash economy, and create generational difference. As is also the case elsewhere in Africa and beyond, increased spending on gifts surrounding weddings puts pressure on men to produce higher amounts of bridewealth, which can delay their abilities to marry (Buggenhagen 2012; Cooper 1995; Kapchan 1996; Meneley 2007; van Santen 2010).

7. This is a good example of how goods can gain value based on their geographic origin (Clark 1994, 36).

8. Anthropologists have demonstrated how exchange is a way through which participants create and make visible their social networks (Buggenhagen 2012; Cooper 1995; Keane 1994; Piot 1999; Strathern 1988; Weiner 1976). Conversely, they also emphasize that it can be a way of marking social difference since participation in these processes puts the receiver in the giver's debt and not everyone has the means to cultivate extensive networks (Bouman 2003; Buggenhagen 2012; Kapchan 1996; Tauzin 2001; Weiner 1992).

9. This is the GDP per capital income. For information on income and other economic statistics on Mauritania, see "Mauritania Data," *The World Bank*, http://data.worldbank.org/country/mauritania. In Nouakchott around the time of this wedding, the average size of a ṣaḍāq for middle-class families was 200,000 to 600,00 (Lesourd 2014, 68), which again illustrates how large this rural gift was. To put the size of Hassan's ṣaḍāq in perspective, given that the average per capita income in the United States in 2011 was close to USD50,000, an equivalent gift here would be almost USD77,000.

10. Jamal itbrīka refers to the fact that in the past the groom would transport his bride to her new home on a camel (Tauzin 2001).

11. The Arabic root of *qaṣṣa* can mean "to follow someone's tracks." This may refer to the gifts following the bride to her in-laws' house. It can also mean "to cut up," and these gifts, which include household items like pillows and plates, are divided and distributed to friends and relatives by the bride's family (Wehr 1994, 896). I was never able to find an explanation for the use of the term *ḥenna* in this context, the same term used for the decorations done on the bride's hands.

12. The Arabic root for *rahīl* means to "emigrate," "resettle," "carry," and "transfer" (Wehr 1994, 383). These goods often accompany the bride when she goes to move in with her husband's family permanently.

13. Marcel Mauss ([1950] 1990) contends that a willingness to receive gifts is an essential element to people's participation in exchange processes and that countergifts are typically presented after a period of time has passed. Similarly, Pierre Bourdieu argues that "in every society it may be observed that, if it is not to constitute an insult, the countergift must be *deferred* and *different*, because the immediate return of an exactly identical object clearly amounts to a refusal (i.e., the return of the same object)" (1977, 5, emphasis in original). As Mauss and Bourdieu suggest, the temporal aspect of exchange is an essential element through which individuals increase their own prestige or further social reproduction. For example, in the case of the kula, the famous serial exchange of necklaces and bracelets between partners in southeastern Papua New Guinea, keeping a valuable gift for a period of time before passing it along is an important means of increasing a man's renown, since it gives him time to become associated with the valued object (Kuehling 2012; Malinowski [1922] 1984). Elsewhere, a temporal gap between exchanges is not limited to extraordinary objects but may be applied to the case of everyday items, such as beer, as a means of waiting until an exchange partner has a need that the giver can satisfy and as a way of extending the relationship into the future (Piot 1999).

14. See Wehr (1994, 947–49) for the Arabic root and its derivatives. Rather than conjugating it, I use the stem form of the verb to avoid confusion for the reader. The noun form, *kbār*, can also mean "notables" (Villasante-de Beauvais 1998, 99).

15. For example, Webb Keane (1994) details how obtaining valuable objects is a way through which people in Anakalang, Indonesia garner prestige; he also highlights the

importance of exploring the role of language in such processes as a means through which people help others (and themselves) interpret exchanges.

16. In her discussion of wedding negotiations in Nouakchott, Céline Lesourd notes that the groom's family typically proposes an amount for the ṣaḍāq that is higher than they can afford as a means of honoring the bride and her family. Her family typically refuses this high offer; the fact that the large gift is actually given in Kankossa suggests people there take this step further by not refusing a portion of the gift until after it has been given (2014, 67–68). Such acts make this wealth visible, even if it is not kept by the bride's family.

17. Anthropologists have shown how this is the case elsewhere, whether it be by Nigerien women displaying household goods provided by the bride's mother and her social networks as they carry them through the town on their heads while moving them to the bride's new home (Masquelier 2004) or by exchange participants in Tanga revealing valuable shell discs to others as a way to "constitute and communicate knowledge about themselves to others" (Foster 1993, 24).

18. E. Ann McDougall (2016) traces concubinage in the colonial period up to practices of sirrīyya today, arguing that these two practices are similar in many forms, including that both are ways of licitly accessing sexual relations outside of some forms of marriage, both produce legitimate children, and both lack the written formalities of other marriage practices. Though Islam allows men to take up to four wives if they can treat them equally, in Mauritania, monogamy is often stipulated in the marriage contract (McDougall 2016). Engaging in sirrīyya is one way men can violate such conditions.

19. Secret marriage among Ḥarāṭīn merits more research to better understand the meaning of this practice and its links with hierarchy and socioeconomic status. This suwāqa noted, for example, that both she and her husband had been previously married at the time they contracted this secret marriage. This could have enabled them to marry while sparing the costs of a larger wedding or helped them ensure control over their union. Their choice to contract a secret marriage could also suggest that her husband was not yet actually divorced; her pregnancy may have forced him to leave his other wife and for the union to become actualized.

20. For more on 50 Cent, see Jethro Nededog and Jason Guerrasio, "6 Ways 50 Cent Says He Tricked the World into Believing He was Rich." *Business Insider*, August 3, 2015. Accessed May 25, 2017. http://www.businessinsider.com/50-cent-trial-testimony-bankruptcy-2015.

6 Embodying and Performing Gender and Social Status Through the *Malaḥfa* (Mauritanian veil)

Rope stretches along the walls of Leilah's boutique, upon which she hangs carefully folded *malaḥfas* (Mauritanian veils).[1] Malaḥfas consist of approximately five yards of fabric that Ḥarāṭīn and Bīẓān women wear by tying one end around their shoulders, making a kind of tunic, then draping the remaining end over their heads and torsos. Since the fabric is not anchored in place, malaḥfas are flexible garments that may slip, revealing women's arms and heads. Women wear them over and coordinate them with long dresses or skirts and shirts, which in Kankossa are often second-hand from Europe. Leilah's malaḥfas come in a variety of fabrics, patterns, and colors: simple cotton cloth in pastels, bright synthetic fabrics covered in whirled patterns, and fluorescent polyester blends decorated with cascading lines and circles. Many of the most vibrantly colored veils are produced locally, with women monopolizing most parts of the production process, including dyeing and sewing them.

Leilah opened her boutique several years earlier after moving to Kankossa when her husband got a job there. She had previously helped with her sister's shop in an urban area, selling clothing and food items. Living in a more rural setting did not excite her, and Leilah often complained that people in Kankossa rarely bought new clothes, saying, "Kankossa doesn't dress up except when there is a holiday or when there is a marriage. Then they will dress up a little. But for us there in the city every weekend all people dress up." Leilah tried to tempt shoppers with new merchandise, occasionally taking buying trips to the capital and having her sister send her new items when she did not have the funds to travel herself. Beyond clothing, these included other products for women, such as lotion, shoes, skin lightening cream, and inexpensive jewelry. During my research year, Leilah also relocated her shop twice, trying to find a location that offered affordable rent and would better attract customers.

The malaḥfa is not just a garment Leilah sells; like many of my other interlocutors, she explicitly connects this garment with Islam and moral personhood. Women frequently discuss the modest dress requirements their interpretations of Islam entail and emphasize how the malaḥfa allows them to keep their arms, legs, and hair covered, though they debate to what extent this is necessary. But

Malaḥfas on display in a Kankossa boutique. Photo by author.

the malaḥfa's meanings extend beyond the religious realm. In the United States, veils are often portrayed as oppressive garments, but in reality veiling practices are complex (Killian 2003; Renne 2013; Tarlo 2010; Watson 1994). Women differ in why they veil and in the meanings these garments have for them—ranging from acting as a form of resistance to a way through which women negotiate "traditional" and "modern" identities.[2] Similarly, the malaḥfa is imbued with multiple meanings and related to a variety of aspects of women's identities. For my interlocutors, the religious nature of the malaḥfa is important but so is its aesthetic character and its economic significance as an object of production. Through their use of this garment, women affirm their piety, create beautiful personas, and garner wealth while asserting their economic independence. These practices are also entangled with how Ḥarāṭīn women claim their social worth. While hierarchy has been a focus of studies of dress outside the Muslim world (Weiner 1989), scholars have only briefly considered the connection between veiling and social rank.[3] In the Kankossa context, dress plays a key role in how Ḥarāṭīn women negotiate and display social rank and difference on a daily basis.

Connections between clothing and social rank make sense in this context since in Mauritania women and men conceive of the distinction between servile and free groups as partly cultural—considering the servile to be linked to a state of "nature" rather than "civilization," which is associated with nobility, moral personal qualities, and particular kinds of comportment (Villasante-de Beauvais 2000, 299). Historically, the difference between slaves and freeborn was thought to manifest itself in their behavior and in how they managed their emotions (Ruf 1999, 259), though, in actuality, behavior among slaves—and elites—varied greatly. The role that particular forms of behavior and bodily comportment play in marking and producing social rank and difference continues today, meaning that "freedom will not be concretized without the acquisition of manners of thinking, being, comportment and speaking, dressing and acting in society" (Villasante-de Beauvais 2000, 300). It is not the case, however, that Ḥarāṭīn aspire to merely mimic elite ideals of dress and comportment in order to become "civilized" or achieve higher social rank. While in some cases they may cultivate behaviors and practices that were historically associated with elites, they also act in ways Bīẓān do not and revalue behaviors that would have formerly been associated with lower social rank. Ḥarāṭīn dress, therefore, can index their claims to elite values and ideologies, but it can also mark their commitment to establishing new value systems. Such contradictions demonstrate how the meanings of social value—and, subsequently, hierarchy in general—are contested and how their engagement with material culture is a way through which Ḥarāṭīn help shape the meaning of social rank more broadly.

Dress, Religious Identity, and Social Rank

One day while we sat in her shop drinking tea, Leilah and I watched a customer examine some *būdis*. These frontless shirts have long sleeves that are connected across the wearer's back with a piece of fabric. They are designed to be worn over tank tops to transform them into modest long-sleeved shirts. When I asked Leilah why būdis had suddenly become so popular, she explained that women like how they cover their arms, which, according to her, is required in Islam. Leilah and other women's connections between Islam and modest dress are not surprising since veiling is strongly associated with this religion in many parts of the world, despite the fact that the central texts of Islam are ambiguous about the kind of modesty required and whether women should veil at all. Scholars argue that it is unclear, for example, whether mentions of veiling in the Qur'an and Hadith (stories about the Prophet's life) apply only to Mohamed's wives or to all Muslim women (Killian 2003, 570).

Leilah continued to explain that, in the past, older women wore opaque malaḥfas, but now, since būdis guarantee their skin remains concealed, they can wear transparent veils. No matter what women wear beneath them, the malaḥfa is a very flexible garment; the free end is not anchored in place, which means they move relatively freely and can reveal the wearers' arms or hair. I asked Leilah how such fluidity affects women's abilities to remain covered. Leilah said this can be challenging but added that Bīẓān are careful to keep their veils in place, fully covering their hair and arms. She then contrasted this to "black" women, describing how "black" women toss the end of their malaḥfas over their shoulders and do not care if their arms are visible to others. She explained that, though she is "*'asūd*" (black) herself, she takes care that her malaḥfa covers her body.

Leilah's emphasis on the importance of modesty aligns with that of Muslim preachers who passed through Kankossa during my research year, emphasizing modest comportment and reformist practices. While residents' feelings about these teachings varied and though the women I knew did not devote much time or discussion to them, women did debate what constituted modest dress. Women disagreed over whether *rgīg* (thin, translucent) veils are acceptable or if pants are appropriate beneath malaḥfas. In general, dress conventions had become more conservative in Kankossa than they were in the early 2000s when I lived there as a Peace Corps Volunteer. Some women still wore tank dresses beneath their veils, but long sleeves were now more common. Similarly, when I first arrived, I had rarely covered my head, even when I was teaching. By the time I returned for my research, people, including strangers, would chide me to cover my hair if I went out with my head uncovered. I subsequently began to wear a sun hat or scarf whenever I left my house.

Dress practices have long been tied to religiosity in Mauritania, and the ability to assert one's status as Muslim has been an integral part of claiming respect and differentiating the freeborn from slaves. Historically, Islam has been used as a basis to both justify and contest slavery (Klein 1998; Ould Ahmed Salem 2013). The Qur'an is ambiguous in regards to issues of social hierarchy since it preaches the equality of all people, but it also allows the enslavement of others if they are subjugated with the intention of bringing them into the faith.[4] Tensions over how Islam articulates with the social hierarchy continue up to the present. The leader of the antislavery organization IRA, Biram Ould Abeid, was arrested in 2012 after burning a text from the Maliki school of religious law, which is followed in Mauritania. He was protesting the role he felt such texts play in justifying and perpetuating slavery—a view shared by other antislavery activists.[5]

In practice, social rank did not neatly equate with religious knowledge and many slaves were in fact Muslim (Ruf 1999, 262). However, they generally did not have as much access to religious knowledge as their masters, and slave owners partly maintained their hegemony through their knowledge of Islam. Slaves should theoretically be freed if they are educated in this faith, so gaining knowledge of Muslim texts and teachings was a way through which slaves tried to secure better social positions, but this did not always work out in practice (Ould Ahmed Salem 2013; Ruf 1999). People's abilities to claim shared ancestry with important religious figures also served as a basis for high social rank and thus excluded lower-status groups who could not claim such genealogy (Brhane 1997; Scheele 2012). Variance in religious practices between free and enslaved people also marked social difference. Because slaves were not considered social beings, they did not have to carry out obligations like paying *zakat* (tithe for the poor)—one of five pillars of Islam (Ruf 1999, 263). Similarly in Islamic law, slaves, unlike free people, are not required to perform Friday prayers (Brhane 1997, 68). Participating in such practices was a way through which men and women could signify their free status.

Dress was also a maker of religiosity. Historically in this region, men and women wore the *guinée*, which served as the precursor to the modern malaḥfa and was produced in the French colony of Pondicherry, India.[6] Guinée consisted of a coarse cloth that was fifteen to seventeen meters long and approximately a meter wide; it was dyed dark blue with indigo and stiffened with rice-water starch (Curtin 1975, 260). It was traded primarily for gum arabic—a natural gum that comes from acacia trees that was used in Europe in the production of cotton cloth, particularly in the dyeing and printing of textile patterns (Roberts 1992). By the late eighteenth century, gum arabic became the most traded item in the region due to the high demand in Europe (Hanson 1992; 1996); in 1838, 240,000 pieces of guinée were imported to be used in this trade (Webb 1995, 126). The popularity of the guinée endured well into the twentieth century; in the 1930s, the French traveler and ethnologist Odette du Puigaudeau noted that women were still wearing this cloth, which they "draped from head to foot like antique statues" ([1937] 2010, 12).

While people of all social ranks wore the guinée, differences in dress visually marked social rank. These aesthetic distinctions, which were also tied to socioeconomic status, helped "sustain social differentiation" (Robbins 1991, 125). For example, in nineteenth-century Walāta, a Mauritanian town that was a popular stop for caravans, veiling was a powerful statement of social class and status (Cleaveland 2002, 184).[7] While slaves also would have worn the guinée, their lack of economic resources meant it was difficult for them to access the quantities of cloth needed to cover fully. Likewise, the cloth they wore often was of lower quality than that of elites as it frequently was obtained secondhand, likely as castoffs from their masters. Elite women's access to expensive beads and other jewelry also differentiated them from their lower-status counterparts. These specifications, though, between quality of dress among status groups did not neatly map onto freeborn versus slave as poor Bīẓān also would not have had access to the same level of cloth and adornment as their elite counterparts.[8]

How a woman wore the malaḥfa also played an important part in indexing status since slaves did not have to adhere to the same modesty requirements as the freeborn. Slave women were only required to cover up to their waists, which would have distinguished them from both elite Bīẓān and their lower-status dependents (Brhane 1997, 72, 324). Travelers to the region noted such differences; the colonial explorer Bourrel remarked that slave women's clothing was more suited to work than that of their elite counterparts (Ruf 1999, 173).[9] While many female slaves would have likely covered more completely when it was convenient, the labor they conducted also impacted how they wore their clothing. For example, slaves might tie their garments around their heads or waists when working in the fields to allow for greater freedom of movement. Slaves' dress thus reflected their social rank not just because of its potential immodesty but also because it was associated with lower-status work, such as agriculture, that elites avoided. While failing to completely cover oneself indexed lower status, beginning to veil or to dress modestly could signify women's respectability and index improved social rank (McMahon 2013; Strobel 1979, 67).

As Leilah insisted, veiling remains an important expression of women's faith in contemporary Kankossa, and both Ḥarāṭīn and Bīẓān continue to wear the malaḥfa. In this sense, unlike among the Ḥarāṭīn elsewhere (Popenoe 2004, 118), Kankossa Ḥarāṭīn's dress does not differentiate them from the Bīẓān.[10] While women do sometimes favor particular colors of malaḥfas based on their skin tone—with darker-skinned women often preferring lighter veils and vice versa—Bīẓān and Ḥarāṭīn wear the same types of malaḥfas. Coverage remains an important criterion in selecting dress; when I asked one Ḥarāṭīn suwāqa what kind of malaḥfa I could bring her from Nouakchott as a gift, she told me to purchase one that had two pieces of fabric stitched together; she explained that this width would make it easy for her to cover herself completely when sitting in the market. Since sexual modesty is situational—mattering more in front of certain people, such as non-relatives (Abu-Lughod 1990, 35)—practicing proper decorum is very important in exterior spaces where women encounter a wide variety of people. Similarly, during dancing at weddings or celebrations, women jump up to fix their friends' malaḥfas if they slide out of place. Women also emphasize modesty in other circumstances, frequently chiding their daughters to cover their heads at home. Of course, not all women always carefully cover. This is deliberate at times—a young teenager who has recently had her hair braided may let her veil slip off to display her new hairstyle—and at others it is not—such as when a poor woman wears a short, tattered veil.

Modest dress is not limited to the malaḥfa; both Ḥarāṭīn and Bīẓān women sometimes wear other forms of Muslim dress, including *abayas*—black robe-like garments that women wear in Saudi Arabia—over their veils like coats (Wiley 2013). When I asked one woman why abayas were becoming popular, she explained it is because they extend to the wrists and ankles and that keeping these body parts covered helps to prevent women from attracting unwanted men. While often seen as signs of radical Islam in the West, women in Kankossa generally consider these garments to be fashionable, and they sometimes favor them because of their popularity in parts of the Middle East—a place some women associate with modernity.[11] Ḥarāṭīn women also publically express piety in other ways, such as by using prayer beads, praying openly in the market, and discussing whether various actions (e.g., applying lotion immediately before prayer and using skin whitening products) are appropriate for Muslims or are *haram* (forbidden).

Women's dress is thus associated with piety and moral personhood. Leilah emphasized this in our discussion of dress when she highlighted that, unlike other "black" people who might casually toss the end of their malaḥfa over their shoulders, she dresses modestly. She thus linked particular dress practices with modest comportment and elite behavior by stating explicitly that this is something Bīẓān do. Leilah thus uses her dress as a way to position herself within the social hierarchy as someone who adheres to elite practices. Her concern with doing so may be due to the continued association of particular kinds of dress with certain social categories. As anthropologist Urs Peter Ruf argues, "While work and clothing were important in constituting and representing the difference between noble or slave women in former times, distinct occupations and individual affluence continue to influence distinguishing patterns of dress among women of different status until the present day" (1999, 173). While socioeconomic standing blurs the line between who can wear what, worn or immodest dress continues to be associated with lower social rank.

Though Leilah self-identifies as "black" and does not call herself Bīẓān, she emphasizes that her pious dress practices are in line with those of the latter group. She thus suggests a hierarchy among those who are not Bīẓān and identifies modest dress as a marker of social worth that can differentiate some "blacks" from others. Leilah's comments demonstrate that dress remains central to individuals' negotiations of rank and status. That veiling and other dress practices index religious identity and moral personhood illustrates how Ḥarāṭīn draw upon social values that would have historically been more available to elites. In this way, they testify to their free status and differentiate themselves from their past connotations with lower-status groups who would not have been able to dress this way. Their dress thus signals Ḥarāṭīn free status, which is assumed for their Bīẓān counterparts. The fact that Leilah critiques "black" women who do not properly cover also suggests that dress and other markers of piety are a means through which Ḥarāṭīn position themselves among other historically lower-status groups and thus potentially claim higher social rank, such as Khaẓarīn.

However, while Ḥarāṭīn women link their dress to Islam and pious personas, they do not simply mimic the comportment and dress of elite groups. One Ḥarāṭīn vegetable seller, Mama, told me Bīẓān women do not sell vegetables because "we, when potatoes have something rotten . . . Look. Look." She paused,

Women in malaḥfas in Atar, Mauritania. By Gerardo Amechazurra. [CC BY 2.0 (http://creativecommons.org/licenses/by/2.0)], via Wikimedia Commons.

holding up her malaḥfa to show me the stains it had accrued that morning in the market. She continued, "I only wore this malaḥfa today. Only today. But a person who still wants men, is going to do this." She proceeded to wrap her malaḥfa tightly around her face, carefully covering her hair, mimicking a Bīẓān woman who is trying to attract a man.

In part, Mama's stained veil indexes her profession, which is associated with lower-status "dirty" work. As Leilah did, people frequently cite dress practices to differentiate between elites and slave descendants. For example, in a discussion about clothing, one Bīẓān woman told me that Ḥarāṭīn often expose their chests and arms in ways that Bīẓān do not because Ḥarāṭīn used to wear shorter veils that they secured around their waists to leave their arms free to perform manual labor. Dressing immodestly or in stained clothes like Mama's thus continues to be linked to certain kinds of work—tending the fields, cooking, carrying water—which are associated with lower social rank. Such stereotypes suggest some Mauritanians continue to view Ḥarāṭīn as a lower-status group regardless of the modest personas they assert.

Mama, however, critiques those who have clean, unblemished clothing. She casts doubt on Bīẓān religiosity, suggesting they carefully cover their heads not because of their faiths, but because of their sexual desire. Such claims destabilize the meaning of pious dress. Mama also indicates that Bīẓān women have clean clothing because they are looking for men, thus highlighting their dependency on others. This contrasts with Mama's own independence, which some women claim to be a valued quality. Mama goes on to describe how her work earns her more money than Bīẓān pursuits, such as selling veils and accessories, claiming "you could go a whole month and not find someone to buy two malaḥfas from you. Not like [selling vegetables] which people eat daily. It will all be bought." Mama highlights the economic benefits of her independence and hard work and frames her stained malaḥfa as a testament to her success. She thus challenges clean, modest dress as a sign of social worth and offers independent labor, with its accompanying stained dress, as a worthwhile pursuit.

Dress, then, does important work in asserting Ḥarāṭīn social rank. In some ways, it does this by affirming Ḥarāṭīn commitment to social values that have long been in circulation in the region, including piety. As Leilah's example illustrates, making their positions as pious Muslims visible also has meaning for Ḥarāṭīn that it does not for Bīẓān; by demonstrating their religiosity, Ḥarāṭīn dress testifies to their respectability and, ultimately, their free status. As Leilah emphasized, how women wear the malaḥfa can also further differentiate between social groups, including among slave descendants themselves. But by wearing the malaḥfa, Ḥarāṭīn do not merely reproduce elite social values. Mama's dirty veil does not, in her eyes, index poverty but rather is a testament to her industriousness and independence. It thus signifies her modernity in the current neoliberal context where labor and individual success is valued and increasingly necessary for women's existence. Ḥarāṭīn women thus draw on conflicting ideologies to make meaning of their dress and, in doing so, offer alternative values for the basis of social rank.

The Malaḥfa and Beautiful Persons

While Leilah connects the malaḥfa and how it is worn to Islam, she also notes that women's dress in Mauritania shifts with fashion trends. During our conversation she told me how some women wear būdis, the garment that makes tank tops long sleeved, just to create a "look" (using the English word though she was speaking Hassaniya). She explained that, while būdis that match the malaḥfa used to be popular, women now prefer it if their būdis are a different color than the accompanying veil. Similarly, different styles of malaḥfas rapidly move in and out of fashion. Although versions of the guinée continue to be available, other kinds of cloth have eclipsed it, but they retain its shape and form (Wiley 2013).

Malaḥfas are available today in a dizzying variety of fabrics—from silk malaḥfas that can sell for as much as USD100 to cheap cotton or polyester versions that may sell for as little as USD3. They come in a wide range of colors—from fluorescents to pastels—and many are decorated with patterns—from geometric designs to pictures of flying twenty dollar bills. Machine-printed veils are imported from around the world; malaḥfas from India, Pakistan, China, Saudi Arabia, and Indonesia are available in Kankossa.[12] Some of these imported veils mimic locally produced styles, which also remain popular. Importing textiles to Africa and the copying of African designs by overseas manufacturers is nothing new (Sylvanus 2016). In the late nineteenth century, European manufacturers produced cloth for the African market that was based upon information provided either by scouts in the colonies or garnered from ethnographies or photographs (Steiner 1985, 98). In the 1990s, Mauritanian women complained that men were taking locally produced veils to Pakistan and making copies, which they would then sell at low prices (Simard 1996, 172). A similar rumor circulated in 2010, which accused Chinese businesspeople of sending digital images of malaḥfas abroad; factories in China would then reproduce the patterns in a few days. While these imported knock-off versions are cheaper than the hand-dyed veils, the local industry continues to thrive.

Like the malaḥfa, Ḥarāṭīn and Bīẓān men's traditional dress also consists of copious amounts of cloth in the form of a flowing, wide-sleeved robe, known as the *darrā'a* or *boubou*. These boubous are similar in shape and style to those worn by men throughout West Africa, including in Senegal and Mali, and are often decorated with elaborately embroidered necklines. Fabric for the darrā'a comes from a variety of places, including West Africa and Europe. Men debate which source produces the highest quality cloth. While historically in Mauritania darrā'a have primarily been blue or white, in recent years, they have become available in an increasing variety of colors. Unlike women who always wear the malaḥfa, some men only wear the darrā'a occasionally, often opting instead for Western style dress. While the meanings of men's sartorial choices are beyond the scope of this book, they deserve further exploration.

After Leilah and I had finished our discussion of the būdi, Moiya, a woman who rents a similar shop near Leilah's, came to chat, leaning against the boutique's doorframe. She and Leilah discussed a woman they saw in the market the day before who was visiting from Nouakchott. Moiya reported that the woman had been wearing pants under her malaḥfa—an occurrence that was extremely rare in Kankossa, though it was becoming more common in the capital—and that she had a cute bag and glasses, which are often non-prescription and worn as accessories. While Leilah and Moiya agreed that the visitor was *mitraqqiyya* (advanced, developed, from the city, fashionable), they also discussed the appropriateness of wearing pants beneath the malaḥfa: Are wide pants acceptable? Is it better to wear pants than a short skirt? Moiya reported that the visitor was married and she had heard her talking to her husband on the phone. They both agreed it is not good for a woman to be dressed so nicely if her husband is elsewhere.

While the malaḥfa signifies a women's modesty and respectability, Ḥarāṭīn women also pay attention to dress as a means of fashioning themselves as beautiful women, which Leilah and Moiya's conversation suggests. This has long been an important way of asserting femininity and engendering social value and cultural capital in Mauritania (Lesourd 2010, 99; Simard 1996; Tauzin 2001). During my research, it was common for Mauritanians in Kankossa and Nouakchott to mention how, in the past (and sometimes in the present), the most valued quality in women was not their intelligence but rather their beauty and adeptness with language, including their verbal wit. Men, on the other hand, were judged on other qualities, such as generosity, wealth, and courage. A Hassaniya proverb captures this idea: *ar-rajul bi-kamālihi lā bi-jamālihi* (a man is a man due to his completeness, not to his beauty). While women did discuss the attractiveness of the male stars of the popular Turkish television serials, when listing qualities that they looked for in a spouse—or that I should look for—they often emphasized wealth and character over looks.

Women's beauty was equated historically with a larger body type. As discussed in chapter two, full figures were a sign of wealth and status since they indicated that women did not have to participate in manual labor and that they had access to the resources needed to maintain their weight. Some Bīẓān who could afford it carried out *gavage*, the practice of feeding young women large quantities of food to help them gain weight. Hassaniya contains many words that reflect preference for larger women, including *fayliḥ*, a beautiful woman who is a bit heavy or, as one interlocutor put it, "someone who has a stomach," and *mjammara*, which one interlocutor explained refers to a woman who is neither thin nor fat and who has well-rounded forearms and calves. I quickly learned that when women asked me why I looked tired or sick they were often asking why I had lost weight, and when they complimented me on looking particularly beautiful it meant that I had gained weight.[13] Practices like gavage are diminishing today due to increasing numbers of women entering the workforce, greater emphasis being placed on health issues, and images of different beauty ideals circulating on television (Fortier 1998; Lesourd 2007; Tauzin 2007). In Kankossa, women debate the ideal body type and many women continue to prefer larger silhouettes, while others, particularly younger women, favor slimmer builds. That Ḥarāṭīn women discuss such issues illustrates that they feel capable of claiming the resources needed to cultivate larger bodies, and some actively did.

Beyond body size, beauty is also linked to women's abilities to dress and accessorize well. Gisèle Simard has argued that the Bīẓān woman is valorized socially not through her maternity but rather through her ability to be *shabība*, "a seductive woman who all men want to woo" (1996, 113). In Kankossa, while people sometimes use this term in the sense Simard discussed, it is more commonly employed to refer to a women who is physically attractive and wearing beautiful clothing and accessories, like the woman Leilah and Moiya discussed who was well dressed and had a cute bag and chic glasses.[14] When used in this sense, being shabība is explicitly linked to dress. Since being shabība is connected to what women wear, it is also a temporary state. Its transitory nature can add to its impact; one man told me it is best when women are not always shabība since then it becomes ordinary. Other words also connect women's dress with their beauty: *matḥafala* refers to women who are dressed up, while *mddafara* refers to those who are not.

I experienced this connection between dress and beauty myself. While in Kankossa, I primarily wore modest Western dress and rarely wore malaḥfas—partly because I found them difficult to move around in since I was not used to them and partly because I felt it was important to maintain a sense of my own culture. When I did wear a malaḥfa for holidays or celebrations, I was always struck by the many compliments I received on my beauty. People's excitement was certainly due in part to their being happy that I was dressed in a more familiar and socially acceptable way that also suggested that I might have converted to Islam, but in some of my interlocutors' eyes, wearing a beautiful malaḥfa literally made me more attractive.

Men's attention to dress is also important. A young man who spent most of his summers in Nouakchott told me about parties there where an award is given to the man who is the *meilleur sapeur* (best dresser, Fr.)—an honor that goes to someone who sets fashion trends by wearing styles that have not yet been adopted by the general public. While this young man did not know the meaning of sapeur in this context, it seems likely that it references young men in the Republic of the Congo who are known for their stylish dress (Ayimpam and Tsambu 2015; Gondola 1999; MacGaffey and Bazenguissa-Ganga 2000).[15] Some older men express anxiety over younger generations' sartorial decisions and their break with "tradition," particularly their tendency to wear styles of Western dress that are associated with rappers. The term "*jenk*" refers to young men who dressed this way. While I was never able to discover this term's etymology, older people often use it in a negative sense, implying a loafer or disrespectful young person. Elders may also be concerned about young men spending money on clothes rather than directing it toward their families. Such behavior threatens social reproduction as young men practice conspicuous consumption rather than saving for marriage or contributing to their families.

Cultivating certain kinds of bodies and donning beautiful dress were important parts of asserting femininity and women's social worth; historically, however, lower-status individuals, including Ḥarāṭīn, did not have access to the same possibilities as their elite counterparts. As previously noted, dress has been one marker of difference between freeborn and slaves since slaves generally only had access to lower-quality cloth and wore it in ways that indexed their participation in manual labor. This related to social conventions regarding the gendered behavior of slaves. Slaves were not as rigidly gendered as Bīẓān and thus were allowed more flexibility in gender performance. For example, while Bīẓān work was segregated by gender, male slaves sometimes conducted women's work, including domestic tasks. Slave women were not expected to adhere to elite feminine comportment, such as practicing chastity and covering themselves in public (Ould Ahmed Salem 2013, 233). Since altering the clothes they wear can indicate a person has shifted social positions (Bouman 2003, 278; Fair 2013; McMahon 2013), contemporary Harāṭīn women's abilities to cultivate beautiful looks through nurturing certain body types and wearing attractive dress asserts their femininity. By highlighting their positions as women, Ḥarāṭīn women's beautiful dress contrasts them with slaves or other lower-status people of the past who would not have been as gendered. Ḥarāṭīn attention to dress and beauty thus serves as a way through which women assert improved social positions and makes them visible to others.

Of course, not everyone dresses well and many Ḥarāṭīn can only afford simple clothing. Women keep track of the value of each other's dress, and many women are knowledgeable about the quality and cost of a wide range of malaḥfas, including how the price of a particular style varies between urban and rural areas. This means the economic value of a woman's clothing is visible to others. Wearing an expensive veil, particularly a new one, is often associated with having access to wealth, as is wearing new clothing in general, even if it is inexpensive. For example, I once jokingly asked a suwāqa to give me money on Tabaski, a major Muslim holiday, which is something children do on holidays and adults tease each other about. She replied that I was wearing a new malaḥfa and should therefore give her money since she did not have new clothes and I did. Women's clothing highlights the ways in which access to income, their own or that of their husbands, allows them to dress well. Women's extensive knowledge about the cost of clothing suggests economic status is becoming an important factor in constituting social rank in Mauritania and their attention to it helps reinforce this.

Beyond signifying femininity and wealth, women emphasize how cultivating beautiful looks is an important way of attracting men. In this context, beautiful dress is thought to literally make women more desirable, thus allowing them to draw men to them. As historian Timothy Cleaveland observed in Walāta, women may veil to cover the body, which has "attractive powers that men cannot resist" (2000, 206).[16] In Kankossa, women also speak of how the clothes they wear can make them more attractive. For example, one day a Ḥarāṭīn friend of mine carefully dressed before she left Kankossa to visit relatives in a nearby village, applying lip gloss and lotion, putting on jewelry, and donning a lovely hand-dyed veil with a matching green dress and būdi underneath. She explained that she had recently been fighting with her husband, but that when he saw her dressed up he would forget their arguments. Furthermore, he had been calling her old, but when he saw her dressed like this, "he will say that I am a young girl." Many Mauritanians consider youth to be an attractive aesthetic attribute.[17]

Conversely, malaḥfas can also make women less attractive. For example, one woman worried that the dark hue of her violet veil would make her appear older, and a pale woman fretted that the light pink veil she had purchased would not compliment her skin tone. Male dress could also attract or repel others. A young man told me if he was going somewhere with his friends and one of them did not have nice clothing, it would reflect poorly on all of them and women might avoid talking with them. To avoid this situation, he said they might tell the shabbily dressed friend to go home or lend him some of their own clothes.

Since a woman's clothing can attract men, women and men both told me that women should not dress up when their husbands were absent, as is also practiced elsewhere in the region (Popenoe 2004, 81). This conviction contributed to Leilah and Moiya's discussion about the propriety of the young, fashionably dressed woman whose husband was elsewhere. Wearing beautiful clothing with no husband present would, in the words of one man, signify that something was "not *waḍḍaḥ*" (clear; correct) since it would suggest that the woman was looking for or already had another man. Since many men migrate at least seasonally to work, women adjust their sartorial choices accordingly.

Women loosely link this principle to Islam and take it seriously, even going as far as to refuse to wear new clothing on holidays if their husbands are not present, despite the fact that even the poorest people try to buy clothing at such times. I could often tell when women's husbands were in town just by looking at them. If they were suddenly wearing beautiful malaḥfas, jewelry, perfume, and henna, it was almost certain that their husbands had returned. While this practice suggests that male sexuality is uncontrollable and places the blame for extramarital affairs on women, it also highlights the perceived power and agency of dress in this context since beautiful dress is able to draw others to it (Banerjee and Miller 2003; Miller 2005).

Women chastise each other for not adhering to this principle, demonstrating the policing that can occur when gender norms are transgressed (Butler 1990).

For example, one day when I was sitting with a suwāqa, she asked a young woman if her husband was in Kankossa. When she replied that he was not, the market trader told her she should not be wearing earrings. The woman insisted that she was only wearing the small, gold-colored earrings because her piercings closed up if she did not, but the suwāqa responded that, if that were the case, she should wear plainer earrings until her husband returned. Before I understood this practice, a woman scolded me for giving perfume to a married friend, telling me this was an inappropriate gift because her husband was in Mali. My gift might entice her to violate these principles or, even worse, suggest that she already was doing so, which would damage her reputation—though another friend noted that she could save it until he returned.

Women's dress, then, also indexes their marital status as they move back and forth between dressing up and dressing down. This means Ḥarāṭīn's dress can index their ability to claim juridical rights that their ancestors could not since slave owners controlled their slaves' abilities to contract (and maintain) marriages. The clothing of women who adhere to these patterns also indexes their economic standing. Since it is common practice to bring gifts for family members, the new finery a woman dons upon her husband's return testifies to his financial success; it transforms his economic capital into cultural capital in the form of beautiful dress and thus makes his wealth visible. While not all women with absent husbands work, many must, so donning simple dress can highlight a woman's economic autonomy and participation in labor, values that Ḥarāṭīn equate with social worth.

While the religious aspects of women's dress in Kankossa are essential parts of clothing's meaning in this context, it extends beyond this. Dress is also a form of cultural capital that helps women to cultivate beautiful personas that attest to their femininity, wealth, and social worth. It can also serve as a means of illustrating their husbands' and women's own economic success and wealth, which are important forms of social value. While dress works in this way for other women as well, including Bīẓān, dress also has unique meanings for Ḥarāṭīn. Its indexing of their marital status, for example, serves as an important marker of improved social rank. Examining the manufacture of locally produced hand-dyed veils also illuminates how clothing plays an important part in negotiations of social rank and how women's social positions are often ambiguous.

Economic Opportunities Through the Production of Malaḥfas

Despite the continuing popularity of imported cloth, over the past forty years Bīẓān and Ḥarāṭīn women have begun participating in the production process of malaḥfas themselves, which was a field formerly dominated by other ethnic groups. Leilah and Moiya, for example, both prepare veils for dyeing and sell the finished products in their stores. Women's entrance into this form of production—versions of which had long been carried out along the Senegal River by Soninke, Malinke, and Wolof women—was linked to severe drought in the region in the late 1960s and 1970s and financial strain from the structural adjustment programs of the 1980s. As economic hardship increased rural-urban migration, commercial opportunities for women expanded, including participation in the dyeing of cloth (Ould-Mey 1996; Ruf 1999, 196; Tauzin 1985–86). The production of hand-dyed malaḥfas was originally concentrated in Nouakchott and the southern town of Kaedi, whose dyers are known for producing bright, vivid colors, including "Kaedi" blue. In 1980, there were 73 dyeing businesses in Nouakchott, and by 1991 that number had grown to 100, showing a steady growth in this sector (Charmes 1992, 54). Women used a variety of resist methods, such as sewing or tying white cloth so that the sewn parts would remain white after dyeing, a process that results in complicated patterns. These locally produced veils quickly became the preferred style because of their durability and the fact that designers could make rapid changes in their patterns and colors in response to demand (Tauzin 1985–86, 87).

In the 1980s in Nouakchott, the production of malaḥfas was both gendered and hierarchical, making this industry a place where gender roles and social rank were reproduced and reinforced (Tauzin 1985–86). Men were minimally involved in this sector, primarily providing women with their supplies, including white cloth and dyes that men sold in bulk. In some cases, particularly among the Soninke and Halpulaar, entire families participated in the dyeing process, with women dyeing the cloth and men removing the thread, washing, and ironing the finished malaḥfas (1985–86, 85–86). However, it was usually women who designed, sewed, dyed, and sold the hand-dyed malaḥfas. The division of labor also built upon and reinforced existing social structures, with the Bīẓān controlling the most prestigious parts of the process such as sewing, as well as most of the commercial aspects. Ḥarāṭīn's roles in this process, particularly their dyeing of cloth, indexed their low social rank since elites consider this task undesirable because of the messiness and bad smells associated with it. In the early 2000s, such divisions remained in the capital, and anthropologist Aline Tauzin, who studied this industry there, noting that its growth "shows both the increase in intense creativity—in the development of motifs, the range of colors, the techniques that are retained—and also the consolidation of the social hierarchy in the divisions of tasks all along the chain of production" (2001, 204). In Kankossa today, women's participation in malaḥfa production demonstrates how such processes continue to contribute to the reproduction of the social hierarchy and also how they provide women with opportunities to rework it.

At the time of my research, the production process in Kankossa remained highly gendered, with the sewing and dyeing of veils done exclusively by women.

Unlike other places where women's participation in the production of cloth has declined or even disappeared (Buggenhagen 2012, 40), the local textile industry throughout Mauritania has become an increasingly important source of income for women (BESCAD 2011, 28). These processes were introduced in Kankossa in the mid-2000s and women's participation in them has since increased rapidly. Despite women's involvement, men continue to monopolize sales of required materials (often in bulk), such as white veils and dye. This echoes other sectors of the market in which men deal in larger quantities of goods than women, which is connected to their ability to access resources. Women's opportunities continue to be limited by the difficulty they have in accessing the large amounts of capital that are necessary for dealing in bulk goods.

Today, many women in Kankossa, including Ḥarāṭīn, sew malaḥfas as part of the production process. To prepare veils for dyeing, women fold white cotton or polyester malaḥfas lengthwise several times, forming long strips that are about eight inches wide and eight layers deep.[18] They then tie or sew parts of the fabric so that it will resist the dye; removing the thread after dyeing results in intricate patterns. During my research, two methods of preparing the cloth for dyeing were used.[19] The first, *khiyāṭa* (sewing), involves sewing tiny stitches in parallel lines or circles with nylon thread. Before it is dyed, the thread is pulled tight to result in linear or circular patterns. The second, *taṣrār* (tying, knotting), involves winding cotton thread around a small portion of the fabric that has been raised by running a needle through all of the layers. While the size of the tied circles varies, they are often quite small, no larger than a nail's head. When dyed, this method produces patterns of small circles. Malaḥfa designs can consist of only one of these methods or a combination of the two.

Before sewing or tying the malaḥfas, women often draw the outlines of their designs in pencil. Some patterns are repeated by many women, while others are created by the sewer and may not be seen elsewhere (Wiley 2013). As is true for other kinds of African cloth, including wax prints (Sylvanus 2016, 92), many of the patterns are named. Wearing a malaḥfa called the "Messaoud" (a Ḥarāṭīn politician), the "Noor" (the star of a popular Turkish television serial), or the "Obama" (the US president), enables women to display their interests and affiliations while also reaffirming their identities as Muslim and Mauritanian since the veils retain the same shape and form (Tauzin 2007; Wiley 2013). Malaḥfa patterns are abstract, and some people gripe that the names are only meant to attract buyers, though others emphasize that wearing a popular design carries social weight and can display the wearer's familiarity with fashion trends. Women keep track of the most popular designs and styles. For example, one woman who bought sewn veils that she then dyed herself told me malaḥfas that involved a lot of the taṣrār technique were currently in demand. Another woman talked about how she asks a friend who is knowledgeable about current fashion trends for help in designing patterns.

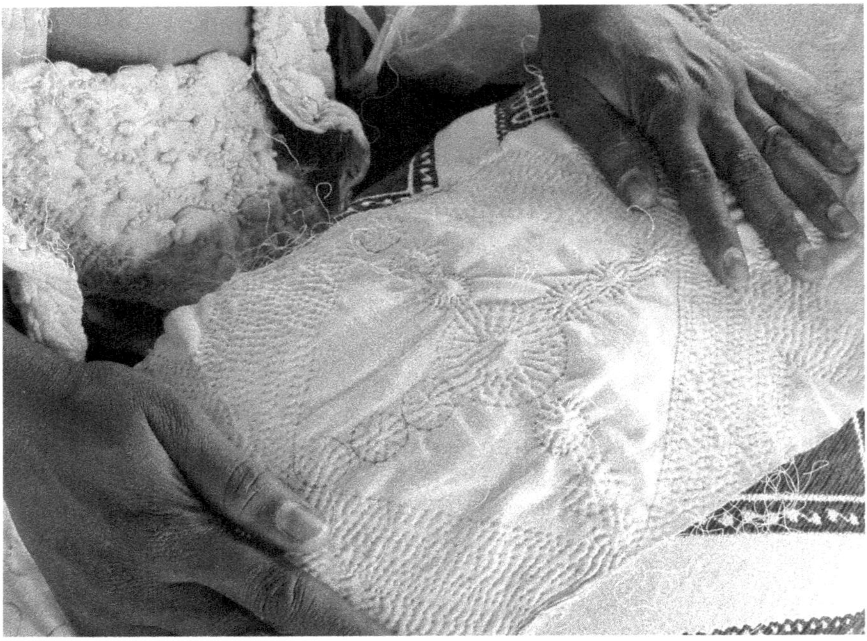

Malaḥfa sewn in the *khiyāṭa* technique, before the threads have been pulled tightly in the final step before dyeing. Photo by author.

Sewing veils is a popular task in Kankossa and most women at least know how to do taṣrār and khiyāṭa. Many of my interlocutors had learned to sew in recent years either locally from other women or during time spent in Nouakchott. Instruction is generally informal; as one woman explained, "Learning the sewing of malaḥfas, I only took [a malaḥfa], that's it. I sat with women, watched what they were doing." Women primarily learn from female friends and relatives who not only teach them the basics of the task but also comment on the size of their stiches, their execution of taṣrār, and their selection of patterns. Their rapid adoption of this task demonstrates women's innovation and willingness to pursue new means of earning income, as well as Ḥarāṭīn creativity.

Sometimes women sew malaḥfas that they intend to keep themselves, perhaps to wear for a major holiday or event, and they thus avoid having to buy expensive veils. Others are commissioned; for example, a woman might pay a friend to sew a malaḥfa for her, perhaps even giving detailed instructions about the design she desires. Other women sew or tie malaḥfas with the intention of selling them to dyers or retailers. Women often carry malaḥfas they are sewing with them and work on them when attending weddings or naming ceremonies, sitting in the market, or visiting friends. Sewing can supplement women's incomes, with prices for sewn veils ranging from between 1,500 and 6,000 MRO, or USD5 and $21, depending on the intricacy of the pattern and the quality of the sewing, though one woman told me she could sell her sewn veils for up to 10,000 MRO (USD35). Women are paid less if someone commissions the malaḥfa and provides the fabric, thread, and needle.

Unlike in Nouakchott in the 1980s, in contemporary Kankossa, both Bīẓān and Ḥarāṭīn women sew malaḥfas, which is also now the case in the capital. Leilah, for example, sewed veils while sitting in her shop and, after paying to have them dyed, sold them there as well. That both Bīẓān and Ḥarāṭīn participate in this activity suggests an equality of status that was absent earlier and also suggests that Ḥarāṭīn now have access to new income possibilities. The task itself, which requires sitting quietly and bending over the work for many hours, requires the stasis that has long been associated with elite status.[20] Such practices thus help Ḥarāṭīn signify elevated social rank.

Similarly, the selling of malaḥfas today is not segregated in Kankossa, and both Bīẓān and Ḥarāṭīn participate in this activity. Women's participation in the commercial aspect is dictated largely by socioeconomic class rather than by race or ethnicity—though the two often overlap—since capital is needed to acquire merchandise. Ḥarāṭīn women's increasing ability to secure the funds needed to begin retail operations suggests that some women enjoy a level of social mobility. Some women have large stores, while others sell a few malaḥfas along with vegetables or other goods at their ṭāblas. Most women sell a mix of hand-dyed malaḥfas and other styles. Some retailers supplement their inventories by sewing (and perhaps even dyeing) malaḥfas themselves. Finished hand-dyed veils started around 3,000 MRO (USD11) in Kankossa, and, during my research, one particularly intricate malaḥfa was rumored to sell for 10,000 MRO (USD35). Such a high price was uncommon, and most high-quality, hand-dyed malaḥfas cost between 5,000 and 7,000 MRO (USD18 and $25). While retailers can make a sizeable profit on good days, finding buyers can be challenging. One shopkeeper said,

> The profit is good with malaḥfas, but they do not always sell. They do not always sell. They only sell when you have Tabaski [major Muslim holiday] or the holiday after Ramadan, then selling will be good. In a day you can sell 15,000 MRO [USD53]. Or sometimes 20,000 [USD70] . . . But if there isn't a holiday or something, [selling] will be rare—[you'll sell] one or two malaḥfas, a little. Sometimes 3,000, sometimes 2,000 MRO [USD11 or $7]. Some also take them and don't pay. Some people take credit and don't pay quickly.

Like Leilah, this seller notes how people rarely buy new clothes, which makes generating sales difficult. Credit can also be a challenge for traders; one woman told me she deals with this problem by only sewing malaḥfas for immediate family members. Despite challenges, Ḥarāṭīn participation in this pursuit provides them with the possibility of increased income and the opportunity to participate in an activity that has been associated with elites and thus demonstrates their social mobility.

While Ḥarāṭīn participation in sewing and selling of malaḥfas illustrates their expanded economic and social possibilities, their role in the dyeing process is more ambiguous. In recent years, several women in Kankossa have started dyeing cloth. Beyond hand-dyed malaḥfas, women also dye other clothing, such as jeans, men's darrā'a, and dresses. The number of dyers in Kankossa is much more limited than women who sew malaḥfas, partly because this task is difficult to learn and involves expensive materials, including protective gloves, metal basins, and dyes. It is also riskier since, while stitches can always be removed and redone, a poor dye job cannot easily be repaired. If the dyes or other ingredients are flawed, which they sometimes are, clothing can be ruined. Many of Kankossa's dyers learned the process through a local NGO, so limited access to its trainings also affected women's participation.[21] Despite the risks of dyeing and the expense of materials, dyers could make significant income; they could charge between 500 and 2,000 MRO (USD2 to $7) per garment and, unlike with sewing, they could dye multiple garments in one session. How much they charged varied based upon the complexity of the dye job and the cost of the dyes, which differed depending on the color.

At the time of my research, it was exclusively black women who dyed malaḥfas, primarily Ḥarāṭīn women, though a few Halpulaar women occasionally did so as well.[22] The relation of their monopoly on dyeing to their social rank is ambiguous. On the one hand, dyeing can be a lucrative profession, and a good dyer can garner significantly more income than she could sewing malaḥfas. One Ḥarāṭīn woman, for example, who dyed malaḥfas and other garments for several hours a week in addition to running a vegetable ṭābla, told me she could make 20,000 MRO a month exclusively from dyeing. This sum was approximately USD70, or USD840 a year, which is close to Mauritania's 2010 gross national per capita income of USD1,140.[23] Though her estimate of income from dyeing was for a busy month, when coupled with her market income, this woman likely earns more than the average Mauritanian. Since garnering wealth has historically been an important part of claiming high social rank, not just through its accumulation but also its distribution to others, such income can help women build social networks and maintain control over resources.

On the other hand, dyeing continues to be considered a "dirty" task, similar to selling vegetables. It thus remains associated with lower-status people, and Bīẓān women avoid it. The undesirable nature of this task is reinforced by the fact that female mu'allimīn, a low-ranking Bīẓān category who are often artisans, also dye cloth (Rasmussen 2013, 96). These artisans occupy an ambiguous status in Bīẓān society; while they are respected for their artistic abilities, they are also looked down upon, and it is common to hear Ḥarāṭīn men and women saying they would never marry a muʿallimīn or reiterating stereotypes about them, such as that they are all liars. Their participation in dyeing further reinforces its standing as a low-status profession.

Despite the connotations of dyeing as dirty work, Ḥarāṭīn's ambiguous social rank allows them to do lower-status tasks like this without risk of as much sanction as when their more elite counterparts participate in them; this can be a real advantage in the neoliberal era. Their flexibility allows them to take on lucrative tasks that others may avoid and thus capitalize on shifting demand and new opportunities. Furthermore, Ḥarāṭīn women's roles in many aspects of malaḥfa production can provide them with the opportunity of displaying their wealth and social worth, partly because the nature of such tasks relies on networks of women. Some women establish informal networks of women who are responsible for different parts of the production process. The person serving as the main organizer of such networks varies; some dyers buy sewn veils themselves and also sell the finished products after they dye them. Likewise, retailers tend to buy sewn veils from the same women and to hire the same dyers. Sewers may also pay a dyer to dye their veils and then sell these garments to a retailer. These networks usually involve the same contacts (e.g., a sewer might always take her veils to the same dyer), but they are not fixed.

Participating in such networks has several benefits, such as assisting women in their efforts to safeguard their economic security by helping them guarantee sales and estimate their incomes. As a newcomer to Kankossa, Leilah cited her lack of social contacts here as the main reason why she was experiencing difficulty in building her client base. While such networks have clear economic benefits, they also have social meaning, and the roles women take on within them may index their socioeconomic status. Women who are central to these networks (e.g., those who buy sewn malaḥfas from many women) not only demonstrate their ability to support others and cultivate relationships but also display their own wealth and resources.

Toutou, for example, knew how to sew malaḥfas, but she no longer did so because the detailed work hurt her eyes. Instead, she bought sewn malaḥfas from others, paying up to 6,000 MRO (USD21) for the most intricate and well-executed designs. She sometimes dyed these malaḥfas herself, selling them in the market along with vegetables and spices or occasionally to a man who bought them in bulk and sent them to his wife in Nouakchott to sell there. Toutou's ability to purchase large quantities of expensive veils not only allows her to expand her earnings but also demonstrates her wealth. It also illustrates how sewing and other seemingly prestigious work can become less lucrative in terms of generating wealth in the contemporary economy.

Women's ability to acquire many malaḥfas to dye or sell makes visible their economic status because a bundle of malaḥfas is physical evidence of their wealth—as malaḥfas can be quite expensive. Similarly, it indexes their relationships with others—as having malaḥfas requires cultivating buying and selling relationships and establishing social networks. These exchanges often happen in the market, a public place where this wealth and social capital can literally be made visible by buying and selling malaḥfas in front of others. Women can thus increase their social capital by extending such networks to include more sewers or dyers. Likewise, women ask other women who sewed the veils they wear. Naming the creator of the veil, which many women can do, also indexes women's social networks since many buy from their friends. These material objects thus help make visible women's relationships to others.

Their ability to display their social networks is important for Ḥarāṭīn since a knack for cultivating relationships has historically indexed social prestige. Toutou, for example, had multiple women from whom she frequently purchased sewn malaḥfas, which helped her to ensure she would be offered desirable goods before others and also displayed her ability to form relationships and support others. Toutou's business also depended on long-distance connections. As holidays neared, she stockpiled sewn veils. When she had acquired enough, she sent these garments to a woman in Nouakchott who had a large dyeing business and was known for producing vibrant colors and complex patterns. Since this woman was Toutou's friend and relative, she did not charge her for this work, though Toutou said she would return the favor in the future. Toutou also often convinced friends and family members who were traveling to Nouakchott to carry undyed malaḥfas for her in their luggage, allowing her to avoid transportation costs.[24] Such long-distance connections between female merchants display women's participation in trade networks and the global economy.[25]

Today, then, the production of malaḥfas does not neatly break down by social group the way it did in the 1980s in Nouakchott. Both Ḥarāṭīn and Bīẓān participate in sewing and selling malaḥfas, aspects of production that were formerly monopolized by Bīẓān. Their expansion into such activities illustrates Ḥarāṭīn women's social mobility and the breaking down of the separation of some economic tasks according to social rank. However, the fact that Ḥarāṭīn continue to conduct dyeing, the dirtiest aspect of production, while Bīẓān avoid this task reproduces a social hierarchy in which Ḥarāṭīn occupy lower social positions. Ḥarāṭīn dyers contest this idea, asserting the value of their activities and emphasizing their wisdom in getting involved early in a lucrative industry. Despite this ambiguity, the income Ḥarāṭīn garner from these activities, including dyeing, provides them with a means to assert valued social personhood by funding their participation in exchange networks and their businesses, both of which would have previously been reserved for Bīẓān women. As with other jobs Ḥarāṭīn do, like selling vegetables, being involved in the production of malaḥfas at various stages simultaneously reinforces and challenges social hierarchy. The social networks women form through such processes compliment and expand other networks and thus make visible their relationships and social worth.

Material Culture, Power, and Social Rank

As Leilah's comments illustrate, the Mauritanian malaḥfa does much more than index a women's religious identity and moral personhood; it also can be a key element in her creation of a beautiful persona, and, through its production, provide her with an important source of income and a means of asserting her social worth. Women's dress thus does important work for Ḥarāṭīn as they negotiate their social rank, helping them emphasize their dedication to Islam, work to meet elite standards of beauty, value their labor, display their wealth in the malaḥfas they both own and sell, and cultivate social networks as they participate in the production and exchange of malaḥfas. While dress can do similar things for Bīẓān women, that slaves were often denied participation in such processes means that such acts signify Ḥarāṭīn's improved social positions. Veils also play a significant role in value production and in the negotiation of such values in the neoliberal moment. Through their debate about appropriate (or fashionable) dress, their embodiment of garments, and their participation in the production of their dress, women conceptualize what it means to be Muslim or beautiful and revalue work that would have been dismissed as dirty in the past. Dress thus serves an important role in helping women to rework the underpinnings of social rank more broadly.

Analyzing this piece of material culture provides important insights about Ḥarāṭīn's places in Mauritania today and the simultaneous malleability and rigidity of social hierarchy in general. Anthropologist Daniel Miller has argued that "the study of material culture often becomes an effective way to understand power, not as some abstraction, but as the mode by which certain forms or people become realized, often at the expense of others" (2005, 19). The previous discussion of the malaḥfa suggests that Ḥarāṭīn, in some cases, are gaining power in Mauritania as they claim modest and beautiful personas and participate in economic activities that were previously denied to them. The fact that women's ability to cultivate social value can depend on their access to financial resources with which they can purchase veils and other essential elements of beautiful dress suggests that economic standing, not just genealogy, is an important element of status today. Likewise, succeeding in opening a shop or setting up a lucrative dyeing business depends on a woman's ability to claim significant economic resources. But the fact that Ḥarāṭīn women also conduct some lower-level tasks like dyeing, which Bīẓān do not, calls into question whether Bīẓān view them as equals.

In times of economic hardship, however, it is worth asking how much of a priority adhering to elite values is for women. While Ḥarāṭīn dyers knew that many people considered this task undesirable, they also emphasized its lucrative nature and how it could help them get ahead. Toutou emphasized how her work as a dyer helped her to improve her children's lives, especially since her husband did not always have money. She described how it was difficult for her children before she worked:

> Children who are older, like [older daughter], couldn't study because I didn't have money. I couldn't send them to school. You've seen how [older son] has left school. Always they go to school and see that there are students who have really nice clothes, who have notebooks, who have money to buy things during their ten o'clock break. They always found this when they went to school . . . I also, if I ended up having a problem, I wanted to do something about it, but I couldn't because I didn't have money. That's all. I said that I would rather go and do something myself because if I always did something myself I wouldn't have to ask [my husband]. And so I entered the market. That's all. [My husband] now, he never gives me malaḥfas. I only buy them myself . . . If the children don't have a notebook, I will buy them one. Those of them who don't have a pen, I'll buy them one . . . Now I can do everything myself. Like now if I wanted land, I would buy it myself.

Toutou identifies a lack of financial resources, not their social rank, as the challenge her children face at school as they compare themselves with their wealthier peers. Similarly, it was money that prevented her from solving her own problems. She thus emphasizes the importance of socioeconomic status and testifies to how her life improved after she began earning her own income, even if that income came from a task that could be viewed as dirty work.

Toutou's income also ensured that her children could remain in school. She hoped that becoming educated could bring them an even better life:

> I want for them to be educated. Not to be like me. Not to be like my husband; he didn't study much. I want them to be educated. I want them to be strong—when they are sitting in meetings to start discussing. They know languages: French, Arabic, English. I want them to be developed, not like us people from the countryside. If a person studies, he will find good work. A person who doesn't study will only go to a ṭābla like me. A person who studies will find good work. I want for them to study. I buy malaḥfas, I buy shoes, I buy lotion, all of that; I only want them to study. I want them to study.

Toutou hoped her children's education would facilitate their finding better work than she had; her funding of their school supplies and clothing helped bring them closer to achieving these goals. Her words suggest that social rank based on ascribed factors like genealogy may not have as much cachet in everyday life as it used to, with factors like a person's socioeconomic standing coming to have more weight. Furthermore, Toutou's equation of education with being "developed" suggests she sees this as an important indicator of status. She thus valorizes her "dirty" work that allows her to finance her children's schooling.

In this time of precarious economic conditions, however, people also noted that economic status is unstable and difficult to read. Many of my interlocutors spoke about how the value of clothing no longer neatly maps onto socioeconomic class. Toutou noted that "there are some people who have a lot of money, but when you see them their darrāʿa are ripped here, ripped here [pointing]. He can only eat beans. He only likes cows and sheep, cows and sheep, cows and sheep ... They really like wealth. They can't give to charity. Honest to God. There are some who can't give charity." As Toutou suggests, some wealthy people might only invest in livestock and wear old clothes to hide their riches and to prevent others from making financial claims on them; however, people also cautioned that individuals who wore expensive clothes might have bought them on credit and that they might not represent any real wealth.

In such a context where social rank—whether stemming from genealogy or wealth—becomes destabilized and difficult to decipher, the work that material objects like clothing can do to index and constitute women's social worth through the display of their religiosity, beauty, and wealth are more important than ever. The very fact that social rank is difficult to interpret means Ḥarāṭīn have an even greater opportunity to challenge hierarchy through clothing and other avenues as they use it to affirm existing values and posit new ones. The multiple meanings of the malaḥfa—as a religious garment, a form of beautiful dress, and a valuable object of production—make it an incredibly rich medium through which to do so.

Notes

1. I use the terms "malaḥfa" and "veil" interchangeably, so "veil" denotes the specific Mauritanian version of this garment unless I explicitly state that I am referencing another form of Muslim dress.

2. The scholarly literature on veiling is extremely rich and explores how the meaning of veiling practices differs between cultural contexts and among individuals. For example, Fadwa El Guindi (1999) analyzes how women's veiling can be a way through which they affirm their cultural identities, express feminist orientations, and resist colonial legacies. In the Sudan, women adopt new forms of Islamic dress in part to make visible their modernity and mark themselves as cosmopolitan (Bernal 1994). Saba Mahmood (2005) shows how women who participate in Egypt's piety movement use Muslim dress as a way to constitute their piety, using it to serve as a constant reminder of their religious orientation. Scholars have also drawn attention to the problematic fact that stereotypes about Muslim women's oppressive dress have been used to justify violence (Abu-Lughod 2002; Ayotte and Husain 2005). The rich meaning of dress in Africa is not limited to veiling. Anthropologist Nina

Sylvanus has argued that wax prints in West Africa "are part of a set of meanings and social practices that have located this object with distinct social, cultural and economic value" (2007, 211), and others have explored the rich meanings of dress in various African contexts (Hansen and Madison 2013; Hansen 2000; Heath 1992; Renne 2013; Rovine 2004).

3. An exception is Fair's (2001) work on dress and its connections to shifting social rank in post-abolition Zanzibar. Other work more briefly touches on this topic (Boswell 2006; Brhane 1997; Cleaveland 2000; Cooper 2005; El Guindi 1999; Fair 2013; Ruf 1999).

4. See El Hamel (2013) for a helpful discussion of the Qur'an, hadith, and Islamic law on slavery. He argues that while the Qur'an makes manumitting slaves a high priority, later Islamic law codified the practice of slavery (2013, 17–59).

5. For an in-depth analysis of this event, see Ould Ahmed Salem (2013).

6. The guinée is also known as *nīla* in Hassaniya (Fortier 2001, 55).

7. This was also true elsewhere, including in the pre-Islamic era Arabian Peninsula where veiling was linked to social class since wealthier women could afford the quantities of cloth needed to veil (Ahmed 1992, 5; Killian 2003, 570; Zahedi 2007, 78).

8. E. Ann McDougall notes that these aesthetic distinctions were not always maintained since sometimes slaves or dependents engaged in lucrative work, such as collecting gum arabic, and were able to obtain better cloth than their masters, especially if these activities occurred in times of drought (personal communication).

9. For example, during Du Puigaudeau's 1933 journey to this region, she was welcomed to a Bīẓān camp by "the strident *you-yous* of the negresses whose bare chests were adorned with amber and glass beads" ([1937] 2010, 54).

10. Popenoe notes that Ḥarāṭīn among the Azawagh Arabs in Niger may still sometimes be distinguished by their dress since they often wear black veils, unlike the people of Arab descent who wear more brightly colored garments. She also notes that this is changing as Ḥarāṭīn move farther away from their slave status and the accompanying clothing and adornment (2004, 118) and that today some Ḥarāṭīn also dress in more sub-Saharan African fashion, something I did not observe in Kankossa. When I asked Kankossa women to compare Ḥarāṭīn and Bīẓān dress, they generally said they were the same, except that darker-skinned women looked better in brighter colors.

11. In the first decade of the twenty-first century, increasing numbers of women in Bamako also wore thin black veils over other garments, suggesting it may be a regional trend. This was an expression of public piety and some people also considered these garments fashionable (personal communication, Maria Grosz-Ngaté). Similarly, in the East African context, such dress is seen as fashionable (Fair 2013), and in Sudan, women also wore similar garments because they were associated with Saudi Arabia, a place they associated with modernity (Bernal 1994).

12. Though the origins of veils may be stamped along the material's edges, sometimes the producers of knockoffs print incorrect origins in the hopes of increasing the cloth's value.

13. Here is an entertaining clip from Oprah's talk show in which a Mauritanian woman tells Oprah about what features are attractive in her country, including thick ankles and stretch marks: https://www.youtube.com/watch?v=PrNcnCFpLno.

14. Note that meanings of some words in Hassaniya vary throughout the country. Thus, it is not unusual to have a word mean something very different in one region than it does in another.

15. For more on the sapeurs of the Congo and images of their dress, see Errol Barnett, "The Fashion Cult Cut from a Different Cloth." *CNN.com*, November 9, 2012. Accessed

January 24, 2013. http://www.cnn.com/2012/11/09/world/africa/congo-sapeur-fashion/index.html and Chris Sullivan, "The Gentlemen of Bakongo and their Cult of Elegance." *Sabotage Times*, October 29, 2012. Accessed January 24, 2013. http://www.sabotagetimes.com/fashion-style/the-gentlemen-of-bakongo-and-their-cult-of-elegance/.

16. Ideas about the power of women's bodies to attract men are also seen elsewhere in the Muslim world (Popenoe 2004, 53–54). In Mauritania, the idea that clothing can literally act on the world relates to discussions of the agency of clothing and materiality. Anthropologists of material culture have argued that dress has a kind of agency, noting that clothing and wearers co-constitute each other (Keane 2005; Miller 2005). They contend that the material properties of clothing impact what people can do with it. For example, the flexibility and easy movement of the free end of the sari allows women to flirt with a suitor by revealing more of the body or, conversely, to hide themselves in ways that would not be possible in a more restrictive garment. It may also, however, trip them (Banerjee and Miller 2003).

17. In the Assaba region, 45 percent of young women in 2007 were married before the age of eighteen. See *UNFPA Child Marriage Profiles: Mauritania.* UNFPA, http://www.devinfo.info/mdg5b/profiles/files/profiles/en/4/Child_Marriage_Country_Profile_AFRMRT_Mauritania.pdf.

18. During my research, plain white malaḥfas cost approximately 1,200 MRO or about USD4 each (less if women purchased them in bulk).

19. Such fabric-dyeing techniques are known by the Indonesian words *tritik* and *plangi* in English (Mbow 1998).

20. Margherita Margiotti has shown a similar process at work among Kuna women who make the mola, a form of Panamanian blouse. The extensive embroidery on these shirts means making them necessitates intense labor, requiring "quietness or tranquility [which] designate highly desirable states of sociability" (2013, 402).

21. World Vision held an initial training on dyeing in Kankossa and then, in September 2010, it sponsored several women to travel to Kaedi, a southern town along the Senegal River that is famous for its dyers, to help them improve their techniques. While a World Vision official told me that work like this was meant to empower women, employees never suggested their work purposely focused upon Ḥarāṭīn, though some NGOs elsewhere in Mauritania did.

22. In the 1990s, Brhane also observed increased numbers of Ḥarāṭīn women dyeing malaḥfas in Nouakchott (1997, 246).

23. See "Mauritania Data Profile." *The World Bank Group.* Accessed March 26, 2012. http://data.worldbank.org/country/mauritania.

24. Taxi drivers usually charge people a fee for transporting merchandise. The cost is usually based on the size and weight of bags or other items.

25. Networks like these have been observed elsewhere in the country (Simard 1996, 183) with some women in Nouakchott traveling to France, Dubai, and China to obtain goods, thus truly participating in global economic networks (Lesourd 2014).

Conclusion: Social Rank in the Neoliberal Era

One warm evening, Toutou and Brahime and I sat on thin mattresses that lined the edges of a plastic mat outside their home. We were discussing weddings in Mauritania because Toutou would soon be traveling to a nearby town to participate in a Bīẓān wedding for which she would "carry the ṣaḍāq." They explained this task involves not literally carrying the goods and money that comprise the bridewealth but rather assisting with the wedding by keeping track of to whom these items should be distributed and helping with that process. Toutou noted that the person who performs this role is often a friend of the groom's mother and that she would be rewarded for her efforts with a portion of the money that is part of the ṣaḍāq and some of the items in the suitcases. Then, in French, a language Toutou does not speak well, Brahime added that, traditionally, the person who carried the ṣaḍāq would be from the "castes." He clarified that this individual would be a muʿallimīn, iggāwen, or Ḥarāṭīn. The term itself may reflect this usage since "carry" implies a form of manual labor, which historically was associated with lower-status individuals. Toutou broke in and, clearly irritated, asked, "Are you telling her that I am the groom's mother's Ḥarṭānīyya?" Given her tone, it was clear Toutou wanted me (and him) to understand that this was not the case.

Toutou's irritation was likely connected to the fact that Brahime, who enjoys speaking French, was, in effect, excluding her from the conversation by using this language. But it also was due to his description of this task. As Toutou signals with her own question, Brahime's explanation of who carries the ṣaḍāq risks implying that Toutou is of slave status since "Ḥarāṭīn" can be a euphemism for slave. At the very least, her question suggests that Brahime had insinuated an ongoing form of dependent relationship between Toutou and the Bīẓān woman, undermining Toutou's earlier claim that they were friends. Toutou is in fact from the same qabīla as the groom's mother, which further supports Brahime's interpretation since many former slaves remain affiliated with the qabīla of their masters, some in semi-dependent relationships with Bīẓān. Furthermore, Brahime describes Toutou conducting a task for a woman who is not part of her close social network, which again suggests this may not be a relationship between equals. Dependents, after all, are people who work for others.

Toutou's offence at her husband's contention undermines his claims and contests his suggestion that she is enslaved or affiliated with this woman as a dependent. Following her response, Brahime quickly explained that people from a variety of backgrounds carry the ṣaḍāq today and that, rather than social rank, certain qualities such as organizational skills make one a desirable candidate for this role since it requires keeping track of the many gifts. He also highlighted the relationships such practices engender, explaining that the groom's family selects someone who they know may later be able to reciprocate, such as when the groom's family experiences financial hardship. He thus casted Toutou not as a dependent, but rather as a respected equal of the Bīẓān family since she would return the gifts she received to them in the future, presumably with increment.

This discussion captures the ongoing tensions that emerge around social rank in Mauritania and the ease with which someone can be associated with lower status. While Toutou was obviously not enslaved or dependent on Bīẓān, the enduring legacy of slavery makes it possible for others to think she was. Some of her anger about Brahime's claims could also be due to my presence; while this conversation happened fairly late in my research year, Toutou likely viewed me, an outsider trying to learn about Mauritanian culture, as someone who might misinterpret her social position.

This incident suggests the complexity of social rank and slavery in Mauritania, issues that also provoke serious debate on the national and international level, with some citizens and government officials contending that this institution has been fully eradicated while others contest such claims. In its first report on worldwide slavery in 2013, the Walk Free Foundation, an international human rights organization, identified Mauritania as having the highest per capita incidence of slavery in the world; the country held this ranking until it was demoted to number seven in 2016, still a significant position.[1] In recent years, Mauritania's government has taken measures to confront the vestiges of slavery and to improve the lives of slave descendants more generally. In 2007, a law was passed that criminalized slavery, and in 2013, the government created the National Agency for the Fight against the Consequences of Slavery, for Reintegration, and for the Fight against Poverty (Tadamoun), which is tasked in part with creating and implementing programs to help eradicate slavery.[2] Two years later, the National Assembly further toughened antislavery legislation, making such practices a crime against humanity and increasing sentences for perpetrators to twenty years. In 2015, the government also created three specialized courts that would try slavery cases; they convicted two people of slave ownership in the spring of 2016.

Beyond the government level, antislavery organizations have worked to draw attention to slavery in Mauritania and to fight for greater equality since independence. In recent years, a new organization, Initiative for the Resurgence of the Abolitionist Movement (IRA), has garnered significant attention both for its radical approaches and its success at exposing these issues internationally. In 2017, for example, the organization's president, Biram Ould Abeid, was named one of Time's 100 most influential people of the year. IRA has worked to draw attention to enduring slavery in Mauritania; for example, during my research, IRA activists freed two young women who they claimed Bīẓān had enslaved in the capital. This event received extensive news coverage throughout the country and beyond, though the details were contested. The girls' father later claimed that his daughters had not been enslaved but rather had come to Nouakchott to attend school and were simply helping with chores as any household member might. After a clash with police surrounding the incident, several antislavery activists were imprisoned. They were released a month later.

As the jailing of the activists suggests, Mauritania's government has not responded positively to IRA's efforts. Biram was also imprisoned in 2012 for burning portions of Islamic texts he contended were used to justify slavery (Thioub 2012, 10; Ould Ahmed Salem 2013). He and two other activists were jailed in November 2014 after organizing a protest concerning the land rights of disadvantaged groups. Many Mauritanians and international human rights groups considered the charges, which included belonging to an unauthorized organization and inciting violence, to be unjust. Despite widespread condemnation of these arrests both within and outside of the country, including from Amnesty International, the men were sentenced to two years in prison and were only released in May 2016. A few months later, thirteen other activists from IRA were arrested while Biram and IRA's vice president, Brahim Bilal Ramdhane, were in the United States accepting the Trafficking in Persons Report Heroes Award from Secretary of State John Kerry.[3]

Both IRA and the government have been criticized.[4] Domestic and international critics of IRA dislike the incendiary actions of its leaders, such as their burning of Islamic texts, and contend that they act partly to further their own interests, such as by exaggerating the prevalence of slavery in Mauritania in order to attract international attention and funds. Others criticize the government for a lack of commitment to truly striving for social equality and slave descendants' rights. Critics argue that the steps it has taken to confront slavery and its legacy are primarily an attempt to appeal to international donors, investors, and foreign governments, citing the low number of slave owners who have actually been prosecuted.

So what do my interlocutors' stories tell us about these issues that have attracted so much attention? What can they add to these debates and discussions? How can they help us to understand contemporary slavery and social hierarchy in Mauritania?

Regardless of the motivations or results of government officials and activists' actions, both approaches rely on classifying social groups in terms of oppositional categories—an approach not unlike that practiced by colonial administrators. They focus on the distinction between freeborn and slaves, suggesting that these categories have distinct boundaries and people can neatly be classified within one; crossing between them is as easy as "freeing" young women. Other categories are also portrayed as oppositional and distinct, including Ḥarāṭīn and Bīẓān as discretely racialized, hierarchal categories. Discourse surrounding slavery's legacy often pits Ḥarāṭīn against Bīẓān and suggests all Ḥarāṭīn are disadvantaged while all Bīẓān are privileged. Such claims thus depict slave descendants (and Bīẓān) as homogenous, erasing their diverse experiences and attributes. They also imply a lack of agency on the part of Ḥarāṭīn and portray these social categories as deeply entrenched and static.

My interlocutors' stories call into question the opposition between freeborn and slave, drawing attention instead to the complexity of social rank and individuals' social positions. They do not view the world in terms of mutually exclusive categories, though they may sometimes describe the hierarchy in this way. Rather, they maneuver between categories and classifications. Indeed, the Ḥarāṭīn I worked with occupy liminal positions: they are members of the Bīẓān social category in part and in part Ḥarāṭīn; they are free but still associated with slave descent; they are "black" but not as "black" as slaves. Toutou, after all, clearly views herself as free, but her continued identification with a qabīla, which is likely the qabīla of her former masters, complicates that position. Others are slave descendants, but their claims to be Khaẓarīn suggest the diversity of social positions within categories. These women's stories thus call into question the opposition between freeborn and slave, Ḥarāṭīn and Bīẓān, and black and white and the usefulness of relying on such distinctions to understand Kankossa's or greater Mauritania's population.

The complexity of women's social positions means that, despite all she has achieved in life, Toutou risks being classified as a dependent; contrary to IRA's actions, there is no neat way to become "free." While my interlocutors identify as free people, they remain marked by their genealogies, perceived skin color, and cultural practices as slave descendants of the Bīẓān. This means they face continued discrimination and challenges and that their social positions are always insecure. All social groups in Mauritania must expend effort to assert and secure their social positions, but the stakes are especially high for the Ḥarāṭīn given their slave past, which remains visible. This means they can always risk being viewed as slaves or lower than Bīẓān, particularly at moments when status becomes especially salient, such as during marriage negotiations or, in this case, when determining roles in family ceremonies.

However, Ḥarāṭīn's flexible social positions and polyvalent identities can also work to their advantage, such as when they allow them to employ ideologies and values of lower-status groups as well as elites. In the market, Ḥarāṭīn women draw on values that would have formerly been the domain of Bīẓān elites, emphasizing their sitting as a way to display their respectability and to justify their work in a very public space. The same women also emphasize the importance of engaging in labor, something Bīẓān elites historically avoided given its association with slavery. Traders argue that their participation in hard work is not only an important aspect of survival in the contemporary economy but also a symbol of their modernity. Rather than viewing categories as mutually exclusive, women maneuver between them. Their adoption of sometimes conflicting values and ideologies that are associated with different social categories allows them to capitalize on new opportunities along with more established practices.

One consequence of this flexibility is that it makes women's social positions difficult to interpret. In the case of the wedding, Toutou could in fact have been capitalizing on older client-patron relations; she did, after all, emphasize the money and gifts she would garner from her participation. However, she also wanted to be perceived as an economic equal, one who could return these gifts at a later date. This reminds us that part of the complexity of social rank is that it is relational; one's social position only makes sense in relation to that of others and it thus fluctuates depending on the social context. Toutou described herself as a friend of the Bīẓān woman and therefore a social equal, but Brahime's assessment illustrates that this woman may view Toutou as a dependent or, at the very least, as occupying a lower social position than herself. Likewise, Toutou clearly does not consider herself to be a slave, but her frustration at Brahime's contention had in part to do with the fact that her genealogy, cultural practices, physical appearance, and, now, her responsibility for carrying the ṣaḍāq at a Bīẓān wedding meant she *could* be construed as a slave—or, at least, as someone of low social rank—despite her insistence to the contrary and her relative success both economically and socially.

Given these ambiguities of women's social positions, language plays an important role in explaining behavior and clarifying social rank, as Toutou's response to Brahime illustrates. Similarly, my interlocutors often rely on speech to explain or justify their behavior, to assert social values, or to extend value generated by exchange into the future. This example illustrates the importance of analyzing language and discourse when considering how people assert, manipulate, and reinforce social rank.

This emphasis on Ḥarāṭīn's liminal positions is not to say that all Bīẓān occupy static social positions or that they adhere exclusively to elite values; many Bīẓān women also work outside of the home and tout the importance of hard work. But Ḥarāṭīn polyvalency makes this group especially flexible and gives them the ability to maneuver between different understandings of social value. Their abilities to move within and between categories suggests the importance of challenging fixed categories and considering how individuals maneuver to better understand the possibilities available to them and how they conceptualize their social positions. The social category of Ḥarāṭīn thus illustrates Rogers Brubaker's contention that it is problematic to view ethnic groups, races or nations as internally homogenous and externally bounded, a conception that leads to understanding "the social and cultural world as a multichrome mosaic of monochrome ethnic, racial or cultural blocs" (2002, 164). Much literature on Mauritania has similarly simplified social categories instead of understanding concepts such as ethnicity as fluid and "contextually fluctuating" (Brubaker 2002, 167).[5]

The focus on slavery in the international media, and the frequent conflation of Ḥarāṭīn with slaves, also suggests a form of helplessness experienced by this group. This is reinforced by the aforementioned government programs and the general approach of IRA, which both suggest that social change comes in a top down fashion. While such acts can lead to change, the Kankossa example demonstrates how women and men make daily efforts to build respectable lives for themselves and influence and shape social rank in the process. Toutou's expression of anger at Brahime's comments shows that she herself is unwilling to be construed in this way. Likewise, the women of this book illustrate that they are not helpless victims; rather, they work to craft their social positions on a daily basis.

The women I worked with do not self-identify as antislavery activists, nor would they describe the actions I explore in the book as overtly political. Rather, they strive to create good lives for themselves and their families, to support themselves in a place where "there is no money," and to create meaningful opportunities for themselves. However, women do impact their own social positioning and the meaning of social categories more broadly, to which the ethnographic examples attest. Women's emphasis on the value of the "dirty" work of dyeing veils attempts to recast such activities as respectable and as indicators of their modernity given their participation in the global economy; such efforts thus expand others' possibilities for claiming social worth. Similarly, the practice and necessity of relying on broad social networks for support, often outside of the family, undermines the importance of genealogy as a determinant of social rank.

People thus challenge the idea that social categories and the social hierarchy are static as they work to alter their meaning or behaviors associated with them. Brahime's final description of the criteria for selecting who carries the ṣaḍāq highlights achieved attributes and virtues: the woman must be well organized—and thus, presumably, intelligent—as well as financially well-off. His comments echo actions we have seen by Ḥarāṭīn women that rework the underpinnings of social rank, basing it upon achieved attributes and downplaying or critiquing ascribed attributes like genealogy or particular forms of static comportment for women. The Kankossa example demonstrates that the meaning of social categories is in flux and that individuals actively shape and change their meanings. While a focus on male leaders provides important insight to the meaning of social rank and how it is constituted, local women's and men's contributions and interpretations are also essential parts of social reproduction and play a key role in constituting theirs and others' possibilities for maneuvering. Ethnography serves as a powerful means of investigating individuals' experiences to better understand how they conceptualize of, move between, and challenge categories like these.

My interlocutors also illustrate how, though the legacy of slavery clearly impacts their lives, so do other global structures, such as global capitalism. The government's and IRA's focus on slavery means they risk overlooking other ways through which particular groups are disadvantaged and exploited across the country. The neoliberal moment has created difficulties for all social groups in Mauritania; the shrinking of the public sector has led to diminishing jobs, rising unemployment, and dwindling government support for its most vulnerable citizens. As a whole, the Ḥarāṭīn and other lower-status groups have been among those hit the hardest by these processes, as such reforms frequently have a negative effect on the most disadvantaged because the poor have fewer possibilities for insulating themselves against economic shocks. It is therefore important not to romanticize a period like this where many people are underemployed and work may be precarious.

However, the neoliberal moment has also created new possibilities for the Ḥarāṭīn. Women's abilities to play a role in constituting social rank are facilitated in part by the fact that shifting economic realities create space for new social configurations. Such shifts have contributed to the altering of gender roles, since rising unemployment and male migration have made it necessary for many women to work outside of the home. Such changes are not always positive and have created tensions between men and women and have strained women's time and energy. They have also, however, expanded women's possibilities for action and have provided them with new possibilities for creating social networks and shaping their social positions.

Neoliberal ideologies have also provided women and men with values that have sometimes been useful to draw upon. As we have seen, this economic philosophy was implemented in Mauritania in a way that valued hard work along with independence and industriousness, qualities that would have formerly been associated with slavery. Ḥarāṭīn women boast of these attributes—supported by national and international organizations—and their touting helps them to justify their participation in lower-status economic activities while simultaneously challenging elite values like stasis as the ideal form of being for women. It also calls into question ascribed attributes as the basis for social rank, instead highlighting achieved attributes such as wealth and participation in labor. Women do not mindlessly parrot neoliberal ideologies, and my interlocutors are well aware that the contemporary economy is often leaving them behind, but these neoliberal ideals help lend legitimacy to a broader range of social values and give women increased support for claiming them. Women's economic strategies in the neoliberal era thus do more than help them get by; they help them challenge and pose alternatives to elite social values and understandings of hierarchy. It is thus important to examine the ways in which different groups are advantaged and disadvantaged by contemporary global capitalism and not to assume they do not creatively harness its policies and ideologies in ways that benefit them.

Furthermore, the effects of neoliberalism and global capitalism are uneven and thus impact particular settings and cultural contexts differently. This can occur at a variety of levels, including, as in Kankossa's case, locally. Kankossa's particular history, in which many Ḥarāṭīn first settled there to work at the French research station, provided them with advantages many of their counterparts have not had elsewhere. These unique beginnings allowed slave descendants to relocate away from their masters, gave them the possibility of claiming land themselves, helped them to form dense social networks, and made it possible to garner income with which they could invest in their futures. Their abilities to harness some of the discourses and ideologies of neoliberalism in ways that reinforce their social worth are therefore unique to this particular setting. Such talk would have been more difficult to act on or bring into being in a community in which slave descendants lived close to their former owners, perhaps even maintaining active relationships of dependence with them. So while it is certainly true that capital is "globe hopping," jumping from place to place and benefiting some while bypassing many (Ferguson 2006, 38), it is also important to acknowledge the pervasiveness of ideologies of global capitalism and to explore how the disadvantaged sometimes creatively harness aspects of its ideologies for their own gain, even in places where global capital itself is severely lacking. The discourse surrounding slavery at the national level risks homogenizing the Ḥarāṭīn and overlooks the unique trajectories of rural places and their effect on slave descendants.

Ḥarāṭīn's experiences are diverse in other ways as well, something the discourses that depict this group as homogenous also overlook. My interlocutors' stories make clear that Ḥarāṭīn women's opportunities differ greatly depending on a variety of factors. For example, women who have greater access to financial resources often have more opportunities to get ahead, both economically and socially. While Toutou complained about Brahime not having enough money, which was certainly true to some extent, he did have salaried work and generally paid for the family's staple food needs. Toutou's income was thus freed up for other necessities and investments. Similarly, her links to relatives elsewhere, especially the woman who dyed malaḥfas for her without charge, helped her to build capital for the future. Toutou's access to significant junior labor in her own household, including a maid, gave her the time to focus on her business and also to attend the family ceremonies that are important to reinforcing social networks and garnering respect. Finally, her own savvy business sense and skills gave her advantages in the market that other women did not have.

Beyond their associations with slavery, then, it is important to consider Ḥarāṭīn's and other slave descendants' gender, socioeconomic status, generation, education level and family composition. While the usage of the term "Khaẓarīn" varies between individuals, its use demonstrates how Ḥarāṭīn are negotiating their social positions not just in opposition to Bīẓān elites but also among themselves.[6] Adopting an intersectional lens that explores a women's history with slavery alongside her many other attributes allows us to avoid painting Ḥarāṭīn as homogenous and to understand not just their opportunities and challenges but also how they conceptualize of who they are. Similarly, it helps us avoid reducing Muslim women to their religious identities, instead highlighting how these are one of many attributes that shape a woman's experiences and outlook on the world.

Through their actions and discourse, the women in this book are doing more than just posing alternatives to particular configurations of hierarchy. Instead they bring new conceptions of social rank into being and expand and alter previous versions. These endeavors illustrate their abilities to enact change; they also call into question who is privileged to enact it since some women are more limited than others in their abilities to participate in such processes. The latter fact has implications for human rights movements and development programs in Mauritania and elsewhere, suggesting that the ability to earn a modest living does more than simply help people get by; it also empowers them to shape the social structure. In this setting, then, women's economic activities form essential parts of not just their ability to support themselves and their families but also their abilities to build meaningful lives. Kankossa women remind us of the importance of exploring and analyzing the complexity between and within groups to better understand our contemporary world and how people creatively employ behaviors, ideologies, and language to generate significant social change.

Notes

1. This report counted both forced marriage and forced labor as instances of modern slavery. It estimates that one percent of the country's population lives in these conditions. For a discussion see Walk Free Foundation. "Country Study: Mauritania." Accessed May 30, 2017. http://www.globalslaveryindex.org/country/mauritania/. The Walk Free Foundation has been criticized for its inaccurate data (Quirk and Broome 2015).

2. For more analysis of these efforts, see Shahinian (2014) and Ould Ahmed Salem (2013). Tadamoun's website can be found at http://www.tadamoun.mr/.

3. For more on this award, see http://www.tipheroes.org/.

4. For a discussion, see Ould Ahmed Salem (2009; 2014) and McDougall (2010). For an example of such debate, see E. Ann McDougall, "The Politics of Slavery, Racism, and Democracy in Mauritania," in *openDemocracy*, June 26, 2015. Accessed May 30, 2017. https://www.opendemocracy.net/beyondslavery/e-ann-mcdougall/politics-of-slavery-racism-and-democracy-in-mauritania, and Alice Bullard, "Letter to BTS: Biram Dah Abeid's Anti-Slavery Activism is Better than Beyond Slavery Thinks," in *openDemocracy*, November 10, 2015. Accessed May 30, 2017. https://www.opendemocracy.net/beyondslavery/alice-bullard/letter-to-bts-biram-dah-abeid-s-anti-slavery-activism-is-better-than-bey.

5. See Jourde (2005) for a critique of simplified social categories in discussions of Mauritania.

6. This is similar to the Halpulaar in Mauritania, whose slave descendants also negotiate their positions in society and pose alternatives to older hierarchies (Leservoisier 2009).

Glossary

ʻabīd	slaves
ʻabūs	frowning, scowling, gloomy, melancholy
ʻāda	customs; also used to signify certain wedding exchanges
ʻaqd	contraction of a marriage
ʻarḍu	reputation
ʻaṣr	social groups composed of women of similar ages
'asūd	black
aurāk	roots; hips, haunches, thighs
bādīya	countryside
bārid	cold
bāriz	prominent, known, important
Bīẓān	group that claims Arab or Berber descent; some members occupy high positions in social hierarchy; Bīẓānīyya (fem. singular)
būdi	open-front long-sleeved shirt designed to be worn over a tank top
darrāʻa	flowing tunic that comprises male Bīẓān traditional dress; *boubou* (Fr.)
dayn	credit
gavage	force-feeding; process intended to help young women gain weight (Fr.)
gendarme	military policeman (Fr.)
giddām an-nās	in front of people
goórjeegan	men who display female qualities; often drummers (from Wolof)
guinée	type of indigo-dyed veil long popular in Mauritania
Halpulaar	black African group that inhabits Mauritania as well as broader West Africa
ḥamara	red
ḥāmi	hot
haram	forbidden
Ḥarāṭīn	generally refers to former slaves or their descendants; Ḥarṭānīyya (fem. singular)
ḥassān	high-status group, historically associated with military strength
Hassaniya	dialect of Arabic spoken by Bīẓān and Ḥarāṭīn
ḥishma	shame, embarrassment
īggāwen	singers, griots; lower-status group under the Bīẓān umbrella

iḥtirām	respect, honor, deference
ijawwaq	to joke
intāj	of the same age, of the same generation, age-mates
kabbara	to make (someone) bigger
ka'ib	dispirited, downcast, sad, melancholy
karāma	dignity, respect, nobility, social standing
Khaẓarīn	slave descendants who claim valued attributes (wealth, long histories of freedom, respect, etc.) and thus differentiate themselves from Ḥarāṭīn; Khaẓarī (masc. sing.)
khādim	slave (female); servant (female)
'kḥal	black
khaẓar	dark colors that are not black (green, blue, dark brown)
khiyāṭa	sewing; method of preparing veils before dyeing
kīş	group savings association
kliyān	clients (Fr.), used to refer to regular customers
kwār	term for black people who are not Ḥarāṭīn (Halpulaar, Soninke, etc.)
limbar	semi-permanent tent many people have outside their homes
malaḥfa	Mauritanian veil
maqdār	rank, social standing, power; social worth, value
marşandīs	merchandise (Fr.)
mashʿūra	person who is funny and adept at language
matériels	household goods, esp. plates, bowls, cups, etc. (Fr.)
matḥafala	dressed up
mawthūqa	reliable, trustworthy
mddafara	dressed down
miswāk	stick that is used for cleaning teeth
mitraqqiyya	fashionable, advanced, developed, from the city
mitṭawwara	developed
mqadārīn	capable, powerful
mtīn	difficult
muʿallimīn	craftspeople; lower-status group under the Bīẓān umbrella (forgerons, Fr.)
mwasakh	dirty
nasab	genealogy
purrī	group savings associations
qabīla	lineage groups organized around shared genealogy (often translated as "tribe" in English)

rahīl	household items and furnishings bride brings with her to husband's home
rgīg	thin, translucent
ṣaḍāq	bridewealth; gifts given by family of groom to bride's surrounding marriage
saḥwa	code of politeness
'ṣfar	yellow
shaqāla	maid
shaqla li'layāt	women's work
shaybanīyya	old woman
shabība	beautiful woman; attractive woman who is dressed and accessorized beautifully
sirrīyya	secret marriage
Soninke	black African group that inhabits Mauritania and broader West Africa
sūdān	term that connotes blackness and encompasses slaves and Ḥarāṭīn
suwāqa	female market trader, small businesswoman (pl., suwāqāt)
ṭābla	table; also used for market traders' short tables
taṣrār	tying, knotting; method of preparing veils before dyeing
'unṣur	origin, ethnicity
valises	suitcases (Fr.)
villages de liberté	liberty villages (Fr.), villages established during colonial period where slaves could seek refuge
waḍḍaḥ	clear; correct
wāgiv	standing; male shopkeeper
Wolof	black African group that inhabits Mauritania; many Wolof live in Senegal
zawāyā	high-status Bīẓān group, associated with religious learning and knowledge
znāga	Bīẓān who occupied dependent positions, often tributaries of higher-status groups

Bibliography

Abu-Lughod, Lila. 1986. *Veiled Sentiments: Honor and Poetry in a Bedouin Society.* Berkeley: University of California Press.

———. 1990. "Shifting Politics in Bedouin Love Poetry." In *Language and the Politics of Emotion*, edited by Catherine A. Lutz and Lila Abu-Lughod, 24–45. New York: Cambridge University Press.

———. 2002. "Do Muslim Women Really Need Saving? Anthropological Reflections on Cultural Relativism and Its Others." *American Anthropologist* 104(3): 783–90.

———. 2013. *Do Muslim Women Need Saving?* Cambridge, MA: Harvard University Press.

Acloque, Benjamin. 2000. "Embarras de l'administration coloniale: la question de l'esclavage au début du XXe siècle en mauritanie." In *Groupes serviles au Sahara: Approche comparative à partir du cas des arabophones de Mauritanie*, edited by Mariella Villasante-de Beauvais, 97–119. Paris: CNRS Editions.

ADB (African Development Bank). 2011. Mauritania: Results-Based Country Strategy Paper, 2011–15. African Development Bank.

AFP. 2012. "Mauritanian Leader Refuses to Resign Amid Protests." *Modern Ghana*, August 6. Accessed May 26, 2017. https://www.modernghana.com/news/410109/mauritania-leader-refuses-to-resign-amid-protests.html.

Ahmed, Leila. 1992. *Women and Gender in Islam: Historical Roots of a Modern Debate.* New Haven, CT: Yale University Press.

Ali, Kecia. 2010. *Marriage and Slavery in Early Islam.* Cambridge, MA: Harvard University Press.

Aliou, S. 2012. "Bagarre au marché 5éme: Deux lourdaudes se crépent le chignon en plein marché." *Cridem.org*, January 9. Accessed January 16, 2012. http://cridem.org/C_Info.php?article=624782.

Appadurai, Arjun. 1986. "Introduction: Commodities and the Politics of Value." In *The Social Life of Things: Commodities in Cultural Perspective*, edited by Arjun Appadurai, 3–63. New York: Cambridge University Press.

Apter, Andrew. 1999. "IBB=419: Nigerian Democracy and the Politics of Illusion." In *Civil Society and the Political Imagination in Africa*, edited by John L. Comaroff and Jean Comaroff, 267–307. Chicago: University of Chicago Press.

Austin, J. L. [1955]1962. *How to Do Things with Words.* Edited by J.O. Urmson and Marina Sbisa. Cambridge, MA: Harvard University Press.

Ayimpam, Sylvie, and Léon Tsambu. 2015. "De la fripe à la Sape." *Revue Hommes et Migrations* 1310: 117–25.

Ayotte, Kevin J., and Mary E. Husain. 2005. "Securing Afghan Women: Neocolonialism, Epistemic Violence, and the Rhetoric of the Veil." *NWSA Journal* 17(3): 112–33.

Babou, Cheikh Anta. 2008. "Migration and Cultural Change: Money, Caste, Gender, and Social Status among Senegalese Female Hair Braiders in the United States." *Africa Today* 55(2): 3–22.

Bakhtin, M. M. 1984. *Rabelais and His World*. 1st Midland book ed. Bloomington: Indiana University Press.
Banerjee, Mukulika, and Daniel Miller. 2003. *The Sari*. New Delhi: Roli Books in arrangement with Roli & Jansen BV.
Basso, Keith H. 1979. *Portraits of "The Whiteman": Linguistic Play and Cultural Symbols among the Western Apache*. New York: Cambridge University Press.
Bayart, Jean-François. 2000. "Africa in the World: A History of Extraversion." *African Affairs* 99: 217–67.
BBC News. 2012. "Mauritanian Protests Against Abdelaziz." *BBC*, April 3. Accessed April 3, 2012. http://www.bbc.co.uk/news/world-africa-17606002.
Bennoune, Mahfoud. 1978. "The Political Economy of Mauritania: Imperialism and Class Struggle." *Review of African Political Economy* 5(12): 31–52.
Bernal, Victoria. 1994. "Gender, Culture, and Capitalism: Women and the Remaking of Islamic 'Tradition' in a Sudanese Village." *Comparative Studies in Society and History* 36(1): 36–67.
BESCAD (Bureau d'Études, Conseils et Assistance en Développement). 2011a. *Étude sur genre et marché de l'emploi en Mauritanie*. Nouakchott: BESCAD.
———. 2011b. *Étude sur genre et marché de l'emploi en Mauritanie*. Nouakchott: BESCAD.
Boddy, Janice. 1982. "Womb as Oasis: The Symbolic Context of Pharaonic Circumcision in Rural Northern Sudan." *American Ethnologist* 9(4): 682–98.
Bond, Patrick. 2006. *Looting Africa: The Economics of Exploitation*. London: Zed Books.
Bonte, Pierre. 1975. "Pasteurs et nomades: l'exemple de la Mauritanie." In *Sécheresses et famines au Sahel*, edited by Jean Copans, 62–86. Paris: F. Maspero.
———. 1989. "L' 'ordre' de la tradition. Evolution des hiérarchies statutaires dans la société maure contemporaine." *Mauritanie: entre arabité et africanité* (54): 118–29.
Boswell, Rosabelle. 2006. "Say What You Like: Dress, Identity and Heritage in Zanzibar." *International Journal of Heritage Studies* 12(5): 440–57.
Botte, Roger. 1994. "Stigmates sociaux et discriminations religieuses: l'ancienne classe servile au Fuuta Jaloo." *Cahiers d'études africaines* 34(133): 109–36.
———. 2005. "Les habits neufs de l'esclavage: métamorphoses de l'oppression au travail." *Cahiers d'études africaines* 179(3): 651–66.
———. 2010. *Esclavages et abolitions en terres d'Islam*. Brussels: André Versaille.
Bouche, Denise. 1968. *Les villages de liberté en Afrique noire française, 1887–1910*. Vol. 28. Paris: Mouton & Company.
Bouman, Annemarie. 2003. "Benefits of Belonging: Dynamics of Iklan Identity, Burkina Faso." PhD diss., University Utrecht.
Bourdieu, Pierre. 1977. *Outline of a Theory of Practice*. New York: Cambridge University Press.
Brhane, Meskerem. 1997. "Narratives of the Past, Politics of the Present: Identity, Subordination and the Haratines of Mauritania." PhD diss., University of Chicago.
Brown, Anthony L., and Marcus W. Johnson. 2014. "Blackness Enclosed: Understanding the Trayvon Martin Incident through the Long History of Black Male Imagery." In *(Re) Teaching Trayvon: Education for Racial Justice and Human Freedom*, edited by Venus E. Evans-Winters and Magaela C. Bethune, 11–23. Rotterdam: Sense Publishers.
Brubaker, Rogers. 2002. "Ethnicity Without Groups." *Archives Europeennes de Sociologie* XLIII(2): 163–89.

Buggenhagen, Beth Anne. 2012. *Muslim Families in Global Senegal: Money Takes Care of Shame*. Bloomington: Indiana University Press.

Bunting, Annie, Benjamin N. Lawrance, and Richard L. Roberts. 2016. "Something Old, Something New? Conceptualizing Forced Marriage in Africa." In *Marriage by Force? Contestation Over Consent and Coercion in Africa*, edited by Annie Bunting, Benjamin N. Lawrance, and Richard L. Roberts, 1–40. Athens, OH: Ohio University Press.

Butler, Judith. 1990. "Performative Acts and Gender Constitution: An Essay in Phenomenology and Feminist Theory." In *Performing Feminism: Feminist Critical Theory and Theatre*, edited by Sue-Ellen Case, 270–82. Baltimore: The Johns Hopkins University Press.

Charmes, Jacques. 1992. *La contribution du secteur informel à l'emploi et au produit national en Mauritanie 1977–1992*. Ministère du plan projet dimensions sociales de l'ajustement. Paris: ORSTOM.

Ciavolella, Riccardo. 2012. "Huunde fof ko Politik: Everything Is Politics: Gramsci, Fulani, and the Margins of the State in Mauritania." *Africa Today* 58(3): 2–21.

Clark, Andrew F. 1995. "Freedom Villages in the Upper Senegal Valley, 1887–1910: A Reassessment." *Slavery and Abolition* 16(3): 311–30.

Clark, Gracia. 1994. *Onions Are My Husband: Survival and Accumulation by West African Market Women*. Chicago: University of Chicago Press.

Cleaveland, Timothy. 2000. "Reproducing Culture and Society: Women and the Politics of Gender, Age, and Social Rank in Walāta." *Canadian Journal of African Studies* 34(2): 189–217.

———. 2002. *Becoming Walāta: a History of Saharan Social Formation and Transformation*. Portsmouth, NH: Heinemann.

Cole, Jennifer. 2009. "Love, Money, and Economies of Intimacy in Tamatave, Madagascar." In *Love in Africa*, edited by Jennifer Cole and Lynn M. Thomas, 109–34. Chicago: University of Chicago Press.

Collins, Patricia Hill. 1998. "It's All in the Family: Intersections of Gender, Race, and Nation." *Hypatia* 13(3): 62–82.

Comaroff, John L., and Jean Comaroff. 2001. "On Personhood: An Anthropological Perspective from Africa." *Social Identities* 7(2): 267–83.

Cooper, Barbara M. 1995. "Women's Worth and Wedding Gift Exchange in Maradi, Niger, 1907–89." *The Journal of African History* 36(1): 121–40.

———. 1997. *Marriage in Maradi: Gender and Culture in a Hausa Society in Niger, 1900–1989*. Portsmouth, NH: Heinemann.

———. 2005. "Reflections of Slavery, Seclusion & Female Labor in the Maradi Region of Niger in the 19th & 20th Centuries." In *Readings in Gender in Africa*, edited by Andrea Cornwall, 156–64. Bloomington: Indiana University Press.

Cooper, Frederick. 1980. *From Slaves to Squatters: Plantation Labor and Agriculture in Zanzibar and Coastal Kenya, 1890–1925*. New Haven: Yale University Press.

Coquery-Vidrovitch, Catherine. 2007. "Women, Marriage, and Slavery in sub-Saharan Africa in the Nineteenth Century." In *Women and Slavery: Africa, the Indian Ocean World, and the Medieval North Atlantic*, edited by Gwyn Campbell, Suzanne Miers, and Joseph C. Miller, 43–62. Athens, OH: Ohio University Press.

Crawford, Mary. 2003. "Gender and Humor in Social Context." *Journal of Pragmatics* 35(9): 1413–30.

Crenshaw, Kimberle. 1991. "Mapping the Margins: Intersectionality, Identity Politics, and Violence Against Women of Color." *Stanford Law Review* 43(6): 1241–99.

Curtin, Philip D. 1975. *Economic Change in Precolonial Africa: Senegambia in the Era of the Slave Trade.* Madison, WI: University of Wisconsin Press.

Daddah, M.O. 2003. *La Mauritanie contre vents et marées*: Paris: Karthala Editions.

Davidheiser, Mark. 2006. "Joking for Peace. Social Organization, Tradition, and Change in Gambian Conflict Management." *Cahiers d'études africaines* 184: 835–59.

de Bruijn, Mirjam, and Lotte Pelckmans. 2005. "Facing Dilemmas: Former Fulbe Slaves in Modern Mali." *Canadian Journal of African Studies* 39(1): 69–95.

de Haas, Hein. 2006. "Migration, Remittances and Regional Development in Southern Morocco." *Geoforum* 27: 565–80.

de Jong, Ferdinand. 2005. "A Joking Nation: Conflict Resolution in Senegal." *Canadian Journal of African Studies* 39(2): 389–413.

de la Brosse, Véronique. 1991. "Dons et contre-dons de mariage en Mauritanie: étude comparative en milieu toucouleur, soninké et maure." *Journal des Africanistes* 61(1): 107–25.

Deubel, Tara Flynn. 2012. "Poetics of Diaspora: Sahrawi Poets and Postcolonial Transformations of a Trans-Saharan Genre in Northwest Africa." *The Journal of North African Studies* 17(2): 295–314.

Diawara, Mamadou Lamine. 1990. *La graine de la parole: dimension sociale et politique des traditions orales du royaume de Jaara (Mali) du XVème au milieu du XIXème siècle.* Stuttgart: Franz Steiner Verlag.

du Puigaudeau, Odette. 2002. *Arts et coutumes des Maures.* Edited by Monique Vérité. Paris: Ibis Press.

———. [1937]2010. *Barefoot through Mauretania.* Translated by Geoffrey Sainsbury. Kilkerran, Scotland: Hardinge Simpole Publishing.

Dugain, Francois. 1958. *Reconnaissance pedologique de la région de Kankossa (Mauritanie) en vue de l'extension des palmeraies.* Dakar: ORSTOM.

Duval Smith, Alex. 2009. "Girls Being Force-Fed for Marriage as Fattening Farms Revived." *The Guardian*, February 28. Accessed May 17, 2017. https://www.theguardian.com/world/2009/mar/01/mauritania-force-feeding-marriage.

El Guindi, Fadwa. 1999. *Veil: Modesty, Privacy, and Resistance.* New York: Berg.

El Hamel, Chouki. 1999. "The Transmission of Islamic Knowledge in Moorish Society from the Rise of the Almoravids to the 19th Century." *Journal of Religion in Africa* 29(1): 62–87.

———. 2008. "Surviving Slavery: Sexuality and Female Agency in Late Nineteenth and Early Twentieth-Century Morocco." *Historical Reflections* 34(1): 73–88.

———. 2013. *Black Morocco: A History of Slavery, Race, and Islam.* New York: Cambridge University Press.

El Hor. [1978]2004. "Charte Constitutive." *L'ouest Saharien* 4: 183–88.

Evans-Pritchard, E. E. [1940]1969. *The Nuer: A Description of the Modes of Livelihood and Political Institutions of a Nilotic People.* New York: Oxford University Press.

Fair, Laura. 2001. *Pastimes and Politics: Culture, Community, and Identity in Post-abolition Urban Zanzibar, 1890–1945.* Athens: Ohio University Press.

———. 2013. "Veiling, Fashion, and Social Mobility: A Century of Change in Zanzibar." In *Veiling in Africa*, edited by Elisha P. Renne, 15–33. Bloomington: Indiana University Press.

Fall, Mohamed Chouaib. 2008. *Rapport: Etude de base pour l'ADP de Kankossa*. World Vision Mauritanie ADP Kankossa.

Ferguson, James. 1999. *Expectations of Modernity: Myths and Meanings of Urban Life on the Zambian Copperbelt, Perspectives on Southern Africa*. Berkeley: University of California Press.

———. 2006. *Global Shadows: Africa in the Neoliberal World Order*. Durham: Duke University Press.

Fortier, Corinne. 1998. "Le corps comme mémoire: du giron maternel à la férule du maître coranique." *Journal des africanistes* 6(1–2): 197–224.

———. 2001. "Le rituel de mariage dans la société maure: Mise en scène des rapports sociaux de sexe." *Awal* 23: 51–73.

———. 2011. "Women and Men Put Islamic Law to Their Own Use: Monogamy versus Secret Marriage in Mauritania." In *Gender and Islam in Africa: Rights, Sexuality, and Law*, edited by Margot Badran, 213–31. Washington, DC: Woodrow Wilson Center Press.

Foster, Robert J. 1993. "Dangerous Circulation and Revelatory Display: Exchange Practices in a New Ireland Society." In *Exchanging Products: Producing Exchange*, edited by Jane Fajans, 15–31. Sydney: University of Sydney.

Frede, Britta. 2014. "Following in the Steps of 'Ā'isha: Ḥassāniyya-Speaking Tijānī Women as Spiritual Guides (Muqaddamāt) and Teaching Islamic Scholars (Limrābuṭāt) in Mauritania." *Islamic Africa* 5(2): 225–73.

Freire, Francisco. 2014. "Saharan Migrant Camel Herders: Znāga Social Status and the Global Age." *Journal of Modern African Studies* 52(3): 425–46.

Geertz, Clifford. 1979. "Suq: the Bazaar Economy in Sefrou." In *Meaning and Order in Moroccan Society: Three Essays in Cultural Analysis*, edited by Clifford Geertz, Hildred Geertz, and Lawrence Rosen, 123–235. Cambridge: Cambridge University Press.

Glenzer, Kent. 2002. "La Sécheresse: The Social and Institutional Construction of a Development Problem in the Malian (Soudanese) Sahel, 1900–82." *Canadian Journal of African Studies* 36(1): 1–34.

Gondola, Ch. Didier. 1999. "Dream and Drama: The Search for Elegance among Congolese Youth." *African Studies Review* 42(1): 23–48.

Grosz-Ngaté, Maria. 1988. "Monetization of Bridewealth and the Abandonment of 'Kin Roads' to Marriage in Sana, Mali." *American Ethnologist* 15(3): 501–14.

———. 1989. "Hidden Meanings: Explorations into a Bamanan Construction of Gender." *Ethnology* 28(2): 167–83.

Guérin, Isabelle. 2006. "Women and Money: Lessons from Senegal." *Development and Change* 37(3): 549–70.

Guyer, Jane I. 1993. "Wealth in People and Self-Realization in Equatorial Africa." *Man* 28(2): 243–65.

———. 2004. *Marginal Gains: Monetary Transactions in Atlantic Africa*. Chicago: University of Chicago Press.

Hale, Thomas A. 1998. *Griots and Griottes: Masters of Words and Music*. Bloomington: Indiana University Press.

Hall, Bruce S. 2011a. "Bellah Histories of Decolonization, Iklan Paths to Freedom: The Meanings of Race and Slavery in the Late-Colonial Niger Bend (Mali), 1944–1960." *International Journal of African Historical Studies* 44(1): 61–87.

———. 2011b. *A History of Race in Muslim West Africa, 1600–1960*. New York: Cambridge University Press.

———. 2011c. "How Slaves Used Islam: The Letters of Enslaved Muslim Commercial Agents in the Nineteenth-Century Niger Bend and Central Sahara." *Journal of African History* 52(3): 279–97.

Hammami, Abdelmajid, Mohamed Elgazzeh, Noureddine Chalbi, and Ben Abdallah Mansour. 2005. "Endogamie et consanguinité en Mauritanie." *Tunisie médicale* 83(1): 38–42.

Hamzetta, Bilal O. 2003. "Solidarité sociale et lutte contre la pauvreté en Mauritanie." In *Regards croisés sur le capital social*, edited by Jérôme Ballet and Roland Guillon, 159–77. Paris: L'Harmattan.

Hansen, Karen Tranberg. 2000. *Salaula: The World of Secondhand Clothing and Zambia*. Chicago: University of Chicago Press.

Hansen, Karen Tranberg, and D Soyini Madison, eds. 2013. *African Dress: Fashion, Agency, Performance*. New York: Bloomsbury.

Hanson, John H. 1992. "Extractive Economies in a Historical Perspective: Gum Arabic in West Africa." *Advances in Economic Botany* 9: 107–14.

———. 1996. *Migration, Jihad, and Muslim Authority in West Africa: the Futanke Colonies in Karta*. Bloomington: Indiana University Press.

Haworth, Abigail. 2011. "Forced to Be Fat." *Marie Claire*, June 20. Accessed May 17, 2017. http://www.marieclaire.com/politics/news/a3513/forcefeeding-in-mauritania/.

Heath, Deborah. 1992. "Fashion, Anti-fashion, and Heteroglossia in Urban Senegal." *American Ethnologist* 19(1): 19–33.

———. 1994. "The Politics of Appropriateness and Appropriation: Recontextualizing Women's Dance in Urban Senegal." *American Ethnologist* 21(1): 88–103.

Hebdomadaire Mauritanoix. 2014. "Faits Divers: Une face cachée de la souffrance des femmes." *Hebdomadaire Mauritanoix*, March 24. Accessed May 13, 2014. http://cridem.org/C_Info.php?article=654376.

Hemmig, Christopher. 2015. "Special Guest Post by Christopher Hemming on Land Tenure and Social Activism in Mauritania." *The Africa Collective*, February 26. Accessed May 26, 2015. http://theafricacollective.com/2015/02/26/special-guest-post-by-christopher-hemmig-on-land-tenure-and-social-activism-in-mauritania/.

Higgs, Johanna. 2017. "Surviving Violence in the Sahara: The Women of Mauritania." *The Huffington Post (UK)*, February 17. Accessed May 17, 2017. http://www.huffingtonpost.co.uk/johanna-higgs/surviving-violence-in-the_b_14807932.html.

Hill, Joseph. 2012. "The Cosmopolitan Sahara: Building a Global Islamic Village in Mauritania." *City & Society* 24(1): 62–83.

Hodgson, Dorothy Louise. 2011. *Being Maasai, Becoming Indigenous: Postcolonial Politics in a Neoliberal World*. Bloomington: Indiana University Press.

Holmes, Seth M. 2013. *Fresh Fruit, Broken Bodies: Migrant Farmworkers in the United States*. Berkeley: University of California Press.

Hunt, Nancy Rose. 1988. "'Le Bebe en Brousse': European Women, African Birth Spacing and Colonial Intervention in Breast Feeding in the Belgian Congo." *International Journal of African Historical Studies* 21(3): 401–32.

Hunwick, John. 1999. "Islamic Financial Institutions: Theoretical Structures and Aspects of their Application in Sub-Saharan Africa." In *Credit, Currencies and Culture: African*

Financial Institutions in Historical Perspective, edited by Endre Stiansen and Jane I. Guyer, 72–96. Uppsala, Sweden: Nordiska Afrikainstitutet.

Hutchinson, Sharon Elaine. 1996. *Nuer Dilemmas: Coping with Money, War, and the State.* Berkeley: University of California Press.

IFAC (Institut français de recherches fruitières outre-mer). 1957. *Rapport annuel.* IFAC.

———. 1974. *Les recherches sur le palmier-dattier: Principaux résultats acquis.* Mauritania: IFAC.

Ilahiane, Hsain. 2001. "The Social Mobility of the Haratine and the Re-Working of Bourdieu's Habitus on the Saharan Frontier, Morocco." *American Anthropologist* 103(2): 380–94.

———. 2002. "Globalization is a Good Thing: 'French Colonial Opportunities' and the Rise of the Haratine in Morocco." *Transnational and Contemporary Problems* 12(1): 109–25.

Ilahiane, Hsain, and John Sherry. 2008. "Joutia: Street Vendor Entrepreneurship and the Informal Economy of Information and Communication Technologies in Morocco." *The Journal of North African Studies* 13(2): 243–55.

Irvine, Judith T. 1989. "When Talk Isn't Cheap: Language and Political Economy." *American Ethnologist* 16(2): 248–67.

———. 1990. "Registering Affect: Heteroglossia in the Linguistic Expression of Emotion." In *Language and the Politics of Emotion*, edited by Catherine A. Lutz and Lila Abu-Lughod, 126–61. New York: Cambridge University Press.

———. 1992. "Insult and Responsibility: Verbal Abuse in a Wolof Village." In *Responsibility and Evidence in Oral Discourse*, edited by Jane H. Hill and Judith T. Irvine, 105–34. New York: Cambridge University Press.

Jackson, Stephen. 2010. "'It Seems to Be Going': The Genius of Survival in Wartime DR Congo." In *Hard Work, Hard Times: Global Volatility and African Subjectivities*, edited by Anne-Maria Makhulu, Beth A. Buggenhagen, and Stephen Jackson, 48–68. Los Angeles: University of California Press.

Jourde, Cédric. 2005. "'The President Is Coming to Visit!': Dramas and the Hijack of Democratization in the Islamic Republic of Mauritania." *Comparative Politics* 37(4): 421–40.

Journal Officiel. 1965. "Ministère de la construction, des travâux publics et des transports." *Journal Officiel de la République Islamique de Mauritanie* 157/158: 141–52.

Kamara, Moctar. 2015. "Lettre au président Mohamed Abdel Aziz." *Cridem.org*, January 4. Accessed May 21, 2015, http://cridem.org/C_Info.php?article=665432.

Kapchan, Deborah A. 1996. *Gender on the Market: Moroccan Women and the Revoicing of Tradition.* Philadelphia: University of Pennsylvania Press.

Kaplan, Robert. 1994. "The Coming Anarchy: How Scarcity, Crime, Overpopulation, Tribalism, and Disease are Rapidly Destroying the Social Fabric of our Planet." *The Atlantic Monthly* 273(2): 44–76.

Kassis, Riad Aziz. 1999. *The Book of Proverbs and Arabic Proverbial Works.* Boston: Brill.

Keane, Webb. 1994. "The Value of Words and the Meaning of Things in Eastern Indonesian Exchange." *Man* 29(3): 605–29.

———. 2001. "Money is No Object: Materiality, Desire, and Modernity in an Indonesian Society." In *The Empire of Things: Regimes of Value and Material Culture*, edited by Fred R. Myers, 65–90. Santa Fe: School of American Research Press.

———. 2005. "Signs Are Not the Garb of Meaning: On the Social Analysis of Material Things." In *Materiality*, edited by Daniel Miller, 182–205. Durham, NC: Duke University Press.

Killian, Caitlin. 2003. "The Other Side of the Veil: North African Women in France Respond to the Headscarf Affair." *Gender and Society* 17(4): 567–90.

Klein, Martin A. 1998. *Slavery and Colonial Rule in French West Africa*. New York: Cambridge University Press.

———. 2005. "The Concept of Honour and the Persistence of Servility in the Western Soudan." *Cahiers d'études africaines* 45(179/180): 831–51.

Kotthoff, Helga. 2006. "Gender and Humor: The State of the Art." *Journal of Pragmatics* 38(1): 4–25.

Kuehling, Susanne. 2012. "They Spear, Hit Again, Bite, Get Engaged and Sometimes Marry: Revisiting the Gendering of *Kula* Shells." *Anthropological Forum* 54(2): 319–32.

L'Authentique. 2012. "Polygamie contre célibat des femmes: Inédite initiative d'une communauté tribale." *L'Authentique*, December 11. Accessed March 27, 2014. http://www.lauthentic.info/spip.php?article2536.

LaFraniere, Sharon. 2007. "In Mauritania, Seeking to End an Overfed Ideal." *The New York Times*, July 4. Accessed May 14, 2014. http://www.nytimes.com/2007/07/04/world/africa/04mauritania.html?pagewanted=all&_r=0.

Launay, Robert. 2006. "Practical Joking." *Cahiers d'études africaines* 184: 795–808.

Lawrence, William. 1999. "Symptom of Crisis or Engine of Development? The Mauritanian Informal Economic Sector." *Praxis—The Fletcher Journal of Development Studies* 15: 1–27.

Lazreg, Marnia. 2005. "Decolonizing Feminism." In *African Gender Studies: A Reader*, edited by Oyèrónke Oyewùmí, 67–80. New York: Palgrove.

Lecocq, Baz. 2005. "The Bellah Question: Slave Emancipation, Race, and Social Categories in Late Twentieth-Century Northern Mali." *Canadian Journal of African Studies* 39(1): 42–68.

Lecocq, Baz, and Éric Komlavi Hahonou. 2015. "Introduction: Exploring Post-Slavery in Contemporary Africa." *International Journal of African Historical Studies* 48(2): 181–92.

Leservoisier, Olivier. 2000. "Les hrâtîn et le Fuuta Tooro, xix-xx siècle: entre émancipation et dépendance." In *Groupes serviles au sahara: Approche comparative à partir du cas des Arabophones de Mauritanie*, edited by Mariella Villasante-de Beauvais, 146–67. Paris: CNRS Editions.

———. 2009. "Contemporary Trajectories of Slavery in Haalpulaar Society (Mauritania)." In *Reconfiguring Slavery: West African Trajectories*, edited by Benedetta Rossi, 140–51. Liverpool: Liverpool University Press.

———. 2012. "Ethnicity and Interdependence: Moors and Haalpulaaren in the Senegal Valley." In *Saharan Frontiers: Space and Mobility in Northwest Africa*, edited by James McDougall and Judith Scheele, 146–61. Bloomington: Indiana University Press.

Lesourd, Céline. 2007. "'Capital beauté': De quelques riches femmes maures." *Politique Africaine* 107: 62–80.

———. 2010. *Mille et un litres de thé: Enquête auprès des businesswomen de Mauritanie*. Paris: Ginko éditeur.

———. 2014. *Femmes d'affaires de Mauritanie*. Paris: Karthala.

———. 2016. "The Lipstick on the Edge of the Well: Mauritanian Women and Political Power (1960–2014)." In *Women's Movements in Post-"Arab Spring" North Africa*, edited by Fatima Sadiqi, 77–93. New York: Palgrave Macmillan.

Lossois, P. 1971. *Etudes du palmier-dattier à la station de Kankossa (République Islamique de Mauritanie). II Problèmes de nutrition*. Institut Français de Recherches Fruitières Outre-Mer.

Lovejoy, Paul E. 1991. "Miller's Vision of Meillassoux." *The International Journal of African Historical Studies* 24(1): 133–45.

Lydon, Ghislaine. 2005. "Slavery, Exchange and Islamic Law: A Glimpse from the Archives of Mali and Mauritania." *African Economic History* 33: 117–48.

———. 2009. *On Trans-Saharan Trails: Islamic Law, Trade Networks, and Cross-Cultural Exchange in Western Africa*. New York: Cambridge University Press.

MacGaffey, Janet, and Rémy Bazenguissa-Ganga. 2000. *Congo-Paris: Transnational Traders on the Margins of the Law, African issues*. Bloomington: Indiana University Press.

Mahmood, Saba. 2005. *Politics of Piety: the Islamic Revival and the Feminist Subject*. Princeton: Princeton University Press.

Makhulu, Anne-Maria. 2010. "The Search for Economic Sovereignty." In *Hard Work, Hard Times: Global Volatility and African Subjectivities*, edited by Anne-Maria Makhulu, Beth A. Buggenhagen, and Stephen JAckson, 28–47. Berkeley: University of California Press.

Makhulu, Anne-Maria, Beth A. Buggenhagen, and Stephen Jackson. 2010. "Introduction." In *Hard Work, Hard Times: Global Volatility and African Subjectivities*, edited by Anne-Maria Makhulu, Beth A. Buggenhagen, and Stephen Jackson, 1–27. Berkeley: University of California Press.

Malinowski, Bronislaw. [1922]1984. *Argonauts of the Western Pacific*. Long Grove, IL: Waveland Press.

Marçais, Philippe. 1951. "Note sur le mot hartani." *Bulletin de liaison saharienne* 4: 11–16.

Margiotti, Margherita. 2013. "Clothing Sociality: Materiality and the Everyday among the Kuna of Panama." *Journal of Material Culture* 18(4): 389–407.

Masquelier, Adeline. 1993. "Narratives of Power, Images of Wealth: The Ritual Economy of *Bori* in the Market." In *Modernity and Its Malcontents*, edited by Jean Comaroff and John Comaroff, 3–33. Chicago: University of Chicago Press.

———. 2004. "How is a Girl to Marry Without a Bed? Weddings, Wealth and Women's Value in an Islamic Town of Niger." In *Situating Globality: African Agency in the Appropriation of Global Culture*, edited by Wim van Bensbergen and Rijk van Dijk, 220–56. Leiden: Brill.

———. 2009a. "Lessons from *Rubí*: Love, Poverty, and the Educational Value of Televised Dramas in Niger." In *Love in Africa*, edited by Jennifer Cole and Lynn M. Thomas, 204–28. Chicago: University of Chicago Press.

———. 2009b. *Women and Islamic Revival in a West African Town*. Bloomington: Indiana University Press.

———. 2013. "Forging Connections, Performing Distinctions: Youth, Dress, and Consumption in Niger." In *African Dress: Fashion, Agency, Performance*, edited by Karen Tranberg Hansen and D. Soyini Madison, 138–52. New York: Bloomsbury.

Mauss, Marcel. [1950]1990. *The Gift: The Form and Reason for Exchange in Archaic Societies*. New York: W.W. Norton & Company, Inc.

Mbow, Marie-Amy. 1998. "African Textile Design." In *The Art of African Fashion*, edited by Els van der Plas and Marlous Willemsen, 133–66. The Netherlands: Prince Claus Fund/ African World Press.

McDougall, E. Ann. 1985. "The View from Awdaghust: War, Trade and Social Change in the Southwestern Sahara, from the Eighth to the Fifteenth Century." *Journal of African History* 26(1): 1–31.

———. 1988. "A Topsy-Turvy World: Slaves and Freed Slaves in the Mauritanian Adrar, 1910–1950." In *The End of Slavery in Africa*, edited by Suzanne Miers and Richard L. Roberts, 362–90. Madison: University of Wisconsin Press.

———. 1998. "A Sense of Self: The Life of Fatma Barka." *Canadian Journal of African Studies* 32(2): 285–315.

———. 2005. "Living the Legacy of Slavery: Between Discourse and Reality." *Cahiers d'études africaines* 45(179/180): 957–86.

———. 2008. "Hidden in the Household: Gender and Class in the Study of Islam in Africa." *Canadian Journal of African Studies* 42(2/3): 508–45.

———. 2010. "The Politics of Slavery in Mauritania: Rhetoric, Reality and Democratic Discourse." *The Maghreb Review* 35(3): 260–86.

———. 2014. "'To Marry One's Slave is as Easy as Eating a Meal': The Dynamics of Carnal Relations within Saharan Slavery." In *Sex, Power, and Slavery*, edited by Gwyn Campbell and Elizabeth Elbourne, 140–66. Athens: Ohio University Press.

———. 2015. "Hidden in Plain Sight: Haratine in Nouakchott's 'Niche-Settlements.'" *International Journal of African Historical Studies* 48(2): 251–79.

———. 2016. "Concubinage as Forced Marriage? Colonial *Jawari*, Contemporary *Hartaniyya*, and Marriage in Mauritania." In *Marriage by Force?: Contestation Over Consent and Coercion in Africa*, edited by Annie Bunting, Benjamin N. Lawrance, and Richard L Roberts, 159–77. Athens: Ohio University Press.

McDougall, E. Ann, Meskerem Brhane, and Urs Peter Ruf. 2003. "Legacy of Slavery; Promise of Democracy: Mauritania in the 21st Century." In *Globalizing Africa*, edited by Malinda Smith, 67–88. Trenton, NJ: Africa World Press.

McMahon, Elisabeth. 2013. *Slavery and Emancipation in Islamic East Africa: From Honor to Respectability*. New York: Cambridge University Press.

Meillassoux, Claude. 1991. *The Anthropology of Slavery: The Womb of Iron and Gold*. Chicago: University of Chicago Press.

Mele, Gianluca. 2014. *Mauritania Economic Update*. The World Bank Group.

Meneley, Anne. 2007. "Fashions and Fundamentalisms in fin-de-siècle Yemen: Chador Barbie and Islamic Socks." *Cultural Anthropology* 22(2): 214–43.

Mercer, John. 1982. *Slavery in Mauritania Today*. Edinburgh: Human Rights Group.

Mianda, Gertrude. 2002. "Colonialism, Education, and Gender Relations in the Belgian Congo: The Évolué Case." In *Women in African Colonial Histories*, edited by Jean Allman, Susan Geiger and Nakanyike Musisi, 144–63. Bloomington: Indiana University Press.

Miller, Daniel. 2005. "Materiality: An Introduction." In *Materiality*, edited by Daniel Miller, 1–50. Durham, NC: Duke University Press.

Ministry of Economic Affairs and Development. 2013. *Report on Implementation of the Third PRSP Action Plan*. Washington, DC: International Monetary Fund.

Mitchell, James Clyde. 1956. *The Kalela Dance: Aspects of Social Relationships Among Urban Africans in Northern Rhodesia*. Manchester: Manchester University Press.

Moore, Clement H. 1965. "One-partyism in Mauritania." *Journal of Modern African Studies* 3(3): 409–20.

Munier, Pierre. 1952. *L'Assaba, essai monographique*. Saint-Louis, Senegal: IFAN.

Munn, Nancy D. 1986. *The Fame of Gawa: A Symbolic Study of Value Transformation in a Massim (Papua New Guinea) Society*. Durham: Duke University Press.

Myers, Fred R. 1979. "Emotions and the Self: A Theory of Personhood and Political Order among Pintupi Aborigines." *Ethos* 7(4): 343–70.

Newcomb, Rachel. 2009. *Women of Fes: Ambiguities of Urban Life in Morocco*. Philadelphia: University of Pennsylvania Press.

Newell, Sasha. 2012. *The Modernity Bluff: Crime, Consumption, and Citizenship in Côte d'Ivoire*. Chicago: University of Chicago Press.

Nicolas, F. J. 1977. "L'origine et la signification du mot Hartani et de ses équivalents." *Notes Africaines* 156: 101–16.

Nikiprowetzky, Tolia. 1962. "The Music of Mauritania." *Journal of the International Folk Music Council* 14: 53–55.

Oliver de Sardan, Jean-Pierre. 1983. "The Songhay-Zarma Female Slave: Relations of Production and Ideological Status." In *Women and Slavery in Africa*, edited by Claire C. Robertson and Martin A. Klein, 130–43. Madison: The University of Wisconsin Press.

ONS (Office National de la Statistique). 2008. *Assaba en Chiffres, 1995–2007*. Kiffa: ONS Service Régional de l'Assaba.

———. 2011. *Annuaire Statistique 2010*. Nouakchott: ONS.

ORSTOM (Office de la Recherche Scientifique et Technique Outre-Mer). 1959. *Elements de bilan des principales activites, 1956–1958*. ORSTOM.

Osirim, Mary Johnson. 2009. *Enterprising Women in Urban Zimbabwe: Gender, Microbusiness, and Globalization*. Bloomington: Indiana University Press.

Ould Ahmed Salem, Zekeria. 2009. "Bare-Foot Activists: Transformations in the Haratine Movement in Mauritania." In *Movers and Shakers: Social Movements in Africa*, edited by Stephen Ellis and Ineke van Kessel, 156–77. Leiden: Brill.

———. 2013. *Prêcher dans le désert: Islam politique et changement social en Mauritanie*. Paris: Karthala.

Ould Cheikh, Abdel Weddoud. 1993. "L'evolution de l'esclavage dans la societe maure." In *Nomades et commandant: Administration et societes nomades dans l'ancienne AOF*, edited by Edmond Bernus, Pierre Boilley, Jean Clauzel, and Jean-Louis Triaud, 181–93. Paris: Karthala.

Ould Cheikh, Abdel Weddoud, and Pierre Bonte. 1982. "Production pastorale et production marchande dans la société maure." In *Contemporary Nomadic and Pastoral Peoples: Africa and Latin America*, edited by Philip Carl Salzman, 31–56. Williamsburg, VA: College of William and Mary, Dept of Anthropology.

Ould Cheikh, Abdel Wedoud, and Yahya Ould Al-Barra. 1996. "Il faut qu'une terre soit ouverte ou fermée: Du statut des biens fonciers collectifs dans la société maure." *Revue du monde musulman et de la Méditerranée* 79(1): 157–80.

Ould Jiddou, Baba. 2004. "La communauté haratine." *L'Ouest saharien* 4: 159–82.

Ould Saleck, El-Arby. 2000. “Les Haratin comme enjeu pour les partis politiques en Mauritanie.” *Journal des Africanistes* 70: 255–63.
———. 2003. *Les Haratins: Le paysage politique mauritanien*. Paris: L'Harmattan.
Ould-Mey, Mohameden. 1996. *Global Restructuring and Peripheral States: The Carrot and the Stick in Mauritania*. Lanham, MD: Littlefield Adams Books.
Overå, Ragnhild. 2007. “When Men Do Women's Work: Structural Adjustment, Unemployment and Changing Gender Relations in the Informal Economy of Accra, Ghana.” *Journal of Modern African Studies* 45(4): 539–63.
Pazzanita, Anthony G. 1999. “Political Transition in Mauritania: Problems and Prospects.” *Middle East Journal* 53(1): 44–58.
Pelckmans, Lotte. 2011. *Travelling Hierarchies: Roads In and Out of Slave Status in a Central Malian Fulbe Network*. Leiden: African Studies Centre.
Pettigrew, Erin. 2016. “The Heart of the Matter: Interpreting Bloodsucking Accusations in Mauritania.” *Journal of African History* 57(3): 417–35.
Pietila, Tuulikki. 2007. *Gossip, Markets, and Gender: How Dialogue Constructs Moral Value in Post-socialist Kilimanjaro*. Madison: University of Wisconsin Press.
Piot, Charles. 1999. *Remotely Global: Village Modernity in West Africa*. Chicago: University of Chicago Press.
Pitte, Jean-Robert. 1975. “La sécheresse en Mauritanie.” *Annales de Géographie* 84(466): 641–64.
Popenoe, Rebecca. 2004. *Feeding Desire: Fatness, Beauty and Sexuality Among a Saharan People*. New York: Routledge.
Quirk, Joel, and André Broome. 2015. “The Politics of Numbers: The Global Slavery Index and the Marketplace of Activism.” *openDemocracy*, March 10. Accessed August 16, 2016. https://www.opendemocracy.net/beyondslavery/joel-quirk-andr%C3%A9-broome/politics-of-numbers-global-slavery-index-and-marketplace-of-ac.
Radcliffe-Brown, A. R. 1952. *Structure and Function in Primitive Society, Essays and Addresses*. London: Cohen & West.
Radcliffe-Brown, A. R., and Cyril Daryll Forde. 1950. *African Systems of Kinship and Marriage*. New York: Oxford University Press.
Rasmussen, Susan. 2013. *Neighbors, Strangers, Witches, and Culture-Heroes: Ritual Powers of Smith/Artisans in Tuareg Society and Beyond*. New York: University Press of America.
———. 1993. “Joking in Researcher-Resident Dialogue: The Ethnography of Hierarchy among the Tuareg.” *Anthropological Quarterly* 66(4): 211–20.
———. 2003. “Gendered Discourses and Mediated Modernities: Urban and Rural Performances of Tuareg Smith Women.” *Journal of Anthropological Research* 59(4): 487–509.
Renne, Elisha P, ed. 2013. *Veiling in Africa*. Bloomington: Indiana University Press.
Rhine, Kathryn A. 2016. *The Unseen Things: Women, Secrecy, and HIV in Northern Nigeria*. Bloomington: Indiana University Press.
Robbins, Derek. 1991. *The Work of Pierre Bourdieu: Recognizing Society*. San Francisco: Westview Press.
Roberts, Richard. 1992. “Guinée Cloth: Linked Transformations within France's Empire in the Nineteenth Century.” *Cahiers d'études africaines* 32(128): 597–627.
———. 1996. *Two Worlds of Cotton: Colonialism and the Regional Economy in the French Soudan, 1800–1946*. Stanford: Stanford University Press.

Roberts, Richard L., and Suzanne Miers. 1988. "The End of Slavery in Africa." In *The End of Slavery in Africa*, edited by Suzanne Miers and Richard L. Roberts, 3–70. Madison: University of Wisconsin Press.

Robertson, Claire C., and Martin A. Klein. 1983. "Women's Importance in African Slave Systems." In *Women and Slavery in Africa*, edited by Claire C. Robertson and Martin A. Klein, 3–25. Madison: The University of Wisconsin Press.

Robertson, Claire C. 1997. *Trouble Showed the Way: Women, Men, and Trade in the Nairobi Area, 1890–1990*. Bloomington: Indiana University Press.

Robinson, David. 2000. *Paths of Accommodation: Muslim Societies and French Colonial Authorities in Senegal and Mauritania, 1880–1920*. Athens: Ohio University Press.

Robinson, Dawn T., and Lynn Smith-Lovin. 2001. "Getting a Laugh: Gender, Status, and Humor in Task Discussions." *Social Forces* 80(1): 123–58.

Rocheteau, Guy. 1991. *L'organisation de la recherche agronomique à l'échelle nationale en Afrique au sud du sahara (pays francophones)*. ISNAR/ORSTOM.

Rodet, Marie. 2010. "Mémoires de l'esclavage dans la région de Kayes, histoire d'une disparition." *Cahiers d'études africaines* 50(197): 263–91.

———. 2015. "Escaping Slavery and Building Diasporic Communities in French Soudan and Senegal, ca. 1880–1940." *International Journal of African Historical Studies* 48(2): 363–86.

Rossi, Benedetta. 2009. "Introduction: Rethinking Slavery in West Africa." In *Reconfiguring Slavery: West African Trajectories*, edited by Benedetta Rossi, 1–25. Liverpool: Liverpool University Press.

———. 2015. "African Post-Slavery: A History of the Future." *The International Journal of African Historical Studies* 48(2): 303–24.

Rovine, Victoria L. 2004. "Fashionable Traditions: The Globalization of an African Textile." In *Fashioning Africa: Power and the Politics of Dress*, edited by Jean Marie Allman, 189–211. Bloomington: Indiana University Press.

Ruf, Urs Peter. 1999. *Ending Slavery. Hierarchy, Dependency and Gender*. New Brunswick: Transaction Publishers.

Saleh, Sidna Ndah Mohamed. 2009. *Migration en Mauritanie: Profil National 2009*. Geneva: Organisation internationale pour les migrations.

Scheele, Judith. 2012. "Shurafā'as Cosmopolitans: Islam, Genealogy and Hierarchy in the Central Sahara." In *Articulating Islam: Anthropological Approaches to Muslim Worlds*, edited by Magnus Barsden and Konstantinos Retsikas, 33–54. New York: Springer.

Scott, James C. 1990. *Domination and the Arts of Resistance: Hidden Transcripts*. New Haven: Yale University Press.

Searle, John R. 1972. "What is a Speech Act?" In *Language and Social Context: Selected Readings*, edited by Pier Paolo Giglioli, 136–54. Baltimore, MD: Penguin Books.

Seddon, David. 1996. "The Political Economy of Mauritania: An Introduction." *Review of African Political Economy* 23(68): 197–214.

Shahinian, Gulnara. 2014. *Report of the Special Rapporteur on Contemporary Forms of Slavery, Including its Causes and Consequences*. New York: UN General Assembly, Human Rights Council.

Shoup, John. 2007. "The Griot Tradition in Ḥassāniyya Music: The 'Īggāwen.'" *Quaderni di Studi Arabi* 2: 95–102.

Simard, Gisèle. 1996. *Petites commerçantes de Mauritanie: Voiles, perles et henné.* Paris: Karthala.
Smith, Daniel Jordan. 2006. "Cell Phones, Social Inequality, and Contemporary Culture in Nigeria." *Canadian Journal of African Studies* 40(3): 496–523.
Smith, James H. 2004. "Of Spirit Possession and Structural Adjustment Programs: Government Downsizing, Education, and Their Enchantments in Neoliberal Kenya." In *Producing African Futures: Ritual and Reproduction in a Neoliberal Age*, edited by Brad Weiss, 262–93. Boston: Brill.
Steiner, Christopher B. 1985. "Another Image of Africa: Toward an Ethnohistory of European Cloth Marketed in West Africa, 1873–1960." *Ethnohistory* 32(2): 91–110.
Stewart, Charles C. 1992. "When Youth Concludes: Changes in Marriage and the Production of Youth since 1890 (in Mauritania)." In *Les Jeunes en Afrique*, edited by Hélène d'Almeida-Topor, Catherine Coquery-Vidrovitch, Odile Goerg, and Francoise Guitart, 103–15. Paris: L'Harmattan.
———. 1989. "Une interprétation du conflit Sénégalo-Mauritanien." *Revue du monde musulman et de la Méditerranée* 54(4): 161–70.
Stewart, Charles, and E. K. Stewart. 1973. *Islam and Social Order in Mauritania: A Case Study from the Nineteenth Century.* Oxford: Clarendon Press.
Stiansen, Endre, and Jane I. Guyer. 1999. "Introduction." In *Credit, Currencies, and Culture: African Financial Institutions in Historical Perspective*, edited by Endre Stiansen and Jane I. Guyer, 1–14. Stockholm: Nordic Africa Institute.
Stoller, Paul. 2014. *Yaya's Story: The Quest for Well-Being in the World.* Chicago: University of Chicago Press.
Strathern, Marilyn. 1988. *The Gender of the Gift: Problems with Women and Problems with Society in Melanesia.* Berkeley: University of California Press.
Strobel, Margaret. 1979. *Muslim Women in Mombasa, 1890–1975.* New Haven: Yale University Press.
Sylvanus, Nina. 2007. "The Fabric of Africanity: Tracing the Global Threads of Authenticity." *Anthropological Theory* 7(2): 201–16.
———. 2016. *Patterns in Circulation: Cloth, Gender, and Materiality in West Africa.* Chicago: University of Chicago Press.
Taine-Cheikh, Catherine. 1989. "La Mauritanie en noir et blance: Petite promenade linguistique en hassâniyya." *Revue du monde musulman et de la Méditerranée* 54(1): 90–105.
Tarlo, Emma. 2010. *Visibly Muslim: Fashion, Politics, Faith.* New York: Berg.
Tauzin, Aline. 1985–86. "Des couleurs et des voiles: Pratique de la teinture chez les Maures à Nouakchott (Mauritanie)." *Littérature Orale Arabo-Berbère* 16–17: 79–100.
———. 1986. "La femme partagé: Contrôle et déplacement de la sexualité féminine en Mauritanie." In *Côté femmes*, edited by D. Champault and J. Jamin, 147–57. Paris: L'Harmattan.
———. 1989. "A haute voix. Poésie féminine contemporaine en Mauritanie." *Revue du monde musulman et de la Méditerranée* 54(1): 178–87.
———. 2001. *Figures du féminin dans la société maure (Mauritanie).* Paris: Karthala.
———. 2007. "Women of Mauritania: Cathodic Images and Presentation of the Self." *Visual Anthropology* 20(1): 3–18.
Taylor, Raymond M. 1995. "Warriors, Tributaries, Blood Money and Political Transformation in Nineteenth-Century Mauritania." *Journal of African History* 36(3): 419–41.

Thioub, Ibrahima. 2012. "Stigmas and Memory of Slavery in West Africa: Skin Color and Blood as Social Fracture Lines." *New Global Studies* 6(3): 1–18.

Thomas, Lynn M., and Jennifer Cole. 2009. "Introduction: Thinking through Love in Africa." In *Love in Africa*, edited by Jennifer Cole and Lynn M. Thomas, 1–30. Chicago: University of Chicago Press.

Thompson, Virginia, and Richard Adloff. 1957. *French West Africa*. Stanford, CA: Stanford University Press.

Thurston, Alex. 2011. "AQIM Kidnappings and Murders in the Sahel, 2007 – present [updated]." *Sahel Blog*, September 13. http://sahelblog.wordpress.com/2011/01/18/aqim-kidnappings-and-murders-in-the-sahel-2007-present/.

Tidjani Alou, Mahaman. 2000. "Démocratie, exclusion sociale et quête de citoyenneté: cas de l'association Timidria au Niger." *Journal des africanistes* 70(1): 173–95.

Toupet, C. 1959. "L'estension récente des palmeraies au tagant." *Notes Africaines* 84: 103–6.

Tourte, René. 2005. *Histoire de la recherche agricole en Afrique tropicale francophone*. Rome: Organisation des nations unies pour l'alimentation et l'agriculture.

UNIFEM (United Nations Development Fund for Women). 2010. *Country Strategy for the Islamic Republic of Mauritania, 2010–2011*. Nouakchott: UNIFEM.

van Santen, José. 2010. "'My "Veil" Does Not Go With My Jeans': Veiling, Fundamentalism, Education and Women's Agency in Northern Cameroon." *Africa* 80(2): 275–300.

van Til, Kiky. 2006. "Neighbourhood (Re)construction and Changing Identities in Mauritania from a Small Town Perspective." In *Crisis and Creativity: Exploring the Wealth of the African Neighbourhood*, edited by Piet Konings and Dick Foeken, 230–50. Boston: Leiden.

Vergara, Francisco. 1979. "L'économie de la Mauritanie et son développement." In *Introduction à la Mauritanie*, 177–234. Aix-en-Provence: Institut de recherches et d'études sur le monde arabe et musulman.

Vermeer, Donald E. 1981. "Collision of Climate, Cattle, and Culture in Mauritania during the 1970s." *Geographical Review* 71(3): 281–97.

Villasante Cervello, Mariella. 2004. "'They Work to Eat and They Eat to Work': M'allemîn Craftsmen, Classification, and Discourse among the Bidân Nobility of Mauritania." In *Customary Strangers: New Perspectives on Peripatetic Peoples in the Middle East, Africa, and Asia*, edited by Joseph C. Berland and Apama Rao, 123–54. Westport, CT: Praeger Publishers.

Villasante-de Beauvais, Mariella. 1991. "Hiérarchies statutaires et conflits fonciers dans l'Assaba contemporain (Mauritanie). Rupture ou continuité?" *Revue du monde musulman et de la Méditerranée* 59(1): 181–210.

———. 1997. "Mauritanie: Catégories de classement identitaire et discours politiques dans la société bidân." *Annuaire de l'Afrique du Nord* 36: 79–100.

———. 1998. *Parenté et politique en Mauritanie: Essai d'Anthropologie historique*. Montreal: L'Harmattan.

———. 2000. "La Question des hiérarchies sociales et des groupes serviles chez les bidân de mauritanie." In *Groupes serviles au Sahara: Approche comparative à partir du cas des arabophones de Mauritanie*, edited by Mariella Villasante-de Beauvais, 277–322. Paris: CNRS Editions.

Watson, Helen. 1994. "Women and the Veil: Personal Responses to Global Process." In *Islam, Globalization and Postmodernity*, edited by Akbar S. Ahmed and Hastings Donnan, 141–59. New York: Routledge.

Webb, James L. A. 1995. *Desert Frontier: Ecological and Economic Change Along the Western Sahel, 1600–1850*. Madison: University of Wisconsin Press.
Wehr, Hans. 1994. *A Dictionary of Modern Written Arabic*. 4th ed. Urbana, IL: Spoken Language Services, Inc.
Weiner, Annette B. 1976. *Women of Value, Men of Renown: New Perspectives in Trobriand Exchange*. Austin, TX: University of Texas Press.
———. 1989. "Why Cloth? Wealth, Gender, and Power in Oceania." In *Cloth and Human Experience*, edited by Annette B. Weiner and Jane Schneider, 33–72. Washington, DC: Smithsonian Institution Press.
———. 1992. *Inalienable Possessions: the Paradox of Keeping-While-Giving*. Berkeley: University of California Press.
West, Candace, and Don H Zimmerman. 1987. "Doing Gender." *Gender & Society* 1(2): 125–51.
Wiley, Katherine Ann. 2013. "Fashioning People, Crafting Networks: Multiple Meanings in the Mauritanian Veil (Malaḥfa)." In *Dress, Performance, and Social Action in Africa*, edited by Karen Tranberg Hansen and D. Soyini Madison, 77–91. New York: Blooomsbury.
———. 2014. "Joking Market Women: Critiquing and Negotiating Gender and Social Hierarchy in Kankossa, Mauritania." *Africa* 84(1): 101–18.
———. 2016. "Making People Bigger: Wedding Exchange and the Creation of Social Value in Rural Mauritania." *Africa Today* 62(3): 49–70.
Zahedi, Ashraf. 2007. "Contested Meaning of the Veil and Political Ideologies of Iranian Regimes." *Journal of Middle East Women's Studies* 3(3): 75–98.

Index

Page numbers in italics refer to figures.

slavery/slaves, 30, 34, 51, 119–20, 177–84; characteristics of, 107, 128–29, 151, 152, 161; diminishment of, 46; expected behavior of, 90, 151, 153; forms and types of, 10, 32, 125n16; justification of, 152; kinship, 33, 128; labor, 6, 32–33, 43, 60, 67, 78n4, 70, 95, 154; marriage, 33, 107, 128–30, 163; means to freedom, 7, 29, 34, 35–36, 43, 44, 152–53; persistence of, 6, 8, 16, 177; post-slavery, 6, 23n6. *See also*, antislavery movements; bridewealth payments (*ṣaḍāq*): slaves'; colonialism: slavery policies; gender: slavery; *Ḥarāṭīn*: connections with slavery; hierarchy, social; independence: slave descendants'; Islam: connections with slavery
slave descendants. See *Ḥarāṭīn*
social rank. *See* hierarchy, social
social value, 18, 59, 49, 66, 75, 115, 120, 122, 123, 127, 130, 134–35, 136, 145–46, 163, 170–71, 173, 180–84; basis of, 4, 5; bestowing on others, 135, 138–41; display of, 9, 133, 136, 141, 169, 171; of education, 51; of femininity, 58–59; generation of, 4, 15, 19, 46, 59, 127, 141, 159; *Ḥarāṭīn* claims to, 41, 46, 51, 52, 66, 70, 77, 102, 122, 130, 150, 155, 157, 161, 180–81; meaning of, 8, 9, 20, 53, 78, 134, 151; of relationships, 102, 107, 110, 121; women's assertion of, 17, 53, 59, 75, 102, 107, 123, 171, 173; of work, 14, 45, 49, 66–67, 70, 72, 74, 95, 102, 121, 157, 163. *See also* elites: values of; generosity; piety; respect: social value of; wealth: social value of
social worth. *See* social value
socioeconomic class. *See* class, socioeconomic
Soninke, 24n1, 72, 78n2, 80n22, 94, 164
status, social. *See* hierarchy, social
Stoller, Paul, 26n28
Strathern, Marilyn, 140
structural adjustment programs (SAPs), 11, 44–46, 72, 164
Sudan, 174n11
Sylvanus, Nina, 173n2

Tanzania, 79n13, 100n9
Tauzin, Aline, 164
taxes, 16, 34, 74
traders, 56–78, 85, 91, 94, 95–96, 101–25, 149, 167–68, 169; conceptions of labor, 60, 180; in gendered space, 91–93; male, 60, 61; women's merchandise, 60–61
Trump, Donald, 15–16
Tuareg, 55n33

United States, 10, 18, 51, 96, 106, 150, 178
unemployment, 11, 44, 129, 145, 182

value. *See* social value
veils (*malaḥfa*, sing.), 12, 117, 130, 132, 133, 144, 149–75; aesthetics of, 150, 157–63; associations with particular social groups, 152–54; connections to Islam, 149–50, 151–57; connections to labor, 155–57; connections to social rank, 150, 153–54, 155, 157, 163; economic value, 150, 161; history of, 153–54; locally produced, 158, 163–71; other forms of Muslim dress, 154–55; varieties of, 158, 165. *See also* clothing; *darrā'a* (boubou); dyeing; men: dress; piety: fashion
villages de liberté. *See* liberty villages

Walk Free Foundation, 6, 177
wealth, 4, 7, 9, 43, 46, 49, 97, 103, 122, 125n10, 133, 135–36, 173, 182; accumulations of, 114, 122, 128–29, 145, 167; display of, 15, 70, 120, 127, 131, 136, 142, 144, 161, 163, 169–70, 171; social value of, 46, 49, 51, 70, 95, 102, 107, 120
weddings, 105, 126–35, 142, 143, 154, 176. *See also* bridewealth payments (*ṣaḍāq*); marriage
wholesalers, 12, 60, 61, 64, 116, 123, 165; credit from, 116, 123; female, 69, 105
witchcraft, 146n4
Wolof, 23n1, 65, 78n2, 80n22, 84–85, 88, 164
women, 18; class divisions among, 110; influence, 63, 181; junior, 102, 110, 112, 115, 132; political influence, 18; senior, 102, 108–10, 115; value of labor, 67–74; work, 12, 13, 64–66, 85, 102–4, 164–71, 182. *See also* class, socioeconomic: impact on women's

KATHERINE ANN WILEY is Assistant Professor of Anthropology at Pacific Lutheran University. Her work has appeared in *Africa* and *Africa Today.*

www.ingramcontent.com/pod-product-compliance
Lightning Source LLC
Chambersburg PA
CBHW052003270326
41929CB00015B/2774
* 9 7 8 0 2 5 3 0 3 6 2 2 3 *